THE UNITED STATES OF
OHIO

ONE AMERICAN STATE AND
ITS IMPACT ON THE OTHER FORTY-NINE

DAVID E. ROHR

TRILLIUM, AN IMPRINT OF
THE OHIO STATE UNIVERSITY PRESS
COLUMBUS

Library of Congress Cataloging-in-Publication Data
Names: Rohr, David E., author.
Title: The United States of Ohio : one American state and its impact on the other forty-nine / David E. Rohr.
Description: Columbus : Trillium, 2019. | Series: Trillium books | Includes bibliographical references.
Identifiers: LCCN 2018038508 | ISBN 9780814255155 (paperback)
Subjects: LCSH: Ohio—History. | Ohio—Civilization. | BISAC: HISTORY / United States / State & Local / Midwest (IA, IL, IN, KS, MI, MN, MO, ND, NE, OH, SD, WI). | POLITICAL SCIENCE / Government / General.
Classification: LCC F491.5 R64 2019 | DDC 977.1—dc23
LC record available at https://lccn.loc.gov/2018038508

Cover design by James Baumann
Text design by Juliet Williams
Type set in Adobe Sabon

THE UNITED STATES OF OHIO

For Mom and Dad

CONTENTS

ILLUSTRATIONS

INTRODUCTION

It was over when they called Ohio.

No matter who you were rooting for in the 2008 election, everyone knew the outcome shortly after 9:30 p.m. on November 4, when several networks announced that Barack Obama had won the 2008 election in the Buckeye State. Presidential elections, as everyone knows, are won state by state and tallied via electoral votes. Although Obama would have won the election even without the state of Ohio, you could tell by the reaction in Chicago's Grant Park (named after Ohioan Ulysses S. Grant) that candidate Obama's supporters had ultimate confidence in his victory. The notion that the election was "over" when the Ohio results were announced was relevant not only to the 2008 election but to countless others before it. George W. Bush could not have won either his 2004 or 2000 elections without Ohio. The camp of his 2004 opponent, John Kerry, was heard to lament many times, "If only we'd changed 75,000 minds in Ohio."[1]

Electoral significance has always distinguished the small- to medium-sized northern state sandwiched between Lake Erie and the Ohio River. Since the Civil War, almost every Democrat who has won the presidency has done so with the help of Ohio's electoral votes. John F. Kennedy and Franklin D. Roosevelt are the only two exceptions to this rule in the last 100 years (Roosevelt won the state in most of his elections). Republican presidents have been elected since the time of Abraham Lincoln, and all of them have had to carry Ohio to do it. No Republican candidate has ever won the presidency without Ohio.

Only twice since the beginning of the twentieth century has Ohio failed to pick the candidate who ultimately won the presidential election. New York, in contrast, has failed to pick the winner four times just since 1988, and California, the nation's most populous state, has been wrong five times since just 1960. While Ohio is among the country's larger states in population, it is by no means large enough to sway results on its own. What could be relevant here is that Ohio's voters serve as such a worthy sample of the nation as a whole.[2]

But presidential elections are only part of the Ohio story. That's because the state has always been an innovator, an incubator, and a bellwether for the American experience. If you have products made by General Electric, thank Thomas A. Edison of Milan, Ohio. Like football? Tip your hat to the Canton Bulldogs, Akron Pros, Cleveland Tigers, Columbus Panhandles, and Dayton Triangles. Ohio is not only the birthplace of the National Football League, it served as the home state of nearly half the league's original teams.[3] You say you're more of a baseball fan? Then surely you know that the first Major League team was the Cincinnati Reds. First known as the Red Stockings, the team got its start in the Queen City in 1869. But if you're more of a Yankees fan, then thank the late Cleveland native George Steinbrenner. (Or not.)

From sports to a century's worth of entertainment superstars to aviation and space exploration, Ohio's best have made for some of America's greatest stories. The same goes for the business world. The country's largest tire company (Akron's Goodyear) and largest consumer products company (Cincinnati's Procter & Gamble) are based in Ohio. The state grows, processes, and builds on a level that far outpaces the size of its population or expanse of its borders. If you have homeowners, auto, or life insurance, chances are good that you're insured by Nationwide, Grange Mutual, Safe Auto, or any one of Columbus's behemoth insurers, or maybe Cleveland's Progressive. Ohio and Ohioans have played a major role in almost everything that defines and distinguishes the country.

This book is intended to be more than a chronicling of Ohio facts and figures. It is this author's opinion that Ohio is the ultimate microcosm of the larger US. The things we like, the accent with which we speak, the values we hold as Americans, and the way we live—day to day—are all influenced in surprising ways by the Buckeye State. This book is about why that is.

Reading something years back put out by, perhaps, the City of Columbus, I recall a saying that Ohio was the "furthest north of the South, the furthest south of the North, the furthest east of the West, and furthest west of the East."[4] That's why—according to my dad's elementary school teacher, whom you will meet in Chapter 1—it is the center of the universe.

Two-thirds of the US population lives within one day's drive of Columbus, the state capital, which sits a stone's throw from Ohio's geographic center. Incidentally, so does half the Canadian population. Despite being smaller than two-thirds of the other US states in terms of landmass, Ohio is a top-five manufacturing state. And it is at the very top in some pretty important areas, including production of rubber and plastics, auto components, trucks, steel, industrial machinery, and jet engines. It not only helps drive the American automotive industry, producing Ford, Fiat-Chrysler, General Motors, and Kenworth and Navistar trucking products, but also is the focal point of Honda's US production operations. Ohio is second only to Michigan in annual car output.[5] If you want to understand America, understand Ohio. If you want to see what's going wrong with the country, chances are very good that Ohio offers the proverbial canary in the mineshaft. Someone who dismisses Ohio as a Rust Belt state would do well to wonder whether we are not soon to be a Rust Belt country.

One thing I can vouch for is that Ohio is an eternally optimistic state. It gets cold in the winter, but Ohioans are perpetually looking ahead to spring. The Browns and Indians have not won their sports' major championships in decades, but Clevelanders and legions of fans throughout the state know that greatness is just a season or two away. At least they hope so. Like Texans, Ohioans have an almost nationalistic pride in their state. Although this attitude seems to have diminished through several decades of marginal economic performance, all it takes is an Ohio State–Michigan game to reawaken the state patriotism.

CHAPTER 1

SISTER THEORY

As a kid growing up in Tiffin and then Toledo, Ohio, I sat in many elementary school classrooms looking at the map that always seemed to be at the front of every room. I always noticed how the outline of Ohio resembled a miniature version of the continental US.

Look at the northeastern corner where Ashtabula and Conneaut are located and you see a stunted New England. Except for the absence of a visible southeastern protrusion that Florida creates, you will see a winding southern border that dips to its lowest point in the center, just as Texas does for the Lower 48. Thanks to Lake Erie, the top border of the state has a natural dip, just like the US as a whole when looking at the country on a flat map and, in particular, in the area of the Great Lakes. And in geographical mimicry of the West Coast, the western edge of Ohio appears straight in the north before rounding to accommodate the Ohio River's bends.

When I shared this youthful observation with my father, he said that I wasn't the only person who looked at Ohio and saw a mini America. He pointed out that when he was a student at St. Joseph's Elementary School in Fremont, his teacher—a Catholic nun—pointed out the same thing to her class. But she went a little further, apparently, suggesting that not only did Ohio resemble the larger nation in its outline, but it also could be a completely self-sustaining country all by itself—without any trade or interaction with other states in the country. Ohio, this Catholic nun told her eager young students, had everything a state could want: the best farming, the best manufacturing, the best schools, and the best roads.[1]

"You could—and should—build a fence around it," she told my dad and 25 or 30 of his classmates. There was really no reason to consider leaving the state. Or letting anyone else in. I have no reason to believe that the good sister actually feared overimmigration from Indiana or Kentucky. She was just darn proud of her native state.

SOUTHEAST OF THE NORTHWEST

Ohio has had three capital cities. First came Chillicothe, from 1803 to 1810, and then again from 1812 to 1816. Zanesville was the state capital from 1810 to 1812—the brevity owing itself to political disputes (what else?). Finally, Columbus was selected as the capital, with full relocation taking place in 1816. It remains the capital to this day and is the fourth-largest state capital in the country.

What many people don't know, however, is that Ohio had another capital city before any of these. Marietta, in the southeastern part of the state, off several bends of the Ohio River and just across from West Virginia, was the first of Ohio's cities to serve as a capital. Marietta was the capital of a larger area known as the Northwest Territory.[2] This land was given to the US as part of the Treaty of Paris, which officially ended the Revolutionary War about two years after Cornwallis surrendered at Yorktown. The Northwest Territory included what eventually became Ohio, plus Indiana, Michigan, Illinois, Wisconsin, and a large portion of Minnesota.

The territory's governor was Revolutionary War General Arthur St. Clair. And it was a distinct, recognized US territory for 15 key years, from 1788 to Ohio's founding in 1803. The founding itself was a product of some intrigue as early politicians in the Democratic-Republican Party, like Thomas Worthington and Edward Tiffin, personally traveled to Washington to lobby President Jefferson to facilitate Ohio statehood. St. Clair, a Federalist, had opposed Ohio's admission as a single state, hoping it could become two—a scheme that he thought would help preserve Federalist control of the area. Jefferson sided with his partisans, signing the Enabling Act and firing St. Clair, thus paving the way for Ohio's admission as a single state.[3]

The area had been claimed at one time or another by the French, by the British, and by the new Canadian province of Quebec. Connecticut, New York, Pennsylvania, and Virginia all viewed portions of the Northwest Territory, particularly Ohio, as theirs.

Northeastern Ohio was also considered Connecticut's Western Reserve. Towns such as Avon, Litchfield, and Kent take the names of earlier established towns in Connecticut. Just to the east of these cities lies an area of the state called the Firelands, where you'll find another Connecticut-named town, Norwalk. I've always found "Firelands" to be a curious moniker, since the area is rather fertile and verdant, but the name apparently comes from its Connecticut heritage. During the Revolutionary War, British soldiers ransacked and burned nine Connecticut towns, and townspeople wishing to move were awarded large portions of Huron and Erie counties as a form of reparation for the damage inflicted by the British.[4]

People in northern Ohio speak with a definite northern accent— otherwise known as the Chicago accent, for which there are dialectic similarities between everyone stretching from Chicago to Rochester, New York. Northeast Ohio is dominated by Cleveland but is also home to large prominent cities like Akron, Youngstown, and Canton. Given its demographics, the area serves as a virtual mirror of the rest of America's blue-collar Northeast, complete with all its ethnic diversity, union ethic, and increasing concerns about the economy.

Northern Ohio is also coastal. Lake Erie connects the land all the way from the point where Ohio meets Pennsylvania to its western edge at Toledo. Ohio's border with Canada sits entirely in the middle of Lake Erie. The lake was an obvious draw not only for people immigrating to the state in the nineteenth century but for industry as well. Entrepreneurs built Cleveland into one of the country's largest and most influential cities, a notion that Clevelanders still have a hard time letting go.

While it's easy for people to associate all things from Cleveland with the city's infamous sporting curses, such as the Browns' latest blown lead or Tony Fernandez's ground ball mishandling (which

FIGURE 1.1. Ohio's north coast. The sun sets over
Lake Erie as seen from Geneva State Park.

cost the Indians Game 7 of the 1997 World Series),[5] Cleveland has
many characteristics and resources for which it can call itself "best
in the world." Ask any Cleveland native and she'll be happy to start
rattling off the list. We'll get to some of those later.

Smack in the middle of the Buckeye State sits the emerging
colossus of Columbus. Once an overgrown farm town content with
its status as state capital and home of The Ohio State University,
Columbus has spent the last 30 years attracting people and companies to its environs, along the way eating the towns that once
surrounded it through aggressive annexation. While the state's
population has been little more than stagnant over the last generation, Columbus has grown significantly.

In fact, this metropolis could well become the Ohio city that
consumes all the rest. In 1983 county planners projected that
Columbus would see its metro population increase to over 900,000
by 1995. It actually increased to 1.04 million. By the 2010 census,
it had grown to nearly 2 million. Columbus occupies all of Franklin County and parts of Fairfield and Delaware counties. Although
Columbus was founded as a town on two small rivers (the Scioto

and Olentangy), its biggest transportation asset is its position at the intersection of interstates 71 and 70.

To the east and south, the state contains Appalachian foothills, and the inhabitants of that region have an accent that is decidedly southern. Southeastern Ohio, while somewhat less hilly, maintains a quasi-southern character. Accents tend to resemble those in Kentucky and southern Indiana rather than their counterparts in Cleveland, Toledo, or even Columbus. Cincinnati, the focal point of this area, is not only one of Ohio's largest metropolitan areas but one of Kentucky's as well.

Ohio is a geographic crossroads for reasons both natural and man-made. The rivers in the northern part of the state flow north to Lake Erie and ultimately empty into the North Atlantic via the St. Lawrence River. Those in the central and southern part of the state (like the Scioto and Olentangy) ultimately empty into the Ohio River, whose waters eventually reach the Gulf of Mexico via the Mississippi. Somewhat north of Columbus, in Crawford County, the paths of the north-flowing Sandusky and south-flowing Olentangy pass just miles from each other for a period. So, an active young guy—whether he's cycling, jogging, or hiking—in Crawford County would have no idea whether his perspiration is destined for the North Atlantic or the Gulf of Mexico.

Ohio, like the country as a whole, experienced its growth in regional spurts, depending on transportation and national economic conditions. Cincinnati had its boom period in the early to mid-1800s. Cleveland's economic party began after the Civil War and continued to roughly 1964, when running back Jim Brown retired from the Browns. Columbus has been enjoying its golden era since the 1950s, buoyed by state government, a huge insurance industry, and its role as a distribution hub to the rest of the state and Midwest.

BLOODLESS WAR

Northwest Ohio, on the other hand, has never really experienced a heyday. Its largest city, Toledo, was settled in the 1830s following the famous border war between Ohio and Michigan. In one of the few examples of states doing battle with one another (except for the Civil War), Michigan and Ohio actually engaged in several, though bloodless, skirmishes over the area of the state between the western edge of Lake Erie and the Indiana border. Both Ohio (then a state) and Michigan (hoping to become a state) wanted the land, and battle ensued.[6] It is a war that many believe continues to this day on the football field.

It is believed that both legislatures viewed the territory as theirs because of a poor understanding of certain areas of the Great Lakes that defined the states' definition of the border. Ultimately Congress intervened and awarded the 468 square miles to Ohio. This was not an insignificant victory. With the development of the Erie Canal in New York, the eastern US had a direct line all the way to the western edge of Lake Erie, which was now in Ohio. This access provided a quick water and land route between the East and points in Indiana and Illinois. It also factored heavily into plans to create a water route via canals and rivers that would link the lake with the Mississippi.

In return, Michigan got the more than 16,452 square miles that form its upper peninsula—an area more than one-third the size of the entire state of Ohio. The deal would turn out pretty well for Michigan in the end, as the "U.P." held some of the country's richest iron and copper deposits. The Upper Peninsula also offers numerous scenic treasures. So, if any state got robbed in this deal it was probably Wisconsin. But it was easy to take advantage of Wisconsin then, since it would not become a state until 1848.

What Ohio gained from the deal was a city, Toledo, that would give the world some of its most prominent industrial and decorative glass companies and become a leading supplier and manufacturing satellite for the Detroit automotive engine. In the late nineteenth and early twentieth centuries, an influx of glass companies spawned a strong and prosperous local economy. Attracted to the area by a rich supply of white Lake Erie sand, these companies quickly established Toledo as the self-proclaimed glass capital of the world. This prosperity produced superb Victorian neighborhoods along with a thriving arts and cultural community, which exceeded expectations for a city of Toledo's size. Prosperity also created an early regional affinity for golf. The first public golf course west of the Eastern Seaboard was opened in Toledo in 1899. Another course, Toledo's Inverness Golf Club is a frequent host to two golf major championships, the US Open and the PGA.

All the development in northwest Ohio also helped drain what had been known as the Black Swamp. Large portions of the area had been uninhabitable and nontraversable because spring and summer rains turned the place into a marshy, mushy mess. After the draining, the land became highly productive farmland. Outside of Toledo, the region is flat, fertile, and full of towns that contain somewhere between 5,000 and 30,000 people. The autumn air anywhere in northwest Ohio is frequently fragrant with the by-products of raising tomatoes, beans, sugar beets, and countless other crops that are grown and often processed in the area. Fremont, where my dad was born and raised, is one of these towns and boasts the world's largest ketchup-processing plant, owned by Heinz. The region also produces in huge volume for other notable labels. The Campbell's plant in Napoleon, Ohio, is the world's largest soup producer, and Dannon makes more yogurt in Auglaize County than any other location in the world.[7]

RIVALS NEXT DOOR

During my stay in Detroit there was an election for city officers. All the officers stationed there at the time who offered their votes were permitted to cast them. I did not offer mine, however, as I did not wish to consider myself a citizen of Michigan.[8]

—Ohio native U. S. Grant, from his *Memoirs*

Getting back to my dad's "Ohiophile" nun, it is important to point out that she is by no stretch of the imagination the only Ohioan with jingoistic enthusiasm for the state. Here, Toledo is again significant because it is located just 52 miles south of Ann Arbor, home to Ohio State's arch rival, the University of Michigan. Legendary coach Wayne Woodrow "Woody" Hayes and the Ohio State Buckeyes were rumored to sometimes lodge in Toledo the night before they were scheduled for biennial road games against Michigan. Hayes frequently felt his boys would play better if they didn't have to spend a night sleeping on Michigan soil. Hayes, it is also said, took his anti-Michigan emotion to extremes in other ways, refusing to stop his car for gasoline in the state to the north.[9]

Woody Hayes obviously had plenty of reasons to disdain Michigan; the two teams' annual epic brawls produced not only drama but also a year's worth of emotional fodder to keep his team perpetually riled. The other reason he might have been in favor of the "fence" my dad's teacher suggested (had he known about it) is that Michigan continually mined the state of Ohio for its rich supply of graduating senior football talent. Like just a few other states, including Texas and Florida, Ohio has a national reputation as an incubator of high school football talent. While many of the state's most talented players go to Ohio State, a fair share end up playing for other schools in faraway states or nearby Michigan.

We can only imagine the possibilities if Sister Mary Isolationist had figured out a way to create her fence and keep all those players in-state.

CHAPTER 2

AMERICA WRIT SMALL

During just about every presidential election cycle, some pundit or pollster will explain Ohio's appeal to the warring campaigns by clearing their throats, thoughtfully adjusting their glasses, and announcing authoritatively that Ohio is simply *America Writ Small*.[1] But they tend to do this by looking at Ohio in terms of content rather than output or influence on the wider American public.

Compress a bunch of fertile farmland between the Great Lakes and the nation's second-largest river and it is easy to envision a mini America of sorts. There are ports and manufacturing centers. It is home to one of the fastest-growing cities in the north (Columbus) and one of the poorest (Cleveland). There are gritty urban streets and suburban sprawl, best represented nowadays by cities like Columbus and Cincinnati. Ohio has plenty of small town America, too. And southeastern Ohio is a little slice of Appalachia, complete with pockets of poverty.

This is a state that distributes its populations in a way that mirrors the nation as a whole. Ohio is exceptionally average in terms of income, demographics, lifestyle, and life expectancy. But what makes it most noteworthy is how the larger nation is influenced both by what has happened in Ohio already and what continues to develop there. Of course, all of this goes far beyond drive-up windows, consumer products, and other manufactured output. And yes, this output includes some pretty significant things: gasoline, the airplane, liquid crystal displays, barcode scanners, cash registers, kidney dialysis machines, aluminum, the birth control pill, and other products we will discuss later.

To see the influence of the little state that kicks off the American Midwest (to a westbound traveler from the East Coast), you have to begin with a look at our ancestors. After six or seven generations of colonial life, the king's subjects had grown significantly in number, up and down the eastern shores. And they gradually came to realize that they were something more than transplanted Englishmen.[2] For example, people in Maine, Maryland, and Georgia came to discover that they had more in common with one another than they had with Old Mother England. They were Americans.

After the French and Indian War and the American Revolution, the Ohio River pointed to the west and willingly served as a main thoroughfare for these "American Americans" moving west. On the north side would emerge Ohio, the first state that had never sanctioned slavery. Nor had it ever been a colony. Formed in 1803, Ohio was the first state carved out of northern territory after the original 13 colonies won their independence from Great Britain. Vermont (sliced off from New York), Kentucky, and Tennessee were admitted as states prior to Ohio entering. Importantly, Ohio was also the only northern or nonslave state residing directly west of the original 13 colonies (Kentucky, Tennessee, and Alabama all being slave states). French historian and political observer Alexis de Tocqueville, writing in about 1830, noted that Ohio's population had grown to a quarter million more people than Kentucky's, despite the fact that the Bluegrass State was admitted to the Union many years earlier.[3] The vibrancy of contrasts between free Ohio and slave Kentucky certainly also caught the eye of Harriet Beecher Stowe, who, as we will see, wrote a novel that awakened a nation.

Ohio funneled the attitudes and ambitions of an enterprising northeastern commercial class, which extended from Massachusetts to Maryland to a western region that was yet to see itself as either northern or southern. Any primary reading of history describes the early Ohio population as being made up of settlers from coastal states like New York, New Jersey, and the New England states, along with influxes of Germans and Irish in the mid-

1800s. Ohio is the place where the American melting pot first began to warm.

Northern merchants and manufacturing and farming classes would come to Ohio in droves. They continued here for several generations too, their numbers swelled by the ever-increasing arrival of European immigrants, who only stayed in eastern port cities long enough to arrange passage west. As the first new state of the nineteenth century, Ohio would grow fast enough to eventually become the country's third-largest in population by the middle part of 1800s. But even before the Civil War, American migration had begun a heavy westward lurch.

Ohio was both a landing place and launchpad for internal migration. The senses and sensibilities of these westbound northerners had been incubated for several generations in what is now the Midwest, Ohio in particular. And during that time, when families were pouring in from the eastern states and Western Europe, the state was connecting its cities through a network of roads, canals, and later railroads.

GETTING DOWN TO BUSINESS

Ohio was always a state considered friendly to business interests. It was where the American Whig Party achieved early and consistent electoral success. Only two Whigs won presidential elections, and the first of them was Ohio's William Henry Harrison (who died less than a month after taking office).[4] The Whigs in many ways were a forerunner to the Republican Party. Although their wavering principles ultimately became the party's undoing, one thing they always remained dedicated to was the cause of advancing business interests—even when that meant using the power of government for such things as roads, bridges, and other infrastructure improvements. In addition, Ohio's status as a young state in the 1800s meant that its governmental and social structure was without deeply entrenched interests for much of the century. People could come to Ohio and make it. Or at least get by.

For pioneering America, Ohio had everything to be wished for in a prospective destination. There was a well-known supply of farmable land. The growing system of canals and railroads, com-

FIGURE 2.1. Even tiny Rushsylvania in Logan County, Ohio, had both passenger and freight service early in the twentieth century. The depot is now gone, but its image remains.

bined with the state's location, made it accessible to the new west beyond the Mississippi as well as to the East Coast. Trains of the nineteenth century might have only chugged along at 20 or 25 miles per hour, but that was considerably faster than any method of transport devised by man up to that point. Ohio was fertile ground for railroad development because so much of its geography was easily traversable and because its rail infrastructure would go largely undamaged by the Civil War.

With rail transport, migration to Ohio was easy, and the transport of goods to and from the state was markedly easier than it would have been a generation or two earlier. Trains and canals were the first transportation modes that began to "shrink" the North American continent, and Ohio was clearly the first beneficiary. And in the mid-1850s, the Baltimore and Ohio Railroad at last linked the state directly to the East Coast.[5]

In considering Ohio's evolution and its importance to the rest of the country, an observer should think not only of the numerous inventors who helped to create the first products of a consumer society but also the early Ohioans who created the kind of state-wide commercial culture that facilitated access to labor, materials, and markets.

Today, 50 years is not even close to a full human lifetime (for most people). Which is why the technological advancements that came to the US between 1870 and 1920 are so remarkable. Civilization had gone some 6,000 years without motorized transportation, artificial lighting, the ability to record and replay sound. Man had never before flown in a heavier-than-air machine. In the space of only 50 years, everything changed.

Ohio played a role—often critical—in achievements that gave us the car, the light bulb, sound recording, motion pictures, and air travel. Think of our world today and the world of the late 1920s and we can see many commonalities. They flew, drove, and watched movies just as we do today. Lights at night? No problem there either. Our immediate ancestors—parents, grandparents, and great-grandparents—lived in a world very similar to our own. But think back to another 50 years before that, and you realize the people of the 1870s wouldn't recognize very much about the way we live today. Like the people of 100, 1,000, or 10,000 years prior, the people of the early 1870s relied on foot and horsepower for most personal transportation. While it is true that the 1850s had brought about the advent of trains, steam-powered boats, and telegraph communications, their world was still without the many "miracles" that began to appear as a result of late nineteenth-century innovation and the safe harnessing of electricity.

Except for black-and-white photos from the 1850s and '60s, the pre-1870 world is dark to people of the twentieth and twenty-first centuries. We see most of those long-past decades only in the words of books, in paintings inside museums, or in any architecture that remains. But through the work of numerous inventors in the incredibly fertile period of the late 1800s, Americans of the early twenty-first century have much in common with those of the early twentieth. During that time, Ohio was not only the country's most productive and centrally located state, it also gave the world countless inventions and produced the vast majority of America's presidents.

THE CONSTITUTIONAL CRISIS NO ONE NOTICED (UNTIL IT WAS OVER)

My father's "isolationist" teacher may have had something else in mind when she shared her pro-Ohio views with the little children at St. Joseph's School in Fremont. When her comments were relayed to my dad and his classmates in the late 1930s or early '40s, Ohio had been an American state for about 135 years. Sort of. Had the Sister been aware of an obscure fact of law (and I suspect she may have been), then she may have been quietly rallying a youth corps for an Ohio independence movement. Why? Sister may have been one of the few to know that Ohio was not, officially anyway, a state.

Few people know that the final step in Ohio's admittance to the Union did not take place in 1803 but in 1953—150 years after the ratification and approval of the state's constitution by the Ohio legislature. It was probably an innocent mistake, but there was no final US congressional vote approving the state constitution back in 1803. Every other state in the Union, from Delaware to Alaska, has had an official date of entry and an official ratification of admission by the Congress of the US.

Apparently, the Ohio oversight never really caught the public's attention until 1953, when people began to research the matter while making plans for the state's 150th anniversary celebration. In getting around to the official business of ratifying the admission, Ohio congressmen were teased by other lawmakers (from opposite parties) about being "illegal" members of the House or Senate bodies. In the end, the situation was corrected, and the state's retroactive admission was approved by an act of Congress and signed by President Dwight D. Eisenhower.[6] Ohio is still counted as the 17th state, rather than the 48th. No need to add arrows to the state seal.

But just imagine the potential disaster if, for some reason, Ohio's admittance to the Union in 1803 had been rendered invalid because of the oversight. Michigan's claim to the "Toledo strip" would have greater validity because Ohio would have no legal basis for its claim on the land. The state would have merely been a territory, unable to field the multiple Whig, Republican, and Democratic presidential candidacies it provided in its first 150 years. And what of Ohio's electoral votes in 32 presidential elections that ran from the time of Thomas Jefferson to Dwight Eisenhower?

Okay, this may be fanciful, but one has to at least consider that the nonadmission technicalities may have had some legal bearing had they been noticed and pursued in the early 1800s. Perhaps if Ohio had made a critical difference in the 1804 election, the losing opponent might have had a legal case that Ohio's electoral votes shouldn't count. But Thomas Jefferson, who captured Ohio's electoral votes in its first election as a state, crushed Charles Cotesworth Pinckney, winning 162 electoral votes to Pinckney's 14. The Ohio oversight continued for another 149 years, never inspiring a legal challenge in presidential politics.

So, all is well that ends well. The official admission date of March 1, 1803, was acknowledged in legislation of August 1953. A stroke of President Eisenhower's pen made everything legitimate, once and for all. There would be no constitutional crisis. The presidencies of Harrison, Grant, Hayes, Garfield, Harrison, McKinley, Taft, and Harding would not be invalidated. There would be no need for fences around the Buckeye State. And every win that Ohio State had over Michigan would still count. Phewwww.

CHAPTER 3

CROSSROADS, THRILL RIDES, AND LUNCH

Longtime New Jersey residents like to identify themselves by what exit they're from. That is, interstate exit. Other states have upstate/downstate identity divisions. Florida has the Atlantic Coast, Gulf Coast, Panhandle, and Keys identities. Residents of states that are oriented north-to-south, like California, categorize themselves as Southern, Central, or Northern. In Tennessee, you are an East, Central, or West Tennessean, and the flag has three stars that formally recognize these distinct regions. South Carolina divides according to Upstate and Low Country. In Michigan, it's the Upper Peninsula and Downstate.

In Ohio, people tend to subdivide themselves into four quadrants, plus a fifth area artfully designated as Central Ohio. People in these areas usually identify closely with the largest nearby city. The only exception to this would be southeastern Ohio, which has no large cities, though in many respects Columbus serves as the anchor city to both southeast Ohio and Central Ohio. The state's compact, interstate- and roadway-rich nature means that Ohio puts nearly 11.7 million residents within four easily driven hours of one another.[1] So it is a relatively quick proposition to travel from Cincinnati to Cleveland or from Akron to Toledo or from Van Wert to Canton, thanks to a well-developed network of interstates and US routes, many of which are also four-lane highways.

Ohioans love to drive. Browns fans who've been transplanted into southern Ohio (Bengals' territory) think nothing of driving to Cleveland and back on game day. Columbus's location in the center of the state makes it easy for Buckeye alums and supporters to get to the capital to watch a daughter play soccer, catch a swimming meet, or witness Buckeye football as they trounce a Big Ten rival like Indiana or Minnesota. You can sit in Ohio Stadium right in between people who have driven up from Marietta on the Ohio River and others who've come down from Lorain, a suburb of Cleveland.

People from Findlay or Portsmouth (193 miles apart) might easily run into one another on a Saturday shopping trip in the Polaris shopping mecca north of Columbus. (If you haven't been to Central Ohio in the last 30 years, you will remember Polaris best for its cornfields and a couple of barns.)[2] When I was a kid, my parents routinely piled my brother, sister, and me into the station wagon at 8 a.m. on a Sunday morning and then drove three and a half hours from Toledo to Zanesville for a four- or five-hour visit with my grandparents. Once my grandparents had had enough of us, we'd load back into the car and be back in Toledo by 8:00 or 9:00 that same evening.

Southeastern Ohio has interesting, curvy, undulating state routes, which are often written up in *Car & Driver* or *Automobile* magazine. But much of the Ohio interstate system is flat, well marked, and divided. Ohio's roads are populated by enough exits or roadside rests that any craving for a Big Mac or potty break can be satisfied within minutes of the impulse first registering with your brain. Four-lane divided highways are not only interstates but also many US and Ohio state routes as well. So, when you're at the family reunion in Cambridge and your friend in Cleveland texts you about an evening of big fun being planned in Cleveland, no problem. You will make it to the festivities. You'll be home in a few hours after a relatively uneventful ride, perhaps stopping in Dover for gas and north of Akron for Starbucks.

If people in Ohio always seem to be going places, people from the rest of the country always seem to be passing through the state as well. If you want to cross the US on I-90 (Boston to Seattle), I-80 (New York to San Francisco), or I-70 (Baltimore to Salt Lake City), you have to spend three or four hours barreling though

Ohio. The Ohio State Highway Patrol is counting on you barreling, too, so watch for them. The great north–south migratory
thoroughfare known as I-75 (Sault Saint Marie, Michigan, to Fort
Lauderdale, Florida) requires travelers to spend about four hours
between Toledo and Cincinnati. There are several long interstates
that begin (or end) in Ohio, including I-71 (Cleveland to Columbus to Cincinnati to Louisville). Interstate 71 is the considered the
state's unofficial Main Street because it links Ohio's three largest
cities. Ohio has other pivotal north–south or east–west interstate
highways: I-77 from Cleveland to Columbia, South Carolina, I-76
from Akron to Philadelphia, and I-74 from Cincinnati to Daven-
port, Iowa.

Ohio has more interstate mileage than any of its neighbors,
including those with larger land areas (Pennsylvania and Michigan).
In fact, Ohio has the fourth-highest number of total interstate miles
in the country despite having a landmass that ranks only 35th.[3] It
also has the fifth-highest total traffic volume, second-highest number of bridges, and third-highest total number of urban areas, trail-
ing only Texas and California.

While Ohio is frequently lumped in with 40 or so other interior
states derisively labeled "flyover country," at least a few people are
in fact flying to the state and landing at one of its 180 public airports. In addition, airports in Cincinnati (oddly enough in northern
Kentucky), Columbus, and Cleveland serve as hubs or feeders for
several major airlines, including Delta. Cleveland's Hopkins is still
bouncing back from losing its status as a United hub in 2014. And
while we're on the subject of air travel, let's not forget where the
country and the world first got the means to fly—Dayton's Orville
and Wilbur Wright. We will get to them later.

Most major freight railroads are run through the state, as are
several Amtrak routes. Ohio's rail strength comes from its settle-
ment and development as America's western frontier during a time
coinciding with the introduction and improvement of the country's
rail transport system. Here again, the state's geography is important. Any east–west flow of traffic in the northern part of the country has to flow through Ohio.

Ohio is a big state for shipping—something surprising to many,
who see Ohio as an inland destination. The state's southeastern
and southern borders are defined by 451 winding miles of Ohio
River shoreline through which passes more commercial freight

FIGURE 3.1. Ohio playing the role of another state: Maine.
Mansfield Reformatory was a major filming location
for the movie *The Shawshank Redemption.*

than through the Panama Canal Zone. (This shoreline would be
much shorter if not for all of the zigging and sagging.) Via the
Ohio River, freight can be on its way any way up or down the Mississippi or other connecting rivers as well as the Gulf of Mexico,
Central and South America, and even the Pacific Ocean and Asia
via the Panama Canal.

Lake Erie, with its 265 miles of Ohio coastline, is an essential commercial thoroughfare, with freight traffic moving to and
from Ohio and the greater Midwest to the Atlantic Ocean and
European markets. Toledo and Cleveland are two of the country's largest nonseaboard ports. Combined, Ohio's Lake Erie and
Ohio River ports are responsible for well over 100 million tons of
freight annually, valued at more than $11 billion.[4] Ohio is not only
a crossroads but an essential junction of road, rail, and lake, river,
and ocean shipping.

It's really almost impossible to be a well-traveled American (or
product or process or cultural institution) without passing through
Ohio.

HOLD ON TIGHT

Highways, runways, and railways all line the Buckeye State in suitable quantity. But one of the most famous ways that Ohio manages to lure traffic is its midways and other attractions. In addition to having one of the country's best-known, best-attended state fairs, Ohio has a couple of legendary amusement parks and other internationally regarded institutions such as the Columbus Zoo, made famous by that famous aficionado of all things furry and crawling, Jack Hanna.

If you mention Ohio to the average thrill seeker, many will quickly develop a gleam in the eye and ask if you have ever been to Cedar Point. Cedar Point, located next to a mile-long stretch of sandy Lake Erie shoreline, is a roller coaster lover's paradise. At 150 years of age, Cedar Point is the second-oldest continually operated amusement park in North America. With over 150 ride attractions, it is best known for the speed, height, and diversity of its roller coasters. Some of these rides are incredible in their ability to stimulate adrenaline or churn the gut. The Millennium coaster, which opened in 2000, reaches speeds of 93 miles per hour. Even higher speeds are obtained by the Top Thrill Dragster, which stands 420 feet tall and produces a top speed of 120 miles per hour. It is one of the fastest coasters in the park. The park has more than 10 miles worth of coasters that produce g-force twists and turns to satisfy most every appetite for speed and thrills.[5]

A recent addition is the ValRavn, which arrived in 2016. Named for a supernatural raven from popular Danish folklore, it is billed by the park as "3,400 feet of thrill-ride innovation." In fact, the coaster broke more than 10 world records with an adventure that begins with a more than 20-story drop (223 feet).[6] That sounds like gravitational forces significant enough for any rider to feel internal organs starting to rearrange themselves. It may be best to wait until you're done riding before you pig out on midway food. In the days of my youth, a huge favorite was the park's famous vinegar-soaked Mama Berardi's French fries. They're no longer available at the park, but they can be found nearby at Berardi's restaurants in Sandusky and Huron.

Despite being closed for the winter months, Cedar Point is one of America's most visited amusement parks. The number-one designation, however, goes to Cedar Point's sister park, Kings Island, north of Cincinnati. Both facilities are owned by Sandusky's Cedar Fair Entertainment. One of the largest such operators in the world, Cedar Fair owns other well-known amusement parks throughout the country, including California's Knott's Berry Farm, Michigan Adventure, Virginia's Kings Dominion, as well as the most frequently visited park in North America, Canada's Wonderland.

In a world where we all seek different kinds of thrills, Ohio appeals to traveler interests that cross the divide from symphonic to rock and roll, from discovery to aircraft, from Major League Baseball to NFL football. The Cleveland Orchestra has for decades been considered one of America's "Big Five" and consistently shows up as a top 10 orchestra in worldwide rankings. It plays in venerable Severance Hall, just a few minutes from a shrine to an entirely different genre, the Rock & Roll Hall of Fame and Museum.

Ohio roads will take you to monuments, zoos, museums, conservatories, halls of fame, and commercial tourist traps of every nature. They will even take you to a museum that celebrates a road: The National Road & Zane Grey Museum. The road, US 40, was originally the "National Road," begun in the early 1800s and originally connecting Cumberland, Maryland, on the east to Vandalia, Illinois, on the west. Known informally as the "Main Street of America" US 40 is Broad Street as it goes through the heart of Columbus.

GETTING OFF THE ROAD

Look closely at the Seal of the Great State of Ohio, and it's clear that the state's founding farmers didn't see much more than agriculture in Ohio's future. The seal shows a rising sun over mountains in Ross County, with light rays representing the 13 original colonies. The foreground is of fields with a neat display of freshly cut wheat next to a display of 17 arrows. Some say that the arrows are an homage to Ohio's indigenous peoples and the fact that Ohio was the country's 17th state. Others among us see the display of grown product and hunting tools as symbolic of the basic food groups, vegetables and meat.

Ohio contains 44,825 square miles[7] of diverse terrain, which includes land that farmers regard as some of America's best. It is a compact, densely populated state. Ohio has the highest population density of any of the interior states and a greater density than many East Coast states. Still, for many, the state considers itself more farm than factory. There are approximately 75,000 farms in Ohio.[8]

Glacier-ground limestone makes the state's soil (especially in the western half) particularly rich and productive. Ohio State University economics professor Bill White points out that if you draw a diagonal line from Ashtabula in the northeast to Cincinnati at the southwest corner, everything north and west of that line is almost perfect for agriculture.[9] These ideal conditions include 35 inches of rain per year and up to 10 feet of topsoil with forest or grassland as native cover. The state has the fifth-highest percentage of prime farmland in the country.[10] Prime farmland incidentally is a designation by the US Department of Agriculture, defined as land best suited for producing food, feed, forage, fiber, and oilseed crops. To be considered "prime" farmland, acreage has to have the soil quality, growing season, and moisture supply needed to produce sustained crop yields economically—when it is properly farmed. After all, even the best farmland is useless under the care of an incompetent farmer. It leads in production of a number of American dairy staples, too (number one in Swiss cheese and number two in eggs, for example).

Population density and high percentage of prime farmland are characteristics that seem a little contradictory, but not to Ohioans. The Ohioan who lives in downtown Cleveland can easily be out in the country in Geauga, Lake, or Summit counties within a half hour. And the fact that many Ohioans live in towns smaller than 5,000 or 10,000 people means that population is distributed rather evenly throughout the state. States like New York, Illinois, and California all have larger populations, but those states also have huge majorities concentrated in just a few metropolitan areas. People inside the metro areas tend to stick with urban lifestyles, while those outside live entirely different lives. One lifestyle involves tall buildings, cab rides, and jobs as investment bankers. The other involves farming or factory work, early rising, and high school football on Friday night.

Metropolitan areas have always risen and fallen on the strength of the vital, sexy industries that draw people and money to them. Denver was a boomtown first because of mining. Silicon Valley first drew people because of the appeal of gold and then diversified into a center for trade, finance, and ultimately high technology. The Seattle area's first lure was salmon, long before it became a center for aerospace and software development. Detroit might look bad to anyone who only sees its early twenty-first century auto economy crumbling. But they forget an era 50 years earlier when that same economy made Detroit one of the country's largest cities and metropolitan areas.

Ohio has had its boom cities too, complete with their relative declines. Akron grew on the strength of its tire making and then declined when most of its tire makers moved headquarters or manufacturing operations. Youngstown boomed with the steelmaking industries of nearby Pittsburgh and Cleveland but has been in decline for 40 or more years. Mostly, however, Ohio has always been comfortable covering the basics of human existence. Growing things. And making things.

Ohio's makeup created the ideal environment for companies that take care of the basic necessities of human life. These include famous long-established names like Procter & Gamble. The state has produced hundreds of manufacturers of other products that Americans use daily and find in their supermarkets. These include makers of meat products and processed foods, such as Dayton Veal, American Sugar Refining in Bucyrus, Smucker's Jams and Jellies in Orville, and Sunshine Soybean Products in West Jefferson. Fleishmann's Yeast, breads, and other products got their start in Cincinnati. The state even feeds the front yards of America thanks to the Scotts Miracle-Gro Company, in Marysville, the world's largest lawn and garden care company. Ohio companies have earned renown regionally and nationally for their contributions to the American diet.

Bob Evans Farm Sausage was started by Bob Evans in 1962 and grew to be a regional sausage and restaurant superpower, thanks in part to its homespun, folksy personality branding. Largely built by Bob and his cousin, Dan Evans, the company grew both on the flavor of its sausage recipe and on the style of its owners.[11] Bob Evans's early commercials were always masterpieces of warm

FIGURE 3.2 A Central Ohio farm awaits the coming growing season.

country cinematography combined with celebrations of even the most mundane family gatherings—all based around the company's flagship sausage. Starting as a 12-stool diner, Bob Evans originally served a few Ohio counties close to Gallia County and its seat, Gallipolis. Under the management of Cousin Dan and the undeniable television appeal of Bob's personality, the chain grew steadily throughout the 1960s and '70s, first conquering store shelves throughout Ohio and neighboring states, and then extending farther through warm, home-style restaurants.[12] Like all things that come from the state, the Evans method of growth (particularly in its restaurant operations) was closely tied to the interstate highway system. Almost all the chain's outlets are located at or near exits off the interstates or major US highways. Bob Evans also distributes packaged food products around the country through its BEF Foods subsidiary, which extends the Evans brand to sausage, packaged gravies, potatoes, and numerous other food products.[13]

The Bob Evans story says a lot about how Ohio's residents make the most of their state's natural and man-made assets. Even though corporate headquarters are now located near Columbus, the company is firmly rooted in the small-town values that typify much of the Buckeye State. It maintains a strong presence in Gallipolis, which has a main street worthy of any Rockwell painting and a population engaged in or the beneficiary of a long agricultural tradition. Life revolves around the kitchen or dining room table. Family is essential. And the automobile is the great facilitator.

HOT 'N JUICY ECONOMICS

Another Ohio icon whose success was facilitated in large measure by American mobility is R. David "Dave" Thomas. Born in Atlantic City, New Jersey, Thomas had a difficult childhood, which included the death of his first adoptive mother, multiple stepmothers, and a lot of traveling with his father. Restaurants always provided a respite where he could watch other families enjoy one another's company. Restaurants were a haven. And with this view, Thomas would find himself in the restaurant business for his entire life. Even his Korean War tour of duty involved mess hall and food service work, including supervision and service. Thomas became one of Ohio's best-known and most famous citizens largely by appearing in more than 800 Wendy's commercials from 1989 until his death, in 2002. But his arrival on the national "eating scene" didn't come until his early thirties, when he arrived in Columbus to manage and run several Kentucky Fried Chicken stores. He'd received a financial interest in KFC thanks to his energetic and innovative tenure with the company in Indiana. In the late 1960s his success with the chain left Thomas with the money to start a venture all his own. He based this new business on his conception of what a hamburger should be. In contrast to the methods of McDonalds, he had a very different idea about how burgers should be sold, too. Thomas opted for more comforting, homey interiors with Tiffany-style lamps, newspaper-clipping-covered tabletops, and carpeted interiors.

Wendy's Old-Fashioned Hamburgers was born in an unused auto showroom provided by Thomas's good friend and Columbus auto dealer Len Immke. The first store opened in 1969, its signage bearing the likeness of one of the Thomas daughters, Melinda Lou, who went by the nickname Wendy. The concept caught on quickly. In just a few years the chain was nationwide, challenging perennial fast-food leaders McDonalds and Burger King. Today, Wendy's is part of Wendy's/Arby's Group Inc., now headquartered in Atlanta.

Not only did people like the Hot 'N Juicy hamburgers that were served with the type of toppings they might get at a family picnic or their mom's dining room table, they enjoyed the service provided at Wendy's. Thomas essentially provided made-to-order burgers with the same speed as his rivals, who made their food ahead of time. It was a fresh idea for the era.

Thomas came up with other innovations that would change the face of burgerdom and fast food throughout the country. He is widely credited with creating the "bucket" concept at KFC prior to joining Wendy's. The snaking line in which one cash register is seemingly able to process more people than multiple cash registers at other fast-food restaurants is another of his inventions. Plus, he introduced the idea of salad in a fast-food restaurant—a novel concept for the time.[14]

But forget the homey interiors for a minute. If anyone deserves credit for making fast food even faster, it should be Thomas. To keep up with a populace that likes being in the car, he came up with an idea to link cars and restaurants like never before. Thomas created the service novelty known as the drive-up window or drive-thru in the early 1970s as Wendy's was just getting started. Soon, virtually every Wendy's had a drive-up window. It wasn't long before Burger Kings and McDonalds everywhere had construction crews retrofitting their buildings to add the window.

Today the drive-up window is ubiquitous throughout the US, Canada, and much of the world. Every chain has it. You can get breakfast, lunch, and dinner from a different establishment every day—all without leaving your car. And while this may not be the most appetizing way of living, it reflects Americans' desire for speed, convenience, and simplicity.[15] Any American scrunched between picking up one kid from ballet at 5:30 and getting another to a soccer game by 6:00 should thank Dave Thomas for making dinner possible.

Wendy's might only be a tasty runner-up in the national burger rankings (behind McDonald's and ahead of Burger King), but it is not the first of Ohio's major hamburger chains. That honor belongs to White Castle. White Castle Systems has been a fixture on the American fast-food hamburger landscape since it created the category back in 1921. White Castle invented the concept of serving foods using fast, easily reproducible practices that could be taught and shared store to store. The preparation process was clearly visible to visitors. And people could get their meals in a matter of minutes. It was, as many have observed, an instance in which what Henry Ford did for car production was applied to meal production.[16]

First headquartered in Wichita, Kansas, the chain has called Columbus home since 1933. White Castle has the unusual distinction of being both a staple of mobile American families and a burger with a sort of cult following. A key part of its marketing strategy is promoting its "difference" compared with McDonalds and other fast-food chains. White Castle initially limited itself to middle-sized metropolitan areas in the Midwest, including Columbus, Cincinnati, Louisville, St. Louis, Minneapolis, and several others. Curiously, it only recently invaded nearby Ohio markets like Akron, Toledo, and Cleveland.

There probably isn't a college student in a White Castle market that hasn't topped off a night of drinking and carousing or cured a bad case of the "munchies" with a dozen or so of the mini-burgers affectionately known as "sliders." These burgers have spawned various imitators, from the big fast-food chains themselves to major regional chains that also make small, square, onion-enhanced burgers, such as Chattanooga, Tennessee's Krystal Company, which has essentially taken the same concept into southern markets. Oh, and White Castle has drive-up windows, too.[17]

With more than 250 million cars on the road, America has an almost equal number of miniature rolling dining rooms as well.[18] Yes, eating and driving is as discouraged as texting, playing with your iPad, or talking on a smartphone. But eating and Coke-slurping have a much longer and more established history. While numerous driving fatalities can be tracked to a texting driver, relatively few are blamed on a driver having his fumbling paw in an order of fries or struggling to unwrap a White Castle jalapeño slider. The ability to gobble a meal and drive is something we owe not only to the singular, all-in-one characteristics of the hamburger but to companies like White Castle and Wendy's, whose founders understood from the beginning that their future success was permanently tied to the mobility of consumers. But of course, most people are only driving through to take their meals home to their own dining rooms. Right? Right.

THE FARE AT THE STATE FAIR

Any trip down Interstate 75 or across US 250 reveals a rich landscape and a wide array of beef and dairy cattle, ranging from Guernsey and Holstein to hulking, striking Angus. Ohio's rural air is redolent with the essence of these and assorted other creatures. Sheep, hogs, steer, as well as duck, geese, and chicken: virtually everything that flies, lays eggs, or can be stuffed with bread and celery has a home on a Buckeye State farm.

The biggest regularly scheduled tribute to Ohio agriculture is the Ohio State Fair, which takes place every August. This is and always has been one of America's grandest state fair celebrations, attracting nearly a million people annually—both participants and fairgoers—and generating millions in revenue.[19] It seems that only states with significantly larger geographical areas (Minnesota), larger populations (New York), or both (Texas and California), consistently generate larger state fair attendance. Held at the 360-acre Ohio Exposition Center in Columbus, the fair is practically a mandatory annual pilgrimage for kids and families who live in the mostly rural counties surrounding the city, including Marion, Fairfield, Muskingum, Pickaway, and Morrow. People living in counties farther from the capital show a nearly equal measure of enthusiasm for the event.

One advantage of a centralized fair location and plenty of interstate miles is that it facilitates not only attendance but also the to-and-fro delivery of those prize-winning heifers, emus, 11-pound cantaloupes, and all manner of crafts, ranging from Amish fudge to the winning recipe for Cincinnati Chili sauce, to quilts and period costumes judged superior in imagination, stitching, and attention to detail. The list of booster organizations represented at the fair reads like a *Who's Who* of local governments, civic organizations, and the 4-H, Boy Scouts, Girl Scouts, church groups, and YMCAs of various counties and towns.

And then there are the vendors. The fair midway is American pop-mercantilism all gussied up and on display. You can "win" a six-foot stuffed gorilla or an eight-gram living goldfish that'll be dead before you get home. You can shoot cut-out ducks and tiny basketballs, for prizes and bragging rights. Have your picture taken with cardboard replicas of the super hero of your choice. Get a hot plastic replica of your kid's hand. Or have her face painted to make her look like a tiger. High-cal, carb-rich foods like ribbon fries, Italian sausage, funnel cake, triple-deckers, and a wide variety of sugar-smothered waffles can be purchased and savored with abandon. There are vendors to satisfy every emotional or intestinal impulse at the Ohio State Fair. And while some are native Ohioans, many are just as likely to pack their trailers and be off to Indianapolis, Syracuse, or another state fair site once this event is done, with a stop or two at a local county fair or town carnival along the way.

The state fair has been an institution in Ohio for well over 165 years, giving the state an annual summertime celebration of its success as a grower, producer, innovator, and celebrator of the American experience. First held in Cincinnati in 1850, the fair moved around the state to locations like Dayton, Toledo, and Zanesville for 25 years before finding a permanent home in Columbus in the 1880s.[20]

In those days, the state fair was a grand celebration of Ohio's work, mostly agricultural. Unlike people in many regions, Ohioans have always had an ethic that saw little difference in types or styles of hard work—whether it involved growing things, making things, or selling things. Early-century Ohio industrial titan companies got their starts in life with the chores and values of the Ohio farm, as did a few well-known "immigrant" companies. When American Honda was engaged in selecting a site for its new US plant, the company was drawn not to the ingrained car-building prowess of the unionized Detroit workforce but to the farm boys and girls who populated rural counties of central and southeastern Ohio. Today Honda, with its world headquarters in Tokyo, is Ohio's largest manufacturing employer.[21]

FAST CASH

Of course, the heralding of Wendy's and the drive-thru window misses the fact that living life in the car began way before Wendy's. The simple premise was to see the car as a way to get you what you needed and along the way wherever you were going as soon as possible.

Ohio companies pioneered this convenient mobility much earlier in other forms. Canton's Diebold Corporation, for example,
predicted accurately that post–World War II Americans would be
increasingly tied to their vehicles. To help its banking customer
base gain a competitive edge in this new era, Diebold (now Diebold
Nixdorf) introduced the concept and equipment of the drive-up
banking window in 1947. It was an idea that meant people could
take care of the most basic and most used banking services without
ever stepping out from behind the wheel. It sped service, satisfied
customers, and helped banks improve efficiency. The concept was
so enduring that it remains a staple of retail banking in a form little
changed since the '40s.

In terms of improving banking service and relationships,
Diebold Nixdorf has been indispensable to American culture in
other ways. The company led the ATM revolution in the 1970s and
'80s and has manufactured more than one-third of all ATMS sold
globally. It has created numerous service and product innovations
to cement itself as an essential supplier to the banking industry.[22]

Banking, food, gas—Americans have run on these for decades.
One thing that happened, starting even before the birth of the
interstate system of the 1950s, was the emergence of a new kind
of American mini-town. Known simply as "exits," these mini-
towns exist within anywhere from a few hundred yards to a mile
of a major highway exit. In urban and highly populated suburban
areas, the exit mini-town is often less recognizable than it is in
more rural or less populated areas. But there is a definite culture,
commerce, and familiarity about exits—usually based around getting gas, going to the bathroom, getting money, and eating.

Ohio companies have been built—and fortunes made and lost—
based on the tens of thousands of highway exits across the US. Of
course, many have Bob Evans, Wendy's, or White Castle restaurants, and there are some in the East and Midwest where you can
get all three. Also consider that several prominent service station
chains have their roots in Ohio, including Speedway and Marathon
(not to mention the numerous descendants of Ohio's Standard Oil),
and it's hard not to see the state as critical to that unique American
quasi-municipality called simply the *Exit*.

CHAPTER 4

MOONDOGS AND ROCK HALLS

The story of one of Ohio's best-known destinations begins in the mid-1980s. I worked at an advertising agency in Northeast Ohio during the time that Cleveland was competing vigorously for the Rock & Roll Hall of Fame. Because I was a native, or "near native," to the area, my loyalty was never in question, though I had a hard time with the notion that Cleveland was a shoo-in for the Rock & Roll Hall of Fame. The competition included nationally known cultural meccas like San Francisco and Boston. Cleveland, on the other hand, was the city of burning rivers and baseball's perennially losing Indians. So, it was tough to conceive of it as beating out the others to become ground zero for rock and roll, a musical phenomenon and soundtrack for several American generations.

But, to the surprise of some, Cleveland rocked well enough and persuasively enough for the selection committee to choose it as the permanent home for the rock hall. With that would come potential tourist income and, hopefully, a better kind of recognition. It would be "the mistake on the lake" no more.

The decision was momentous for the area. The advertising agency I worked for at the time, Hesselbart & Mitten in Fairlawn, even paid for a full-page ad congratulating Cleveland on the feat. It said, in simple, bold, gigantic type: YOU'VE ROCKED THE WORLD! The headline was upside down. Pretty clever, I thought.[1]

But it would take years of wrangling, financing wizardry, civic gamesmanship, and controversy to finally get the hall built. Sparing no expense, the powers behind the project agreed on internationally renowned designer and architect I. M. Pei. Apparently, Pei was "not a rock and roll person" and had to spend some time getting a feel for the music before embarking on the project.

In the end, Pei's observation that rock is "all about energy" resulted in a glittering glass pyramid, not unlike some of his other designs in Europe and Asia, but certainly unlike anything in Cleveland or on the shore of any of the Great Lakes. The Rock & Roll Hall of Fame and Museum opened finally on September 1, 1995.[2] It is a shining tribute and monument to the musical art form. There have been 323 inductees admitted since Ray Charles, Elvis Presley, Sam Cook, Buddy Holly, and 13 others entered in the 1986 inaugural ceremony. In all, as of this writing there are more than 750 honorees, inducted either as members of bands, as solo acts, or as important "non-performers" (producer/executive David Geffen, for example). But one pioneering performer is conspicuously absent from the Rock & Roll Hall of Fame.

His name is Wynonie Harris.

STARTING UP THE '50s

Harris had been called a shouter, a practitioner of "jump" music. His sound was a highly charged rhythm and blues (both a precursor and a contemporary of popular rock and roll). Those familiar with both performers say that when it came to portraying sexual energy in a performance, Elvis Presley was simply a tamer version of Wynonie Harris.

In 1947 Harris signed an agreement with a little-known production company, King Records. This would bring him into a small Ohio recording studio in December of that year for a series of songs, one of which was called "Good Rockin' Tonight." Listen to it and you will hear many of the beat and arrangement conventions that would soon infuse the musical releases from names like Chubby Checker, Fats Domino, and others in the first wave of R&B legends from the 1950s. "Good Rockin' Tonight" was also

FIGURE 4.1. The Rock & Roll Hall of Fame in Cleveland.

the first popular hit in which the words *rock* and *rockin'* were used in a context that suggested music and dancing.[3]

"Baby bring my rockin' shoes
because tonight I'm gonna rock away all my blues."
(Source: The song, "Good Rockin' Tonight" by Roy Brown, performed by Wynonie Harris)

You could say that Harris put the rock into the rock and roll equation. It was bass, piano, sax, and percussion along with Harris's boisterous, bluesy enthusiasm. And he had a hit. It was a genuine chart topper in the limited cultural confines of "race" music that was played on radio stations catering to African American audiences and on jukeboxes in the clubs frequented by many— juke joints.

It is unlikely that very many white kids heard this song in its early days, but in June of 1948 the song reached number one on Billboard's charts for jukebox-played records and records sold at retail. Harris spawned numerous imitators who would include *rock* or *rocking* in their titles or lyrics. That his music featured double entendre, sexual edginess, and alcohol references no doubt added to the appeal. Consider some Harris titles: "Lovin' Machines," "Blood-shot Eyes," "Keep on Churnin' ('Til the Butter Comes)," and "I Love My Fanny Brown." The music hinted at rebellion, misbehavior, and sex. This was music that enabled people to say one thing, think another, and share in the enjoyment of the verbal subterfuge. No wonder it caught on.

By the way, King Records and the studio where Harris recorded his hits were located in Cincinnati, Ohio, not Cleveland.

A CULT OF MILLIONS

As for Cleveland, its claim to musical fame could come from many places. No stranger to what Shakespeare called "the food of love," the Cleveland area's ethnic and cultural diversity brought varied sounds from around the country and the world. It is home to a rich musical tradition ranging from popular sounds like the singing of Dean Martin (from Steubenville, Ohio) to the loftiness of the Cleveland Symphony. It had its own soul music tradition anchored in its east side. But rock and roll was really born in many places—blues halls up and down the Mississippi, Harlem jazz clubs, Tennessee honky-tonks, and small recording studios like King Records in Cincinnati. Cleveland, like other northern cities, including Chicago and Philadelphia, had benefited musically from the northern migration of jazz and blues. But despite such broad ancestry, the actual paternity of the entire rock genre is credited to a 29-year-old broadcaster and promoter named Alan Freed.

The birth occurred in an era when the music business was driven by the sale of records: 45s and 33s were selling by the millions, driven primarily by demand from a rising youth culture. Radio, the recording industry, and the musicians had created a triad of profit. Big bands, the blues, and golden-throated crooners like Frank Sinatra, Bing Crosby, and Rosemary Clooney were solid gold. Native Ohioan singer-actors Doris Day and Roy Rogers also caught the public's ear. All of these performers were selling records briskly, but the rising generation of that time—teenagers born in the mid-to-late 1930s—wanted their own music.

That music already existed, of course, in the R&B of Harris and in other interpretations such as Paul Williams's Hucklebuck and the Memphis sound. What Freed did was to make this not just the choice of Cleveland's minority youth but also the music of white kids in places like Pepper Pike, Hudson, and Lakewood, Ohio.

Soon after he joined Cleveland radio station WJW, Freed visited the Cleveland area's biggest music seller, Rendezvous Records, located downtown near Playhouse Square. It was there that he took notice of a fact previously observed by the store's owner, Leo Mintz. Large numbers of white teenagers were showing a high level of interest in race records. They weren't always buying (presumably because they were afraid of parental disapproval), but they were enjoying the sounds they heard in the store's listening booths. The years 1950 and 1951 were part of an era when even musical tastes were segregated, but Mintz convinced Freed and ultimately WJW management to begin a late-night show featuring this edgy race music.[4]

Freed started airing his nightly rock and roll celebration, "The Moondog Show," in 1951 with an idiosyncratic style that became the perfect accompaniment for the music he played. He pounded on a phone book in time to the music, drank and promoted beer, rang a cowbell, and shouted his approval of the music and artists he played. Most of all, he exhibited a sincere, soulful appreciation for the music and for his ever-growing audience.

CROWDED CORONATION

Freed is credited by music historians with being the first to use the term *rock and roll* to broadly describe this emerging form of music. Perhaps just as importantly, he is also known for the world's first rock and roll concert.

Billed as the Moondog Coronation Ball, the event was scheduled for March 21, 1952, at the Cleveland Arena on Euclid Avenue. A fraternity of thousands of late-night-music-loving hipsters, all largely anonymous to one another, would gather to pay tribute to Freed, their "king," and revel in the sounds of their kingdom. Featured acts would include the Rockin' Highlanders, Paul Williams's

Hucklebuckers, the Dominos, and many others. Tickets were $1.50 in advance, $1.75 at the door.

It was an absolute disaster.

The arena, which could hold 10,000 people, was packed to capacity when the doors were finally closed and locked. But people kept showing up, tickets in hand. Thousands were outside clamoring to get inside when the first act, Paul Williams's Hucklebuckers, began playing. The crowd inside, predominantly African American, was surprised to discover that Freed was white. Festivities were cut short when the frustrated outside crowd finally breached the entrance. In swarmed a rush of hundreds of additional people. A riot broke out and police struggled to control the situation. The event ended just as it began, disappointing thousands and becoming one of rock's first scandals.[5]

As in future years, a little scandal proved beneficial to the musical form. Freed and his program became more popular than ever. It spawned imitators in cities everywhere. The sound, born of southern blues, R&B, and infused with the musical playfulness of country and western, was now *rock and roll*. It was no longer the sound of African American youth but the musical passion of young people of all races.

Freed would soon get a national megaphone, moving his show to New York and syndication. But his career didn't move in an entirely upward direction. After a few years he lost his job at WINS in New York. A failed TV show, scandals involving payola, numerous radio firings, and alcoholism were just part of Freed's problems to come. He died in 1965 at the age of 43.

Rock and roll, however, was here to stay. DJs everywhere began playing it. Freed had inspired many imitators, including Dick Clark and *American Bandstand*. The music moved easily into middle- and upper-class neighborhoods. It became the music of Friday and Saturday night dances—the hops. It also continued to connect itself to scandal. Bill Haley and the Comets' famous song "Rock Around the Clock" was the lead-in music for a dark 1956 movie about juvenile delinquency in high schools: *The Blackboard Jungle*. The association was enough for older folks to connect rock with a culturally decaying American youth. Elvis Presley and his gyrating hips came along and caused parents to cover their daughters' eyes.

Then there was Jerry Lee Lewis and his child bride, his 13-year old cousin.

Soon enough the Beatles brought a charming English interpretation that would evolve dramatically over the next six years. There were other British acts, like the Yardbirds and the Rolling Stones. From the west came the Beach Boys and then the Mamas and the Papas. The rest is history. Rock's inherent flexibility and creativity-inspiring energy would see it change over time from the jumping, bluesy style of the '50s to a more guitar- and percussion-based style that would dominate in the '60s and '70s.

There would also come infinite interpretations of the genre, including Motown. The Muscle Shoals influence played well to the voices of Etta James and Aretha Franklin and helped to birth the southern rock of the Allman Brothers and Lynyrd Skynyrd. California would deliver still more musical poetry popularized by artists like Jackson Browne, Linda Ronstadt, and the Eagles. There was disco, punk, heavy metal, and "new wave," and the hyperproduced sounds of the '80s, '90s and beyond.

Rock and roll is like a father with many children, but it all harks back to the youthful notions of freedom, rebellion, and the longing for love that were evident from rock's earliest days. This was the music joyously and tirelessly promoted by Cleveland's Alan Freed and grasped eagerly by a country that was beginning to see itself as forever young.

ROCK AROUND THE STATE

Huey Lewis and the News had a mid-'80s hit that charged musically through a list of cities wherein the artists sang "The heart of rock and roll was still beatin'." The final time through that refrain is followed by a pregnant pause.

Now the old boy may be barely breathing,
but the heart of rock and roll,
heart of rock and roll is still beatin'.' . . .

(PAUSE)

In Cleveland.[6]
(Source: "The Heart of Rock & Roll" by Huey Lewis and the News)

The song then quickly mentions Detroit before instrumentals carry you the rest of the way out. Apparently, the song was originally supposed to be titled "The Heart of Rock & Roll Is in Cleveland," because band members had fond memories of an exceptional concert they had played in the city. And it was released about the time Cleveland was making its play for the world's Rock & Roll Hall of Fame. But even if Cleveland were only vying for an *Ohio* Rock & Roll Hall of Fame, the city and state alone could legitimately fill a large exhibit space. Ohio artists have covered a very wide range of the rock spectrum. The iconic Motown sound of the Isley Brothers began in Cincinnati. The funky-weird sound of Devo is the product of Akron. The unmistakable progressive and harmonious sound of the '70s and '80s band Boston began with a kid from Toledo, Tom Scholz. Here is a sampling of well-known Ohio performers variously defined as rock, pop, Motown, or R&B:

Screamin' Jay Hawkins ("I Put a Spell on You")
Ruby and the Romantics ("Our Day Will Come")
Bo Donaldson and the Heywoods ("Billy Don't Be a Hero")
O'Jays ("Love Train")
The Outsiders ("Time Won't Let Me")
James Gang
The Raspberries ("Go All the Way")
The Ohio Players ("Love Rollercoaster" and "Fire")
Devo
Wild Cherry ("Play That Funky Music")
Eric Carmen (also of the Raspberries)
Isley Brothers
Joe Walsh (James Gang, Eagles, and solo career)
Tom Scholz (founder and leader of Boston)
Chrissy Hynde (founder and lead singer of the Pretenders)
Marilyn Manson
Michael Stanley Band
Macy Gray
Boz Scaggs

Benjamin Orr (bassist for The Cars)
John Legend

Ohio has also given birth to country acts with wide crossover appeal. You probably know of Pure Prairie League, Rascal Flatts, and Johnny Paycheck (best known for "Take This Job and Shove It").[7]

One example of the enduring presence of rock in Ohio can be found in its radio stations. Stations I listened to years ago, including WIOT Toledo, WMMS Cleveland, and WLVQ (QFM 96) Columbus, are still playing the same music they were in the mid-'70s and still drawing listenership that keeps them near the top of their markets' ratings charts. It's been amazing permanence for a music genre that my grandfathers thought (and hoped) would soon fade away.

If not their actual birthplace, Ohio has helped launch many famous music acts, particularly in the Cleveland area. A major concert destination since the first Moondog Coronation Ball, Cleveland was the site of David Bowie's first US appearance and Otis Redding's last performance before his death. Elvis Presley played some of his earliest northern concerts in Cleveland. At the start of their journey to worldwide stardom, Bruce Springsteen and the E Street Band played no fewer than 10 northern Ohio concert dates during 1974 and 1975. Meat Loaf's "Bat out of Hell" first took flight via Cleveland International Records.

ICONICALLY CLEVELAND

Some of the country's most familiar, popularized sounds have their roots in Ohio. Listen to the Isley Brothers' "That Lady" or the O'Jays' "Love Train" and you hear a clear bridge from rock's early R&B roots to popular nightclub sounds of the '70s and '80s. "Love Train" is familiar to middle-aged and older Americans as a song they danced to in their youth as well as to their kids, who know it as a backdrop to Coors Light commercials.

The lyrics to the Pretenders' "My City Was Gone" might not be known to many, but a 20-second instrumental opener to the song will be familiar to the 20 to 25 million who regularly tune in to the Rush Limbaugh radio show. The song was written to reflect Chrissy Hynde's frustration over the decay of her hometown, Akron. While most radio shows change their intros regularly, Limbaugh has been conservative in keeping with the Pretenders opener for three decades. The Pretenders are best known for the mid-'80s hits "Back on the Chain Gang," "Middle of the Road," and "I'll Stand by You."

The movie *Dirty Dancing* spawned a number of top hits including Clevelander Eric Carmen's "Hungry Eyes." Carmen is also familiar through '80s songs like "Make Me Lose Control" or '70s songs like the Raspberries' "All the Way."

Cleveland and Ohio have some sounds they've been able to keep for themselves. The Michael Stanley Band, for example, received incredible airplay and concert attendance throughout the state in its heyday from the late 1970s to the late 1980s. Songs like "He Can't Love You," "Lover," and "Heartland" became regional anthems that I assumed were playing everywhere. Then I moved to upstate New York, where hardly anyone had heard of the band. So, one way to verify the authenticity of someone's claim to being an Ohioan is to ask him or her to name a favorite MSB song.[8]

One of the most iconically Cleveland songs wasn't even written or performed by a Clevelander, or even an American for that matter. "Cleveland Rocks" is the product of British musician Ian Hunter (formerly of Mott the Hoople). As if to completely package the whole rocking Cleveland experience, the song begins with a brief clip of Alan Freed introducing his radio show. And it culminates in a repeating echo of the word "Ohio." For many years a cover version of the song was also the musical lead-in to *The Drew Carey Show*. Hunter, also well known as the vocalist behind "All the Young Dudes," gives a particularly compelling rendition, owing partly to his Shropshire accent and the grittiness of his vocalization:

Mama knows but she don't care
She's got her worries too
Seven kids and a phony affair
And the rent is due

All the little chicks with their crimson lips
Go "Cleveland rocks, Cleveland rocks!"

Livin' in sin with a safety pin
Goin'
Cleveland rocks, Cleveland rocks!
Cleveland rocks, Cleveland rocks![9]
(Source: "Cleveland Rocks" by Ian Hunter)

"Cleveland Rocks" is the unofficial anthem of the city, surrounding suburbs, and almost all Cleveland-area sports teams.[10] It's a celebration of urban turmoil and the energy to get through it all, just like this music has always been. "Cleveland Rocks" is shouting, jumpy, and bluesy. And just like the songs Wynonie Harris introduced the country to in the late '40s, it makes for "good rockin'" wherever it is played.

CHAPTER 5

HARRIET AND
THE GENERALS

Almost every moderately well-educated American knows that the US was once divided geographically, north from south, by the Mason–Dixon line. The line actually begins and ends with the Pennsylvania–Maryland border. Once Pennsylvania's southern border disappears, the physical divide takes the form of the Ohio River. Though the river starts inside Pennsylvania, its political function was to separate the northern states of Ohio, Indiana, and Illinois from Virginia (West Virginia) and then Kentucky. All of which means that at the country's narrowest point, the state of Ohio *was* the American North—smack dab between the Canadian border that bisected Lake Erie and the Kentucky border in the middle of the Ohio River.

Ohio has always been a sliver of north that was close to the south, geographically and sentimentally. Mount Vernon, Ohio, was home to Daniel Decatur Emmett, famous for the Southern folk anthem "Dixie," first published as "I Wish I Was in Dixie's Land." The song was written by Emmett while he was in New York in 1859.[1] Note also that Mount Vernon is not far from where abolitionist John Brown first pledged himself to a fervent, unrelenting campaign against slavery while attending an Akron church service.

Northern language characteristics, culture, mercantilism, and slavery-free economic values flowed from west to east, funneled through Ohio. Sometimes families would stay for a generation or two in a slow progression toward the west. Generations that didn't remain in Ohio took their values to Indiana, Illinois, Michigan, Wisconsin, and beyond. The North–South division and questions over the future of our national character defined the country long before the start of the Civil War in 1861. That war remains the most transformative event in US history. Transformative and bloody. Originally called the "the rebellion" by Northerners,[2] the war kept the US from splitting into two separate countries. At the same time, it preserved long-standing divisions that would continue for another whole century.

Both sides seemed to have been prodding each other toward the Civil War since the early part of the nineteenth century, even though everyone dreaded the thought. Avoiding war gave jobs to politicians from every state for many, many years. Ultimately, the war put to an end the question of slavery, but it amped up, perhaps permanently, the notion of how different social and economic classes would coexist in the US.

The war also took my great-great-grandfather, Charles Roahr. Before he died, one of his letters home to his wife asked her to tell his father that guns were firing not sausages but "lead and iron bullets that did make rough music."[3] One can only speculate about the origins of this discussion. Perhaps Charles's father, in previous correspondence, had referred to some benign German war in the family's past.

A PECULIAR INSTITUTION,
SEEN FROM THE QUEEN CITY

One thing that Northerners knew at the middle part of the nineteenth century is that they did not like the way the South was dealing with its black population. Most Northerners hated slavery. The other thing that Northerners knew is that they also didn't like the idea of the whole black population itself. Harriet Beecher Stowe wonderfully captured the national ambivalence related to slavery and the African American population in her 1852 novel, *Uncle Tom's Cabin; or, Life among the Lowly*. Stowe, a daughter

FIGURE 5.1. Cincinnati gave Harriet Beecher Stowe a unique vantage point from which to study the problem of slavery. Courtesy of the Ohio History Connection (AL04184.tif).

of abolitionist Lyman Beecher and sister of Henry Ward Beecher, spent her formative years in Cincinnati, where she got up close and personal with the practice her family had so ardently campaigned to end. Cincinnati is where she met her husband, a professor at the Lane Theological Seminary, where her father also worked. Cincinnati is where she learned firsthand about the horrors and abuses of the slave system from both fugitive slaves and those active in the Underground Railroad.

Part of Stowe's account includes the story of Eliza, a slave woman desperately fleeing Kentucky by walking across the thawing Ohio River with her young son in her arms. That account was inspired by a story told to Stowe by Reverend John Rankin, one of Ohio's best-known abolitionists. Rankin's home on the Ohio River provided an ideal gateway to the freedom offered by the Underground Railroad. The white participants in this network spoke in modern railroad terminology, using words like *stops, sta-tions, schedules,* and *cargo* so that their talk wouldn't reveal them as transporting and hiding slaves. More than 2,000 fleeing slaves made it safely to freedom with Rankin's Ripley home as their first "station."[4]

Stowe observed the attitudes she saw expressed about race and communicated them through her widely read book. It is said that Stowe's time in Cincinnati afforded her the opportunity to inter-view people on all sides of the issue—white and black, Northern and Southern.[5] The book also presents differing sides of the slav-ery debate. Though it is decidedly antislavery, Stowe's tale never-theless takes plenty of shots at Northern attitudes about race as well. In one memorable scene, a woman from Vermont is visit-ing her Southern cousins. Along with her luggage, she carries the prevailing Northern disdain at the idea of slavery. But even more revolting to the proper Vermonter is the notion that her plantation cousins touch, hug, and kiss their slaves as though they were fam-ily members.[6] In the final analysis, *Uncle Tom's Cabin* is as much about healing, forgiveness, and the power of Christian prayer as it is about the ills of slavery. It found a ready and receptive audience in nineteenth-century America and is said to have helped flame the passions that would lead to war.

Uncle Tom's Cabin was a remarkable phenomenon in its day— part news, part pop culture event, part political awakening. It cap-tured the country's attention in a way that may not be achievable today, when attention spans are split between so many different directions and so many different media. Stowe's book became the second-best-selling book of the nineteenth century, after the Bible.[7]

Surprisingly, it is one of the most misunderstood—and prob-ably least read—books of the modern era. That fact is evident in the way *Uncle Tom* is misused as a metaphor for an obsequious black man, one thought to be appropriated by white culture. Any-one who's read the book knows that Tom was a rock: true and sup-portive to friends of both races and willing to lay down his life in defiance of "the man" when the man was truly evil. Stowe herself would probably consider it a compliment for someone to be called an "Uncle Tom."

Slavery also imprisoned the South in an almost feudal "work avoidance" culture for generations. That is an issue that French diplomat and historian Alexis de Tocqueville saw from a unique, economic perspective. He noted the contrast between the two banks of the Ohio River in the early 1830s:

> On the left bank [Kentucky] of the river the population is sparse; from time to time one sees a troop of slaves loitering though half deserted fields; the primeval forest is constantly reappearing; one might say that society had gone to sleep; it is nature that seems active and alive, whereas man is idle.
>
> But on the right bank [Ohio] a confused hum proclaims from afar that men are busily at work; fine crops cover the fields; elegant dwellings testify to the taste and industry of the workers; on all sides there is evidence of comfort; man appears rich and contented; he works.[8]
>
> (From Alexis de Tocqueville's *Democracy in America*)

Slave owners looked down on labor as being the chore and responsibility of their slaves. Most believed that the "gentlemanly" way to live was in pursuit of reading, hunting, and other forms of leisure. Many poor Southern whites absorbed this attitude, too, seeing hard work as the business (or the problem) of slaves. The term *free labor* means essentially that free men are able to sell their skills freely to whomever they wish. It was becoming the driving ethic of the time. All but perhaps the Southern merchant class failed to understand what free labor was achieving in the North. They didn't hear the "hum" described by Tocqueville.

WITHOUT OHIOANS, WHERE WOULD WE BE NOW?

Geographic importance is mentioned throughout this book, but it is particularly noteworthy in understanding the War between the States. Ohio, because of its location, provided the routes by which real slaves and the fictional slaves of *Uncle Tom's Cabin* fled to the safety of Canada. It was also the essential gateway between the eastern Union states and those in the west throughout the Civil War. Later, in Republican and Democratic party politics, there were those in the East who feared their fellow partisans from the West, and vice versa. Ohio—and Indiana to a lesser extent—was an ideal state for compromise candidates during a time when regional self-interest was a primary political driver.

Even at the time of the Civil War, Ohio was quickly becoming the heart of America's growing industrial might, producing everything from soap to wagon wheels, barrels, tractors, tools, and artillery. My great-great-grandfather was hard at work in Petersburg, Ohio, as a cooper (barrel maker) before joining the Union cause with the 105th Ohio Volunteer Infantry in 1862. Ohio delivered impressive numbers of volunteers for the Union either as regular army or as militia. It also produced military leaders perhaps at a number better than any other state, including Virginia, with its contributions to the Confederate Army. Among the state's contributions to the military history of the Civil War were, of course, U. S. Grant, plus William S. Rosecrans, Phillip Sheridan, and William Tecumseh Sherman. Rosecrans was distinguished for his command of the Army of the Cumberland up to and through the Battle of Chickamauga.

Rosecrans, although a Democrat and Catholic, was so highly regarded that at one time he was considered a possible 1864 running mate for Lincoln. Sheridan was one of the youngest and certainly most diminutive of the Union generals. At a little over five feet tall and only in his early thirties, the Somerset, Ohio, native impressed U. S. Grant so much in western campaigns that he was transferred to command of the Army of the Potomac late in the war. There, head-to-head with Lee's forces, Sheridan erased a long record of Northern failures in the Virginia theaters as his men laid waste to Confederate armies in the Shenandoah Valley and campaigns leading to Lee's Surrender at Appomattox. Sheridan's life was not without controversy.[9] His efforts in the Shenandoah campaigns had been criticized as harsh, as were some of his efforts in western Indian campaigns after the war. He is, however, also widely recognized as being key to the preservation and establishment of Yellowstone, the first national park, during the Hayes administration.[10]

Then there is Sherman. He, of course, is best known for the sacking of Atlanta and the infamous March to the Sea. Those events are not his only claim to fame. He distinguished himself earlier in the war in service to Grant at Vicksburg and elsewhere in Mississippi, leading up to the destruction of Confederate forces in Tennessee.[11]

Sherman and Sheridan are memorialized along with Grant as the most important Union generals. There have been numerous stamps and other official recognitions featuring the three. Sherman is said to be the inventor of "total war," a concept that acknowledges the idea that breaking the spirit of the civilian population (or those in safe areas) is as important as defeating armies on the battlefield.[12] In breaking those spirits, his troops inflicted more than $100 million in damage on the South—in 1860s dollars.[13] In many ways, the notion that war between armies is connected strongly to the sentiments of civilian populations was born with Sherman.

Ohio's Civil War military honed five US presidents. Grant, who stood at the head of Lincoln's army at the war's conclusion, is the highest-ranking and first-serving of these. Known as a hard-driving, hard-drinking general, Grant succeeded where numerous others failed. Once Grant took complete command of the Union forces, it was only a matter of time before the "rebellion" was crushed.[14] When he became president three years later, Grant was enormously popular early on, even drawing converts to the Republican Party in the formerly adversarial South.

Ohio provided other presidents with military credentials, too. Rutherford B. Hayes, who served as president immediately after Grant, was a brevet major general ("brevet" meaning that the appointment did not include the pay or permanence of a fully commissioned major general). James Garfield also achieved the rank of major general.[15] Benjamin Harrison, born in Ohio but an Indianan much of his life, was a brigadier general. William McKinley, who was considerably younger than the previously mentioned and who served as a mere captain, nevertheless saw combat at some of the war's most notable battles, including the Battle of Antietam. McKinley actually served under and was promoted by Hayes.

These Ohio-born presidents all played roles in the greatest, deadliest human drama ever to take place on the North American continent. And that was an important "résumé enhancement" (to use a twenty-first-century term) for the politics of their era. The war was a defining life experience for them. Their participation ensured that they would always have something in common with the largest, most powerful part of the American electorate at a time when the country was getting over the war and getting on with business.

   Before the Civil War, relatively few American presidents had military experience, Washington being a major exception. Others, like Lincoln, had relatively minor experience in uniform. But after the Civil War and a long succession of Ohioans with substantial experience in that war, the country began a long tradition of demanding or at the very least applauding the military credentials of its commanders-in-chief. Presidents of that time also certainly needed to be from the North, and Ohio was a perfect northern state, centrally located, at a proper distance from the East, close to the deeper Midwest, and just a train ride away from the rest of the country. When Ohioans weren't serving as president during the 60 years following the Civil War, they were running for it. One little noticed streak is that Ohioans were on Republican or Democratic presidential tickets in 11 of 13 races between 1868 and 1920. This includes Ohio-born Democrat Thomas Hendricks, who served as Grover Cleveland's first vice president.

   Let us turn again to Mrs. Stowe for a moment. An often repeated but unconfirmed story holds that a bemused President Lincoln once met the author and said, "So this is the little lady who started this great war."[16] Other than a few raids from the Confederate Cavalry's General John Hunt Morgan, Ohio's role in the war was in troops, supplies, and support facilities. But Ohioans played key roles before, during, and after the country's bloodiest conflict. Grant, Sherman, and Sheridan ended what Mrs. Stowe "started," and Ohioan presidents carried the momentum forward.

CHAPTER 6

PORKOPOLIS

Ohioans have always known how to get the most out of an acre of land. And how to use an animal—dead or alive—for all its worth. One of the most noteworthy examples of agricultural product meeting commercial success relates to the magic of rendered animal fat. More specifically, it is the story of candle maker William Procter, an English immigrant, Irish soap maker James Gamble, and the Norris sisters, who brought them together. In Ohio.

Today, this fortuitous union is reflected in almost every mass merchandiser, grocery store, drug or convenience store in the country. Indeed, it is entirely possible that there isn't a single soul on the planet who hasn't eaten, shaved, showered, shampooed, or "gone potty" without the help of Cincinnati's Procter & Gamble. Easily the world's largest consumer products company, P&G brands are almost always the number-one player in their respective categories—true of everything from Crest toothpaste to Tide laundry detergent, Gillette razor blades, Downy and Bounce fabric softeners, Always maxi pads, Head & Shoulders shampoo, and Puffs tissues. P&G makes and sells hundreds of different brands, from Febreze air freshener for your teenage son's smelly closet to Old Spice deodorant for the boy himself. Some names, like Pepto-Bismol, were purchased from other companies, but most began with P&G and have been with us for quite a few years. P&G brands sell well everywhere from Vienna, Ohio, to Ho Chi Minh

FIGURE 6.1. Cincinnati as seen from Covington, Kentucky.

City, Vietnam. P&G's worldwide workforce numbers 100,000. That figure is truly worldwide, with the company doing business in almost every country on the planet.

The company's image in its state and across the country has always been conservative, even stodgy. Even so, it has been a marketing powerhouse for generations. Its early adoption of market segmentation strategies gives it not only the leading brand in many product categories but often the number-two and number-three brands as well. For example, walk down a supermarket aisle, and you'll see the names Dawn, Cascade, Pampers, and Charmin. And if these are the only brands you see in your store, just consider what it means that P&G owns them all.

Of course, P&G has also had a fair share of product failures, but the more than 180-year-old company's story has largely been of one success building on success. It all began with Messrs. Procter & Gamble being in the right place at the right time. Cincinnati was that place.

THIS TALLOWED GROUND

Born initially of post-Revolution land speculation activities, the town was originally called Losantiville. Later, the name Cincinnati was adopted to honor both the Roman warrior Cincinnatus and the Order of Cincinnati, a Revolutionary War veterans' organization. Cincinnati is set near the point where the winding Licking River empties into the Ohio River. In its early days spanning the 1780s and '90s, Cincinnati was a relatively lawless, rough-and-tumble town. By the 1820s it had grown to a city of over 10,000. Year after year, the town became more and more impressive. In the 1830s it was one of the great boomtowns in what was then the "west." A large German population settling along the Miami and Erie Canal referred to that waterway in an ironically homesick way as "the Rhine." They designated their neighborhood as "Over-the-Rhine." Today "OTR" is significant as one of the nation's largest, intact urban historic districts, notable for its residential and industrial architecture from an era when beer brewing helped fuel the city's growth.

Cincinnati was strategically located on ideal ground at a midpoint of the Ohio River, with rail and canal connections to hundreds of points throughout Ohio, Indiana, Illinois, and the South. It became a mecca for immigrants and enterprising young men who'd moved west to escape problems or seek opportunity. Cincinnati drew westward-bound adventurers looking to lodge for a few days and speculators eager to turn a fast buck. Hardworking but haggard Europeans simply too tired to go farther would stop in Cincinnati for a couple of days or the rest of their lives. By far the largest influx of Cincinnati immigrants came from the armies of desperate laborers who could and would change their lives and prospects. And by the time of the Civil War, Cincinnati would be the premier "western" city, with over 160,000 people.

The partners, Procter and Gamble, found success in no small measure because of Cincinnati's location. It was not only Ohio's largest and fastest-growing city but also the commercial gateway to the rest of Ohio and the Mississippi. Before the Civil War, Cincinnati was a major point in southern trade as well. Along with the rivers, Cincinnati's manufacturing and commercial interests were fed by a vast network of canals such as the Miami and Erie and the country's growing rail system. Accessible transportation made Cincinnati a nexus for many young and growing companies.

Slaughtering houses abounded, too. Pigs were skinned at hundreds of places near where the Cincinnati Bengals now engage in pigskin pursuits on autumn Sundays. Those pigs were packed and prepared for shipping across the country at places throughout the city. And with the butchering trades came the valuable rendering facilities that made sure no good animal fat went to waste. Rendered fat, of course, was a key ingredient in both soap and candles. The young entrepreneurs could rely on a plentiful, easy, affordable supply from local vendors as well as from those as far away as Chicago, St. Louis, and even New Orleans.[1] It is said that the routine efficiency of these slaughtering and disassembly lines, which could process hundreds of thousands of hogs per year, would one day become the inspiration for Henry Ford's automobile *assembly* lines.

Hogs were part of the city's landscape for decades. During much of the nineteenth century, the animals could be seen being driven through the streets. And many wandered freely. In his diary, a young man named Cyrus Bradley visited Cincinnati and observed the omnipresence of its porky inhabitants: "The very gutters are congested with them, as the dull monotony of pigs is visible everywhere."[2] Even the best of Cincinnati's neighborhoods were infested with the meat of the city's success.[3] Dayton Street, home of some of the richest of Cincinnati's nineteenth-century millionaires, still stands today. Its bold and complete system of wrought-iron fences is a visual monument to an era when homeowners wanted to keep pigs out of their yards and gardens and away from their houses.

It all began with the first local pork packer, Richard Fosdick, who in 1810 developed methods for successfully curing and packing pork in a way that would keep the meat sound for long-term storage and shipping. During three months beginning in 1826, productivity had grown to the point where 40,000 hogs were slaughtered and packed. Pork production created a relatively efficient way to convert vegetation to protein.[4] Southern Ohio was a great place for all that to happen. Annual production would remain in the hundreds of thousands for decades. In 1860 a *London Times* reporter noted:

> It was Cincinnati that originated and perfected the system which packs fifteen bushels of corn into a pig and packs that pig into a barrel, and sends him over the mountains and over the ocean to feed mankind.[5]

This was the Cincinnati that awaited the young Procter and equally young Gamble. Procter had come to the US in the 1820s after his English woolens shop was destroyed by fire and burglary. After a brief period working as a candle maker in New York, Procter and his first wife, Martha, moved west in search of new frontier opportunities. Cincinnati was not their destination but was rather an emergency stop precipitated by Martha's illness. She would die there of cholera.

Gamble, born in Ireland, had established his soap business in Cincinnati in 1826. Mr. Procter and Mr. Gamble met one another because they courted and married the Norris sisters. Company legend suggests that along with Elizabeth and Olivia, the girls' father, Alexander Norris, was the catalyst in the men's friendship and ultimate partnership. His recommendation was based on the fact that both candle making and soap making required large quantities of lye and meat products (fat) and that the two could save significant money by pooling their resources and purchasing power.

The Procter & Gamble Company opened for business in 1837, at a location near the Ohio River as well as major rail lines. Location and opportunity came together beautifully for the two. Nearby water and rail transit facilitated lye shipments as well as shipments of rendered meat fat from places up and down the bustling Ohio River. Mr. Procter and Mr. Gamble were soon thick in the fat themselves. By 1859 Procter & Gamble had used lye and animal fat so effectively that the once struggling candle maker and soap maker now employed more than 80 people. The company's sales also exceeded $1 million for the first time—a stunning figure in 1860, just before the Civil War.[6]

By this time, Cincinnati had gained the nickname "Porkopolis" because of its substantial and prosperous hog-butchering business. Nowadays, the city embraces another, more flattering nickname, the Queen City, but so do dozens of other American cities, including Buffalo, New York, and Charlotte, North Carolina. No one is fighting Cincinnati over the "Porkopolis" moniker.

CHAPTER 7

THE SOAP THAT FLOATS

If war was good for arms makers, it was also very, very good for the soap and candle business. During the Civil War (1861–65), Procter & Gamble won generous Union contracts to supply the armies of the North with soap. The company's location at one of the southernmost points in the nonslave North put it in an ideal position to distribute its products. Martial law was declared in Cincinnati—a town in which a significant portion of the population held pro-Confederacy sentiments. However, Procter & Gamble's soap- and candle-making capability was considered so vital to the Union cause that its plant was allowed to remain open.[1]

Ultimately, the war delivered an incredibly valuable marketing opportunity for the company. Whether intended or not, the conflict between North and South also begat the modern era of branding.

THE MOON AND THE STARS

Illiteracy was common throughout the general population. So, to distinguish its products and shipments, Procter & Gamble developed and imprinted its recognizable "stars & moon" logo to aid buyers of its Stars brand soap in the 1850s. During wartime, P&G benefited from widespread distribution of the product to soldiers

FIGURE 7.1. An Ivory Soap package from the 1940s.
Procter & Gamble's "moon and stars" logo was a more
prominent feature of brand packaging in that era.

who were then using the company's candles for nighttime illumination at a time well before electricity was used for lighting.

Eventually kerosene and gas lighting—and then electricity a few short years later—would reduce Procter & Gamble's candle business to nearly nothing. The company's core product quickly went from a household mainstay to a quaint, occasionally used item. Not good news for a company that was used to turning tallow and lard into sales and profits. But Procter & Gamble proved its resiliency by developing into an even more aggressive competitor in the soap market. It learned to anticipate and adapt to change.

That ability is critical. Any business era is littered with the names of companies who went from "great to gone," primarily because they failed to adjust themselves to changing consumer tastes, technological shifts, or other forces that prove more powerful than even the best green-eyeshade managers can manage. For Procter & Gamble, the answer to the future would come again from the fruit of agrarian innovation and industry. By the 1870s and '80s, P&G had become much more studied and scientific in its approach to every aspect of business. Then, under the leadership of a second generation of Procters and Gambles, the company was hiring chemists to help improve products and processes.

Early research led the company to greater reliance on vegetable oils for its products, which had once been based solely on animal by-products. Not only did this help the company with materials expenses, it also proved more cost effective in the long run. In 1878 the company brought out the pure but unimaginatively named White Soap. The name didn't last long, but the product has continued for well over 130 years. Soon after its introduction, the product was renamed "Ivory."

The story of Ivory began a corporate culture that would make Procter & Gamble one of the most research-driven companies in history. Research would permeate every operational area, from the way P&G developed and manufactured products to marketing, sales, and continuous innovation. It would be P&G's driving ethic for many generations, making it a virtually unbeatable competitive force.

Then, as today, a bar of Ivory does more than get little Johnny clean. The soap's floating characteristic makes it a bit of a play toy as well. Any Cub Scout who has carved Ivory into canoes, ducks, or other floating creatures should appreciate the mistake of a P&G employee in 1890. The story says that a worker accidentally left a mixing machine on before going to lunch. This in turn caused more air than normal to be whipped into the mixture. Combined with a vegetable oil base that already made Ivory light in weight, the product had surprising in-water buoyancy. The floating characteristic wasn't discovered until customers who'd bought bars from the over-whipped batch contacted the company. But instead of complaining about the soap that floated, they wanted more of it.[2]

P&G had a hit. And that product differentiation exists to this day, with Ivory still one of the most revered P&G brands. Procter & Gamble has followed Ivory with thousands of products. Many have been blockbusters, permanently on the scene of American commerce. Brands like Tide changed the way people did laundry. More recently, the Swiffer has revolutionized the way people clean and dust. Of course, Procter & Gamble has produced its share of duds, too. One of the most famous flops was Olestra, a synthetic substitute for fat. Olestra was accidentally discovered in 1968 by P&G researchers investigating fats that could be more easily digested by premature infants. It was introduced to the public in the late '90s with much fanfare, predicted to be a future substitute for fat in all kinds of foods, from staples of the American table to chips and snack cakes. The product never caught on with the consuming public due to documented and reported digestive difficulties among some. So, ironically, more than a century and a half after making it big in fat, P&G's biggest flop was in fat substitutes.

THE BIRTH OF MODERN MARKETING

P&G has done so many things right that it gets credit for creating many long-accepted practices in marketing. It was the first to engage in long-term, wide-scale national brand advertising for a specific product. The $11,000 that its board approved for advertising Ivory Soap was an investment in an era when print advertising for consumer products was largely viewed as a suspicious activity undertaken by soulless hucksters. Dr. Goode and other phony miracle cures come to mind. Today, P&G spends millions annually for its Ivory Brand products. How many other companies spend so much on a brand that goes back more than 130 years? However, the company is not averse to changing with the times. Even as it continues to support the brand, P&G is said to be considering a sale of the Ivory line-up of products in an effort to focus on stronger competitors.[3]

Procter & Gamble's success at using consumer advertising to build trial, acceptance, and loyalty for specific brands is the stuff of marketing legend. Back in the early part of the twentieth century, most companies considered themselves makers of products first and foremost. This "build it first and then find a way to sell it" mentality was still prevalent. P&G was moving toward a different viewpoint and a more innovative approach even then. It decided that it was not primarily a product *manufacturer* but a *marketer* of brands. With this viewpoint came an organization to manage the individual brands as distinct and separate businesses.

If you dislike telephone or shopping mall surveys, you can probably blame Procter & Gamble. But if you have a favorite soap opera, you also have P&G to thank. It was the first company to engage in market research. A desire to build a loyal customer base for its growing line of soap products drove the company's early investments in the new medium of radio during the 1930s. When P&G introduced its first soap opera, *Ma Perkins,* it realized it had discovered a way to uniquely tie the entertainment of a primarily female audience with the products to make their lives easier. The combination proved powerful. Naturally, the approach was expanded by P&G and imitated by competitors. Regular, serialized dramas—tales of elusive love and ever-present woe—would remain a daytime staple and elements would work their way into evening entertainment. The genre has survived nearly 90 years, morphing naturally from radio to television—the first successful TV adaptation being the 15-minute *Search for Tomorrow* in 1951. One constant has been the continuing presence of household products—including soap—as sponsors.[4]

Whether it identified the philosophy as such, P&G had taken steps toward becoming the country's first large consumer-driven, marketing-oriented company. It was building a business around the notion that the best way to grow is to thoroughly know and understand customers and then create products, brands, and strategies designed to meet their needs.

Of course, plenty of people see evil in the consumerist approach to life, just as misguided zealots saw occult symbolism in P&G's ancient moon and stars logo.[5] Anyone who might malign the notion of marketing and consumerism, hate "Mr. Whipple," or cling to the notion that everything that contaminates waterways or landfills was originally conceived in a P&G lab has to look at the most important parts of the Procter & Gamble story. They should also try to remember life before Pampers or fluoridated Crest.

One way to look at P&G and its focus on products for the home is as a sort of "handmaiden" to the progress of the Industrial Revolution. People needed effective, convenient ways to keep their daily toils off what was hoped could be a clean, enjoyable home life. Anything that could simplify life and bring convenience to Mom was sure to be warmly received.

Tide detergent is an example. This product significantly improved cleaning performance and reduced the time that Americans—mostly women—were required to spend on laundry chores. Take a mental trip back to the laundry room of the 1920s and '30s, and you'll find antiquated machines and curiosities like wringing

FIGURE 7.2. Procter & Gamble's unique two-tower headquarters in Cincinnati.

wheels. You'll also find that there was nothing like Tide liquid or dry detergent but rather something called simply soap flakes, made by P&G and a host of other companies.

These flakes were barely more effective than plain old water. Washing may have helped to separate dirt from fabric but it also let the same dirt settle elsewhere in the load. Tide began as a secret man-hour-intensive effort known as Product X. At first the effort failed and the team disbanded, but one participant continued to work on Product X, unbeknownst to P&G management. And from this secretive continuation of an abandoned company project, Tide was born, in 1947. Tide's two-part concept (revised and improved countless times over the last 70 years) lifts the dirt out and then keeps it suspended in the wash water, unable to settle on another fabric.

Water, soap, and problem solving remain central to the P&G mission. P&G remains obsessed with perfecting Tide many decades after introducing the brand. Each year the company tests the product by doing over 50,000 loads of laundry with water from all over the country so that Tide's performance can be evaluated against the mineral content of different municipalities' water. Today, Tide (and its imitators) makes detergent products to meet every need for convenience, from powder to liquid to a new variety that combines detergent plus stain remover plus brightener in tiny one-ounce pods.[6]

Procter & Gamble's corporate heart remains firmly implanted in Cincinnati, where its headquarters are two adjoining towers, each flanked by long flat buildings. These buildings are said to represent a gateway to the Queen City. Over more than 17 decades, P&G has been part of the Cincinnati economy. The benefits provided to the people and culture of the area have been enormous.

P&G-driven innovations extend well beyond commerce. In 1915 one of the founders' sons, James N. Gamble, created the first community-wide charitable program to coordinate fund-raising and share proceeds among member charities. The early effort was known as the Community Chest (remember the Monopoly card?). Today it is known throughout Cincinnati and the rest of the country as the United Way.

CHANGING TIDES

Today, the company retains its long-standing position as the world's largest consumer products company, with reach that extends from the most advanced countries to those that are underdeveloped or emerging. The universal desire for convenience and cleanliness that has created demand for its products comes with a price, however. Competition demands growth and economy of scale, something the company has pursued aggressively.

Because its products are universally accepted, P&G's status as a global company means that it can suffer greatly when emerging countries' economies teeter or when the dollar gains significant strength against international currencies. This has been the case recently, as P&G has been experiencing declining earnings and a decreasing stock value.[7] Such challenges and a huge portfolio of brands are at the heart of management's efforts to pare its product roster. Being a global company means that the world can affect your fortunes. Still, you can be pretty sure that somewhere P&G has a team of researchers working on a solution to that basic fact of life.

CHAPTER 8

RUTHLESS

It is one of those words that is almost always bad. Except when it's associated with the concepts of sports teams or business efficiency. And because of the latter, *ruthless* is the perfect way to describe the first of America's late nineteenth-century "robber barons": John D. Rockefeller.

Born in 1839, Rockefeller lived nearly a full century, dying in 1937. His lifetime seems perfectly timed to the ages of exploding industry and emergence of the automobile—developments he influenced enormously and profited from handsomely. He was a disciplined, efficient, Baptist bean-counter. The legacy he left includes descendants who themselves made huge impacts in industry, politics, and philanthropy. Some have been senators or governors. Others have left their mark as benefactors of large historical restoration projects, such as the massive restoration of Williamsburg, Virginia, which began in the 1930s and now preserves an important part of American history

Every time you fill up your tank, curse the smog, or ponder the complexities of modern corporate America, you can also thank John Rockefeller. It was he, more than any other American, who ushered in both the industrial age and the first "era of big oil." Ohio, most notably Cleveland, played a central role in his decision-making.

Rockefeller came to the small Lake Erie port town as a teenager during one of his family's many moves during his youth. He was born in south central New York State, the son of a devout and charitable mother and a father who achieved small success as a traveling medicine man. Young Rockefeller seemed to inherit the characteristics of both parents, too, as would be exhibited throughout his life. As a youth, he exhibited a great aptitude for numbers and the ability to quickly perform calculations in his head. It was that and his persistence that led to his first job as an accountant, gained after persistently walking Cleveland's tiny business community.

The company was Hewitt & Tuttle, a commission merchant—essentially a business that might be viewed today as a combination broker and distributor. Hard work, attention to detail, and unswerving honesty put Rockefeller immediately in good standing with his employer. He quickly became involved in other matters related to transportation and other elements of what might be called "logistics" in modern business nomenclature. But there was clearly not too much room to go far beyond the bookkeeper's desk. So, with his neighbor, Maurice Clark, Rockefeller formed his own commission merchant business, Clark & Rockefeller.[1]

At that time Cleveland was well positioned for companies involved in the buying and selling of agricultural and dry goods products. It was becoming a major Great Lakes port at a time when the lakes were seen as essential to American transportation and commerce. The Erie Canal had been built in New York State to connect the lakes to New York City and the Eastern Seaboard. Rockefeller and Clark did well in their initial years largely due to Rockefeller's accounting and business acumen and to the fact that their revenues were tied to commissions. They were in a largely inflation-proof position.

Brokering products to meet common needs was competitive. It was easy for a person to get into the business, thus assuring a crowded field of rivals. Rockefeller was restless for something significant, unique, and profitable. The answer came gushing from the ground in the form of oil. Discovered first in western Pennsylvania, an oil boom had begun throughout eastern Ohio at a time when the future of the business was yet unsure. Clark and Rockefeller were approached by an innovative chemist named Samuel Andrews,

FIGURE 8.1. An early Standard Oil agent hauls a 350–500 gallon tank in the 1890s. Courtesy of the Ohio History Connection (AL07668.tif).

who convinced the two to invest $2,000 each in "oil refining."[2] It is worth noting that the immediate future of what would become the world's indispensable natural resource came first as a source of light rather than as something that would power internal combustion engines. Both uses require the refinement of crude oil.

Refining would help the company avoid what Rockefeller saw as the one big problem with the oil business. Most companies focused on drilling. It was easy for people to enter, and those willing to drill wells were also quickly becoming a business commodity. The answer, he felt, lay in refining. To do that work well required more investment and business acumen, something that would surely be an entry barrier for many. And Cleveland was a city perfectly situated for such a venture. It was close to the fields that were making eastern Ohio the Middle East of the time, and it was served by several lines in the fast-growing railroad business. It would be a significant rail transport deal with Vanderbilt-controlled rail lines that proved instrumental to Rockefeller's early success.[3]

Refining was the specialty that would turn black oil into unprecedented wealth. Along with rail transport, Rockefeller had the geographical advantage of building close to Lake Erie and the network offered by the Great Lakes. With such transportation advantages, Cleveland became the hub of a business empire never before created in history. It made the teetotaler the wealthiest man in the world by the time he reached his early thirties.

At that time, the immediate future of oil lay not in gasoline but in kerosene—a new product that would help turn back the night by providing bright, relatively clean indoor illumination far brighter and more economically than either whale oil or the candles of Procter & Gamble. It took entrepreneurs like Rockefeller to create and satisfy a demand for kerosene lighting. Rockefeller's entry into the oil business was not without challenges, however. There were enormous costs associated with refining, a process that was far from perfected at the time. Samuel Andrews's expertise helped the company use the key refining ingredient, sulfuric acid, effectively and efficiently. In addition, each aspect of building and operating a refining business required the expertise of outside contractors, from barrel makers and metal workers to experts in chemistry. Then too there was the issue of transportation. You can't light the world without getting your kerosene to willing purchasers. Rockefeller had this issue well in hand not only with willing rail partners but also with those who paid a fee to Rockefeller for every barrel of competitor's oil that they hauled.[4]

Rockefeller approached business with ruthless efficiency. His solutions for virtually every obstacle lay in what modern MBA students know today as "vertical integration." By owning or controlling more of the processes that went into the procurement of crude, refinement, and ultimate delivery to customers, he was able not only to get a handle on costs but also to build his concept of efficiency into every part of the process. He hired his own chemists, coopers, and skilled tradesmen so that his company embraced far more job types than those of a typical refiner of the day.[5]

This gave him better control not only of costs but also of product quality. Quality was important, too, particularly in an era in which kerosene was not only a new source of lighting but also one with flammability and volatility problems. As more and more people embraced the convenience of the bright warm light, the number of house fires soared. Consumer accidents were making local newspapers wherever kerosene was being put to use. Like many new technologies, kerosene was having a "PR problem."

THE STANDARD

Rockefeller turned consumer fear and suspicion into a marketing opportunity. Using his chemists to perfect and "standardize" manufacturing and formulas, he reduced accidents and gained consumer trust. Then, by naming his oil and later the company "Standard," he created an early branding and marketing edge to accompany his business efficiency. *Standard* came to connote safety, reliability, consistency, and every other quality folks wanted in the kerosene they were putting into their lamps. The move showed marketing acumen that paralleled the other inventive capabilities of Rockefeller's enterprise, which eventually became known as Standard Oil.[6]

Rockefeller controlled so many of the processes that went into refining that he had insurmountable pricing and strategic advantages. Still, he was unrelenting in his pursuit of financial and functional efficiency. When Standard began making its own barrels, the cost per barrel declined by more than 50 percent. And when Rockefeller identified better ways to package and ship his product (tank cars and pipelines), Standard Oil quickly adopted them.

His distaste for waste meant that in spite of the fact that 60 percent of the average barrel of crude could be refined into kerosene, Rockefeller wanted more. This led to selling by-products, which other refiners would turn into other products like naphtha, paraffin, or gasoline. Later the Standard Refineries would refine for all of these and more. Then, as demand for gasoline began to grow, Standard chemists perfected a way to change the molecular content of crude oil, or to "crack it." And this process dramatically increased the gasoline yield.

Standard Oil maximized human productivity by allowing, encouraging, and nurturing specialization long before such practices were commonplace in business. The company also pioneered the art of diversity and management of far-flung operations. The early Standard is perhaps most famous in history for being the target of early antitrust legislation. In another light, Rockefeller's trust could be viewed as a very inventive way to operate in multiple US states in spite of archaic and arcane incorporation laws. Such laws largely forbade significant operations based in other states from forming corporations outside the state of their incorporation. The laws did not forbid ownership of corporations by citizens of other states. The Standard Oil trust meant that Rockefeller and eight others shared ownership of numerous separate corporations that engaged in multiple enterprises in multiple states.

Over more than 20 years, Ohio and other states along with the federal government made it their business to bust the trust. It took a while. The effort, which began when Standard controlled more than 90 percent of the refining of kerosene, finally concluded when kerosene was fast becoming passé as a lighting method (in favor of Edison's incandescent light bulb) and when other oil refineries where effectively competing with Standard. The result was that Standard Oil was busted as a trust and forced to spin off into 34 separate companies under separate ownership.[7]

Soon these companies would be known by different names like Mobil (Standard Oil of New York), Exxon (Standard Oil of New Jersey) and Chevron (Standard Oil of California). They would grow, reinvent themselves, and merge with each other or other oil concerns. Sohio (Standard Oil of Ohio) itself grew to be one of the country's largest industrial corporations in size and revenue through the 1980s. It eventually acquired part of BP (British Petroleum) and then was itself acquired by BP. This put the headquarters of BP America in Cleveland and then Chicago where it retains the Midwest rights to use the name "Standard Oil" if it so chooses.

As he grew much older, Rockefeller set another life goal for himself: to live to 100. He unfortunately fell short of this by a little over two years, dying in 1937 at the age of 97. He was buried in Cleveland, next to his wife, who had died 20 years before.[8] A *New York Times* feature following his death cited his $1.5 billion fortune as "probably the greatest amount of wealth that any private citizen had ever been able to accumulate by his own efforts" and also lauded his charity:

> Mr. Rockefeller, who had been the greatest "getter" of money in the country during the years he was exploiting its oil resources, became, after his retirement from business, the world's greatest giver. He gave even more than Andrew Carnegie, whose philanthropies amounted to $350,000,000.[9]

Whether you view the definition of Rockefeller's "ruthlessness" as the epitome of personal and corporate greed or as an example of efficiency and innovation, we still live its effects every day. That is especially true for those of us who fill up at Exxon, Mobile, BP, or any of the other gas station brands spun from what was once simply Standard. Those who wanted to break up big business 100 years ago might be disappointed in the results achieved with the 1911 Supreme Court ruling that "destroyed" the old Standard. Two children of the breakup—Exxon and Mobil—eventually married during an FTC-approved merger in 1999. Today, depending on the month and market conditions, ExxonMobil is frequently the world's largest company in terms of market capitalization. One therefore has to ask how much has really changed since the entrepreneurial uncertainty of oil, the geographic opportunity of Cleveland, and the ambition of a young resident all came together to form ExxonMobil's forerunner more than 150 years ago.

The idea of a departed one rolling over in his grave may not apply to this accountant turned titan as he rests in Cleveland's Lakeview Cemetery. But wherever the Lord he so fervently adored took him, John D. Rockefeller must certainly be rolling his eyes at the irony.

CHAPTER 9

MOTHER OF INVENTION

Maybe someone at Procter & Gamble should have paid a little more attention to the young man from northern Ohio.

In 1869 the soap and candle maker hired a 21-year-old telegraph operator who grew up near Milan, on the Lake Erie shore. The young employee joined P&G to work with one of the company's second-generation leaders, James Gamble, on improving the company's internal communications. You could say that he created the first enterprise-wide system for the company. He made it clear that the company's system of pouches and horseback couriers was a highly inefficient way to communicate in an era when telegraph technology could make intercompany communications so much more efficient. Thomas Edison spent just a year at P&G before moving on to bigger and better things. His rudimentary office-to-office telegraph system (a forerunner of the modern communications enterprise, perhaps) was left in a somewhat unfinished state when he departed. Procter & Gamble was a brief résumé note for the man who would one day be known as the Wizard of Menlo Park.[1]

Ironically, Edison's light bulb, patented on January 27, 1880, would ultimately extinguish the candle-making business of his former employer. Edison then went on to become the most famous inventor of the nineteenth and twentieth centuries. His light bulb—

FIGURE 9.1. Thomas Edison was born in this tiny Milan, Ohio, house in 1847.

though currently in the midst of a gradual phase-out in use—burned brightly for well over 135 years. In addition, his genius produced the first phonograph and other sound-recording devices along with the precursor to the film projector. Edison, perhaps more than any single inventor, changed the world in the most profound ways. Like Procter & Gamble, Edison's business enterprises were always the product of intense research and development efforts—the likes of which had never been seen but which would come to define business success in an increasingly industrial world.

Edison's route to adulthood was not through school but was rather the product of a patient and loving mother. In fact, he spent only three months in school, his instructors deeming him "addled." This, however, is believed to be related more to Edison's hearing problem, as he would conclusively prove that he didn't have a "thinking problem."[2] As a young adult, he developed a keen interest in telegraph work as well as electricity. Lasting nearly 65 years, his career would be marked by stunning success in science, technology, and corporate management. He founded at least 14 companies in his lifetime, the most famous being General Electric, which remains an American cultural and corporate icon. Thomas Edison is immortalized not only by GE and his many inventions but also by the many other companies that have carried his name—Southern California Edison, Commonwealth Edison, and Consolidated Edison of New York, to list just a few.

Procter & Gamble's candles and Standard Oil's kerosene may have lit America, but Edison relit it, brighter than ever. He delivered not only the light of his bulbs but the bright promise of motion pictures and recorded sound. Edison's impact reached around the world and has extended over many generations. Quite an accomplishment for an "addled" boy from Milan.

THE GLOW OF EDISON'S LIGHT

I don't know how many times our car whizzed by the exit nearest to Milan, Ohio, when I was a kid on a family trip. It has probably been hundreds of times that I have seen the sign proclaiming Edison's birthplace. Always, however, I took the home, the history, and Ohio Turnpike (Interstate 80–90) Exit 118 for granted. I guess I figured that every state had an Edison or two as part of its historical legacy. Imagine the world we would have if that were true.

Edison had strong competition from others, too. This included Cleveland inventor and scientist Charles Brush—recognized for inventing arc lighting and for being the first to use electricity to light a city's streets (yes, in Cleveland).[3] For Edison, Brush, and others, Ohio was a wonderful place to create, tinker, and invent life-changing machines or launch hare-brained schemes.

In the mid- to late 1980s, I wrote advertisements and brochures for General Electric. One ad showed a European city (cleverly, Milan, as I recall) lit two different ways. One scene showed a row of old buildings in the light of ordinary bulbs. The other was an identical shot but taken in the light of a new kind of street light from GE that was clearer, truer, and brighter. My headline for the ad was simply "See Your World in a Better Light." Today, there are 17,000 people helping with that chore in the headquarters of GE's lighting division located in Cleveland.

Back in the era of the late 1800s and early 1900s, Ohio was literally the heart of a nation muscling its way to its full potential. The state produced presidents almost as a trade crop during this period. It was also a decidedly friendly state for anyone or any company looking to innovate. As the nucleus for American industrialization, it is also natural that the state helped launch the modern labor movement. It was the birthplace of many powerful unions, including the United Mine Workers and the American Federation of Labor (the first half of the AFL-CIO).

Ohio was drawing restless hearts and new ideas westward from the East. It drew Edison's parents, along with Procters, Gambles, Firestones, and Rockefellers. Some assert that Ohio even deserves credit for inventing the automobile, said to be the creation of Ohio City in 1891. Ohio was definitely the ideal place for Cyrus McCormick to invent the reaper and for Obed Hussey to create an early version of the mower, both of which, in turn, changed farming across the land.[4] Inventor and aviator Wilbur Wright summed it all up in a speech 1910: "If I were giving a young man advice on how he might succeed in life, I would say to him, pick out a good father and mother and begin life in Ohio."[5]

In addition, the Buckeye State was a magnet for immigrants looking to farm or make more out of their trades or artisan skills than they might have in the European "old country." Plus, it was the only Northern state in the first westward tier. So, while the South spent much of the late 1800s recovering from the Civil War, Ohio had a decided economic advantage. The manufacturing-oriented North had defeated an agrarian South. And Ohio companies clearly profited from much of the manufacturing necessity generated by the Civil War, from soap and candle making in Cincinnati to clothing manufacturing in Columbus. The Columbus Blue Jackets hockey team takes its name from the city's role as uniform provider to the Union Army. Ohio sustained the momentum as the reunited country healed and got down to business.

OHIO USED TO BE CALIFORNIA

Because of Silicon Valley and other West Coast technology centers, California is often seen as the place from which innovation flows in twenty-first-century America. But it is worth noting that for the first years of its time in the Union, California was a sparsely populated wilderness. It would be decades into the twentieth century before California's inventive mojo really caught hold. By the same token, there was a time when Ohio was the nation's epicenter of innovation. And much of this innovation related to the business of business. Here is just a sampling of what got its start in Ohio or from Ohians:

Jet engines
Liquid crystal display
Kidney dialysis
Crosley radio
Washerless faucet
Traffic light
Vacuum cleaner
Automobile (also claimed by several other states and countries)
Teflon
The Richter scale
Birth control pill

There were also cash registers and other business machines, all designed, manufactured, and marketed by Dayton's National Cash Register Company (NCR is now headquartered in the Atlanta area). Ubiquitous today as collectibles sold by antique shops, old NCR machines serve as large masterpieces of nineteenth-century inventiveness and reminders of a bygone commercial world. At the same time, NCR has remained at the forefront of cash and credit transactions at the point of sale since the time of the first mechanical cash register, which the company introduced in 1885. Numerous innovations brought out by NCR include the first successfully commercialized barcode technology.[6]

From NCR's first tests in a Troy, Ohio, store in the mid-1970s, barcode technology has evolved to the point where it is now used worldwide as a method for product identification and point-of-sale cash transactions.[7] It is difficult for anyone born after 1970 to remember a time when the checkout was done solely by a clerk reading tags and keying in prices. The control offered by this technology has meant billions in savings and efficiency at all levels in the supply and delivery chain.

Other business machine achievements include the products of companies like Canton Ohio's Diebold Company. Diebold has been in existence since 1859, making it one of a few American companies to last more than 150 years. Founded in Canton by Karl Diebold, the company focused early on an essential need for merchants and other enterprises of the time: storing and protecting cash. In an era that predated credit and electronic exchange, the safe was one of the most important pieces of business equipment that a company could have. Diebold purchased Germany's Nixdorf Corp in 2016. Today it remains a little-known name that is nevertheless omnipresent in many aspects of American life. It is one of the country's largest suppliers of transaction equipment for banks, including the equipment used in drive-up windows and the ever-present automated teller machine. It was Diebold that first pioneered the ATM back in the mid-1960s.

The cash register, the safe, the ATM. As some of the most essential pieces of business equipment, these products have made millions of dollars for their companies' owners. They've created hundreds of thousands of jobs and generations' worth of new achievements in areas related to counting, storing, computing, and managing business assets. The achievements of NCR in computing, point of sale, and inventory management go largely unnoticed because of the behind-the-scenes nature of its products. That is probably just as the company would have it. Other Ohio companies that are in business for the sake of business include Cincinnati's famous Milacron, known worldwide for its plastic extruding and molding equipment.

Toledo Scale is another iconic business brand. It took the notion of accurate commercial weights and measures and turned it into not only products but a name recognized by business customers as well as consumers everywhere. Toledo, it should be mentioned, is a now a brand of Mettler Toledo, LLC, which is headquartered in Columbus. Technology that helps other companies has long been developed in the state. Over a century ago, a Fremont, Ohio, inventor delivered the ultimate business and consumer convenience when he invented the machine that quickly formed paper into the brown paper bags that many of us still prefer when we go to the supermarket.

The fact that so many Ohio-created business essentials remain with us today (some in more advanced form) testifies both to the necessity of invention in the late nineteenth and early twentieth centuries and to the ability of these inventions—think gasoline, ready-mix paint, tubeless tires, and more—to so perfectly meet many of humans' long-held needs.

Charles Brush became the first to light an American city using electricity when he illuminated the roadways of Cleveland's Public Square in 1879. This took place years before his company would be merged with Thomas Edison's to form what we have since known as General Electric.[8] Today, it is difficult for many people to fully appreciate the inventiveness of these Ohioans and the way they changed the world. But if you are one of them—and happen to be reading this on a plane—look out the window to your right or left. That jet engine mounted to the wing was likely designed and built by GE in Cincinnati.

ELECTROSTATIC CATS IN COLUMBUS

Today, the epicenter of innovation in many fields is a quiet non-profit firm in Columbus, Ohio. With more than 20,000 scientists, engineers, and other technical staff members, Battelle Memorial Institute has played a role in perfecting countless technologies in just about every area of endeavor, from space exploration to compact discs and from golf to fighting heart disease. Clients include governments around the world, among them branches of the US military and the Department of Energy as well as the United Kingdom. Battelle co-manages national laboratories, including Oak Ridge National Laboratory (Tennessee), Brookhaven National Laboratory (New York), Idaho National Laboratory, and Pacific Northwest National Laboratory (Washington), in addition to serving hundreds of commercial clients and partners.

Perhaps one of the most famous Battelle achievements involves the technology that went into Chester Carlson's Xerox machine.

Carlson, a New York patent attorney and inventor, had conceived and demonstrated a dry, no-chemical method of transferring images from an original to a second substrate—the process now widely known as photocopying. Carlson called the process "electrophotography." It had five key components: (1) electrostatically charging a surface to make it light-sensitive, (2) exposing the surface to printed or written material, (3) dusting the surface with powder that adheres only to "charged areas," (4) exposing the surface to paper, and (5) "fixing" the image with heat. The science sounds very basic, almost crude. For example, charging the surface could be achieved by rubbing a surface with fur. His first "copied" image, created in 1938, was unpretentious, reading simply "10-22-38 Astoria."[9] And for years going forward, Carlson was unable to develop the idea further or to generate interest from any of the many firms he approached.

Then, in 1944, his law firm received a fortuitous visit from a Battelle representative in New York who was there on a legal matter that involved another client. One thing led to another and soon Carlson was in contact with Battelle. The institute agreed to fund further research and develop the idea with an eye toward commercialization. It also acted as Carlson's agent. Ultimately the vital third component came in the form of Rochester, New York's, Haloid—a photo paper maker hungry for revenues and eager to set itself apart from the city's industrial behemoth, Eastman Kodak. Sol Linowitz, an attorney and close associate of Haloid (later Xerox) president Joseph Wilson, recalled that "we went to Columbus to see a piece of metal rubbed with cat's fur."[10]

But the rest, as they say, is history. Carlson's invention would become the cornerstone for multibillion dollar photocopying and laser printing industries. As for the name "Xerox," it would come several years later as an adaptation of the term *xerography*. That linguistic gift was the suggestion of an Ohio State professor who combined the Greek words for dry (xeros) and writing (graphein).[11] Xerox of course went on to become a major research leader itself, investing around the world in facilities like PARC—the Palo Alto Research Center—which ultimately developed technologies employed in the development of Apple's early computers.

Research, science, and other components of innovation are themselves additive processes. Nothing happens in a vacuum or without either purpose or precedent. In the case of Battelle Memorial Institute, the precedent was its founder and initial benefactor, Gordon Battelle, who built it with his steel fortune and conviction that science and research applied to industry could uplift both industry and the common individual. The story of Carlson and the once struggling Haloid Company certainly help to prove Battelle's point.

CHAPTER 10

HENRY FORD'S
FRONT LAWN

The inventiveness of the late nineteenth and early twentieth centuries came on many fronts and at many levels. Key to an expanding industrial base was the ability to discover, produce, and sell the materials that would form consumer and commercial products. This meant the taming of natural obstacles, and the use of raw materials and compounds leading to the production of steel, oil, glass, rubber, aluminum, and other materials. It was an enterprise that made possible almost everything we rely upon today.

In many cases, these materials are essential to making every car on the road and every building that lines the skyline. They are so omnipresent in everything that we make and do that it is hard to imagine a time when their production was difficult, impossible, or simply nonexistent.

By the late nineteenth century, Ohio had established itself as the nation's second-largest steel-producing state. It achieved this distinction because of iron ore delivered via the Great Lakes and furnaces powered by Ohio's own rich coal preserves. A number of the industry's most impressive innovations in steel production were implemented in Cleveland-area steel companies, including the open-hearth furnace and the Bessemer converter. The Bessemer converter revolutionized steelmaking by reducing cost and greatly increasing manufacturing speed and scale while also decreasing labor requirements.[1]

In Toledo, Edward Libbey, Michael Owens, and others took previously "artisan" industries and relocated them to a place where nature merged perfectly with industrial invention. It was an early example of one region working to attract business from another through the use of incentives. Back in Massachusetts, Libbey's struggling New England Glass Company had to face declining glass prices at the same time that his laborers were striking for higher wages.

Toledo's city leaders thought they might have a solution for the young businessman: bring himself and his 250 jobs to Toledo. In a manner similar to today's regional development efforts, they offered what were then "big time incentives" for relocation. These included a factory site, lots for worker housing, plus $100,000 to build the factory. Libbey took the deal. Eager to transform the business founded by his father into a profitable operation once again, he renamed it the Libbey Glass Company. The Toledo area had many advantages, including strategic positioning on the nation's rail network as well as plentiful natural gas resources—essential to the high-heat requirements of glassmaking. Lake Erie provided the other key ingredient. The beaches on the western end of the lake yielded one of the world's largest resources for white sand silica, the key raw material in glass.[2]

In an early installment of an often repeated industrial-era drama, Libbey's reborn company became a world leader in various forms of cut and mass-produced glass used in a variety of commercial, food service, and consumer applications. The company, which for a time was part of Owens-Illinois, continues today as one of the nation's premier glass companies. It has operations throughout the country and numerous international locations.

Every time you raise a bottled beer or soft drink to your lips, be sure to toast Michael Owens, one of Libbey's early Toledo hires. During his 64 years, Owens would hold or have a share in no less than 45 patents. These included what is perhaps his most ingenious "game changing" machine, which automated the production of glass bottles. Today, the Owens name lives on in several Toledo-based companies, all tied to glass production. These include Owens-Corning (fiberglass insulation and building materials) and Owens-Illinois (the descendant of Owens's bottle-making innovations and a major producer of consumer, industrial, and scientific glass). Owens also encouraged the invention and innovations required to mass-produce sheet glass for industrial, building, and automotive use. That company continued for decades as Libbey Owens Ford. Its corporate descendants continue to produce glass in Toledo along with various smaller glass firms, fiberglass insulation companies, and other glass product manufacturers.[3]

Innovation in glass continues in Toledo, which still calls itself the "Glass Capital of the World," and Owens-Illinois is still developing new technologies to advance quality and production processes. In addition, the company sells itself as being "in step with the times," citing glass as the most "sustainable packaging material" on earth. Glass is, after all, sand.[4]

Industrial success in Ohio came from the growth of companies that benefited from the earth's bounty. These were fed by the emerging US transportation system. Steel relied on the iron ore mined farther north in the Great Lakes region plus the rich supply of coal prevalent in southeastern Ohio and southwestern Pennsylvania. Glass was manufactured from Lake Erie sand. All could be easily shipped via rail, water, or the interstate highway system.

Thanks to private and public universities that were growing in accomplishment and output, Ohio was also producing people who could think their way around what had been difficult scientific obstacles. One of these individuals was Charles Martin Hall of Thompson, Ohio. Hall discovered a new process for easily extracting aluminum in a tale reminiscent of the stories often told of Silicon Valley computer pioneers. Fresh out of Oberlin College and aided by Oberlin professor Frank Jewitt, Hall worked day and night on his idea. His workshop was a small, rustic shed behind his parents' home. Unable to partake or uninterested in exploring the employment opportunities around his small community, Hall persisted tirelessly on experiments designed to use electrolytic principles for the extraction of aluminum from base rock. The process basically involved an electrical charge and 1,000-degree temperatures to separate aluminum out of a molten solution of aluminum oxide in molten cryolite.[5]

Hall's patent application ran into some difficulties when it was discovered that France's Paul L. T. Héroult was granted a patent in his country for a similar approach. Ultimately, Hall received the US patent after proving that he had made his discoveries prior to Héroult's. Because of the remarkable and virtually simultaneous discovery in an era when neither man could know of the other's

FIGURE 10.1. Thomas Edison, Henry Ford, and Harvey Firestone, pictured in the 1920s. The three were good friends, often working and vacationing with one another. From the Ohio History Connection (AL02918.TIF).

work, the method is today known as the Hall–Héroult process. There has been much discussion over how two people working in two very different parts of the world—a small town in Ohio and Paris, France—came up with the same idea at virtually the same time.[6] One might have thought the inventor from Paris would have a distinct advantage in the quest to separate aluminum from its ore—on the hot list of scientific objectives during the period. However, Hall had great resources at his disposal. He was close to an excellent educational institution and a great library. He also had quick and easy access to some of the materials and innovations available in Cleveland, such as the products of Brush Electric.

Prior to Hall's Oberlin experiments, aluminum cost a small fortune and was practically considered a "precious metal." Years later, at the height of Alcoa's (in which Hall became a partner) success, it was down to 18 cents a pound. Importantly, this mainstreaming of aluminum produced an alloy that would form the basis for America's windows, building components, cookware, and other products. Incidentally, it is from Hall that the American English version of the word *aluminum* comes. The British, and theoretically more proper spelling, *aluminium,* fell victim to a simple typographical error on Hall's part.

RUBBER AND THE ROAD IT MEETS

Anyone who remembers the Ford Explorer rollover controversy of the late 1990s knows that in later phases news coverage was dominated by a flurry of accusations and rebuttals between Ford Motor Company and Firestone Tire and Rubber. Each blamed the other for the rollover of the vehicles—mostly all of which were fitted with Firestone tires. And it was frequently pointed out that the lawsuits and PR assaults between the companies were ending a 90-year corporate marriage dating back to the personal friendship between Harvey Firestone and Henry Ford.

Though often forgotten, the American rubber industry actually had its origins in New England and New York's Hudson River Valley, where hundreds of entrepreneurs experimented with, produced, and sold various products fashioned from rubber. The practice became dramatically more practical once Massachusetts native Charles Goodyear invented the process of rubber vulcanization.

Although it's a word that may conjure comic book images in some minds, vulcanization solved the previous problem of rubber melting in warm weather and getting hard and brittle in cold. This process required a combination of rubber, white lead, and sulfur. By the 1860s vulcanized rubber was being used to manufacture products ranging from clothing and household items to covering for telegraph wire and other cabling.

Frank Sieberling, Harvey Firestone, Benjamin Franklin Goodrich, and other industrial adventurers found themselves in northeastern Ohio via different routes. All three, however, built powerful companies that would be essential to the northeast Ohio economy and critical to the emerging automobile industry. Dr. Benjamin Franklin Goodrich, a Civil War surgeon, settled in Akron, where he started BF Goodrich after spending several years as a

New York businessman. His earlier medical training at what is now Case Western Reserve and subsequent service as a Civil War surgeon seemed to bear little relationship to his pursuits after the war. He first worked in Pennsylvania before working in real estate in New York. It was there that he became the largest stockholder of the Hudson River Rubber Company.

Firestone grew up in Ohio and began an early career as a merchant, which took him to a number of cities, including Detroit. Cities of the late 1800s were experiencing a boom in the presence and use of bicycles. Along with these two-wheeled, human-propelled machines, the streets were crowded with various forms of carriage, buggy, and other horse-drawn conveyance. Rubber had recently been discovered as an effective way to soften the ride of hard, metal and wood tires used on bikes and buggies. Those first solid rubber tires needed improvement, which came quickly with the invention of the pneumatic tire. Filling tires with air made the ride in any bicycle or buggy much smoother. This kept the vehicles of the time from literally shaking apart. Most importantly, they kept human bodies from getting injured when simply out for a ride over the rough roads of the time.

Rubber and tires meshed perfectly with another emerging technological application that would soon overtake the US and the rest of the world. That, of course, was the effort to build and perfect the automobile. Akron's rubber makers would remain forever linked to Detroit and the rest of the car-making industry—a fact that has been both a blessing and a curse. It gave Akron's tire companies a unique role in American commerce as marketing innovators.

Originally, Akron had numerous tire and rubber manufacturers, but by the 1980s the numbers had been reduced to just four: Goodyear, Firestone, BF Goodrich, and General. Today, only the biggest and strongest of these—Goodyear—remains headquartered in Akron, with its core business devoted to tire making. But the fact that the General, Firestone, and BF Goodrich brands live on (owned now by other corporate entities) says something about the marketing and branding that created such strong consumer franchises that they could outlive their original corporate creators.[7]

Goodyear always has been and always will be an aggressive marketer. From its application of trademark and branding techniques during its early years to the universally recognized Goodyear Blimp, the company has displayed a talent for marketing

FIGURE 10.2. Production at Goodyear Tire and Rubber Company in Akron during the 1940s. Courtesy of the Ohio History Connection (Om3084 3675638 001.tif).

that some say exceeds the technical achievement of its tire making. Founder Sieberling displayed this flair from the beginning with his decision to name his company after the long-deceased inventor Charles Goodyear. This choice gave the company immediate credibility and recognition in the world of rubber manufacturing. Goodyear is a dominant player in virtually every category of tire and many other product lines. It is omnipresent in the world of motor sport racing and a leading producer of tires for everything from heavy equipment to aircraft and aerospace.

Today Goodyear is a main component in northeastern Ohio's claim to being the world's polymer innovation leader. Polymer engineering is the key activity behind the development of rubber, plastics, adhesives, paints, sealants, and other essential materials.

It should be noted that even northwest Ohio rubber firms such as Cooper Tire have roots that can be traced back to Akron. And as it did with other industries, Ohio offered fertile ground for growth. The state's location put it close enough to the East Coast as well as to the expanding West. The state's transportation assets made it a nexus for interstate commerce, something vital to any company wanting to serve a large portion of the US. Still a relatively new state after the Civil War, Ohio pulled in the country's enterprising classes like a vacuum. It drew the types of individuals that would create tire companies or found paint companies like Sherwin Williams and Glidden.

It doesn't take too much concentration of the mind to realize that rubber, steel, glass, and aluminum make pretty good materials for a lot of different products, especially cars. Along with Michigan and several other midwestern states, Ohio has been at the heart of auto manufacturing since the industry's first days. Seeing trains and steamships power themselves inspired many imaginations to come up with automobile-style transport.

But the concept of a large, heavy, free-moving vehicle was impractical at that time. Who would feed the wood or coal into the steam engine while driving? That's where gasoline comes in. We know about Rockefeller and Standard Oil, but it was William Burton, a Standard Oil employee, who invented "cracking"—the process of refining petroleum in a way that maximized the gasoline yield.[8] First a rarity in any town, the gas station grew with the popularity of the automobile. Starting out as only one or two per town, their numbers increased to a point where many intersections have one on every corner. Today, the US has nearly 200,000 gas stations, many connected to convenience stores or fast-food restaurants and often part of that ubiquitous American mini-town: "The Exit."

Fuel is only one of the many things Ohio contributed to the automobile. Almost from the beginning, the state of Ohio has been a top producer of cars themselves, usually ranking second, just behind Michigan. Importantly, it usually ranks first in the production and distribution of automotive parts and components. All this talk of steel, petroleum rubber, glass and putting it all into motion might be moot if not for another Ohioan: hardware store owner and part-time pharmacist George Bartholomew. Bartholomew lived in the late 1800s in what was then and still remains the small town of Bellefontaine (pronounced "bell fountain" by the locals). With the resources of limestone and clay in nearby marl pits, Bartholomew believed that the Ohio earth had given him superior materials with which to work. And he believed that his variety of Portland cement would make the ideal concrete when mixed with nearby sand and stone material.

Fortunately for Bartholomew, Bellefontaine was willing to take to take a risk on the novel concept of cement-paved streets. At first the paving was limited to a tiny eight-foot strip next to some horse hitching posts. Then came an entire street, followed by blocks around the town square. Fame and trial by other municipalities quickly followed, especially when the paving technology received a first-place award at the Chicago International Exhibition.[9]

Bartholomew's achievements developed a superior surface for horse hooves and wagon wheels at a time when all these items were becoming both more sturdy with the use of steel and harder on the roads themselves. Most Americans still had not heard of nor imagined automobiles in 1891. They would follow quickly, however. And so you could say that although he had nothing to do with inventing cars, Bartholomew was certainly instrumental in *paving* their way.

KEYS TO AUTOMOTIVE GROWTH

From Toledo-made Jeeps to giant General Motors facilities in places like Warren and Lordstown, Ohio has long been a giant factor in both the domestic and the international auto industries, including in the manufacturing of some of the world's most famous muscle cars, like the Chevrolet Camaro and Pontiac Firebird. Honda's groundbreaking decision in the 1980s to build an American automaking presence was a first for a Japanese firm. Ohio is still the focal point of the company's US operations and has served as a model for other auto companies (Japanese, German, and Korean) looking to build cars close to their customer base. Honda's US output eventually grew to a point where its American-built exports outstripped imports of Honda vehicles from abroad.[10]

Beyond the natural and human resources available in Ohio for automaking lie countless tales of imagination and invention. Charles Kettering is just one of many of these, but with a résumé of achievements that makes him particularly noteworthy. He was one of the foremost researchers and inventors of the first half of the twentieth century.[11] He made contributions to the auto fuel business, namely the invention of anti-knock fuel. And although this leaded variety of gasoline was later replaced by unleaded because of important environmental considerations, the addition of lead proved tremendously beneficial to engine performance and longevity. Unleaded formulations were never feasible until they could replicate the properties of Kettering's formulation. Note propeller airplane fuels still use lead.[12]

Kettering also invented the automatic ignition, which eliminated the torturous chore of hand cranking. His development of a lightweight diesel engine led to the development of the Zephyr: a fast, stylish streamliner that dominated American rails in the mid-twentieth century. Kettering is credited with hundreds of other inventions as well. He was, after Henry Ford, the foremost American automotive engineer. His is a classic tale of what can come to an enterprising kid when personal ingenuity meets up with the opportunity provided by emerging industries.

Kettering's early career at National Cash Register saw him rise to become head of research at a time when the field was just beginning to drive the thinking of modern business. Later, he would employ research in great measure in the development of Delco. Its name originally an acronym for Dayton Engineering Laboratories Company, Delco spent decades as the country's pre-eminent auto parts supplier. Kettering's achievements include more than 140 patents in all, not only the electronic starter and leaded gas but also the Freon used in auto air conditioning and other cooling units. When Delco merged with GM, Kettering became one of the company's most important contributors. He led GM research operations for more than 25 years.[13]

Kettering's important life would come to be memorialized via the Dayton suburb of Kettering, Ohio, and at institutions like Memorial Sloan Kettering Hospital in New York, one of the nation's premier medical institutions.

CHAPTER 11

UP FROM THE BICYCLE SHOP

In the early twenty-first century—100 years after the fact—there emerged a quiet war of words, played out via license plates. With more and more states making use of their plates as marketing tools, North Carolina adopted the slogan *First in Flight*. This slogan touts the first airborne success of the Wright brothers, which took place December 17, 1903, on the sandy and wind-whipped beach of Kitty Hawk. Ohio's plates trumpeted a similar but conflicting message: *Birthplace of Aviation*. You can just imagine all the auto vacations where kids lean toward the front seat to query their parents about which state is telling the truth. The answer is that both are.

North Carolina may be where the first powered flight took place. But there is no doubt that Ohio gave the world flying—more specifically, the powered heavier-than-air flying associated with planes, helicopters, and spacecraft. There is a popular saying in the Dayton area that attempts to answer the Tar Heel State's "first in flight" claim: "Kitty Hawk provided the breeze, Dayton provided the brains."[1]

WIND BENEATH THEIR WINGS

Heavier-than-air flight had long eluded humanity, even though it had tantalized us for millennia. Da Vinci's famous drawings of gliders and birdlike flying machines, created around the year 1500, were fairly accurate representations of what human flight might resemble.[2] Drawings in caves and other ancient interpretations show humans flying either with the aid of makeshift wings or via contraptions that provide the wings. There are many depictions of angels and devils throughout the history of the Catholic Church. Most show flying forms that combine humanlike beings with birdlike wings.

"Winged man" was the conception of human flight held by most people prior to the twentieth century. It was also the basis for ideas first pondered by the Wright brothers, Orville and Wilbur. These enterprising, nattily dressed young Ohio gentlemen were already at the crest of late nineteenth-century enterprise and inventiveness. The two had tried and met with varying degrees of success in several other industries that were enriching Americans in that era, including printing and bicycle building.

It was their bicycle business that would provide the brothers the financial wherewithal and mechanical understanding to aid and propel their discoveries. The Wrights were bicycle-building innovators. Working out of their shop on West Third Street in Dayton, they invented pedals that would not unscrew as you pedaled and the self-oiling hub. All of their bike shop resources, from financing to skilled employees, tools, and mechanical know-how, would prove invaluable from 1898 to the point around 1906 or 1907 when the brothers' pioneering work gave critical mass to their airplane business.

The Wrights were also blessed to come from a literate, curious, and perpetually enterprising family. Their father, Milton, was a clergyman and leader in his church. This fact ensured that the Wright family library was fuller than most. The Wright children were all encouraged to read, discover, and aspire to higher education. Curiously for the time, when few women attended university, only the Wrights' sole daughter, Katherine, would earn a bachelor's degree. Like many great inventors and innovators, including Thomas Edison, Alexander Graham Bell, and, more recently, Steve Jobs and Bill Gates, college education would prove unnecessary for Wilbur and Orville.

The brothers extended, revised, and improved on the achievements of others. In short, they were giants standing upon the shoulders of giants. Humanity's first adventures aloft actually began in the late 1700s with the tethered Paris balloon flight of Jean-

François Pilâtre de Rozier, Jean-Baptiste Réveillon, and Giroud de Villette, as well as the untethered flight of the Marquis François d'Arlandes, which both took place in 1783. Throughout the nineteenth century, flight became real and practical but in a way that was always tied to the concept of lighter-than-air flight—for example, free-flying or tethered balloons.

Balloon flight was employed by Union troops for reconnaissance purposes during the Civil War. The Union's Thaddeus S. C. Lowe used tethered balloons to gain an aerial view of Confederate troop encampments and strategic movements.[3] This activity attracted the curiosity not only of military personnel but also of others like a visiting German, Ferdinand Graf von Zeppelin, who would eventually guide the German airship company bearing his name. Even into the 1920s and '30s, many people clung to the idea that humankind and flight would best be served by lighter-than-air flight, which had by then become most common through blimps and other dirigibles. But the Hindenburg disaster in 1937 ended that idea rather quickly.

Although there is no sight more exciting than that of a Goodyear blimp flying overhead or the colorful airborne pageantry of a weekend hot-air balloon race, flight is now associated with wings. Aviation borrowed the idea of wings from the birds but added the power of engines. However, it was necessary to bring power and physics under control so that man's flying machines could rise, descend, cruise, and turn at an operator's will. These are the elements provided by the bicycle builders from Dayton.

HEAVIER THAN AIR

The curious, adventurous Wright boys came upon their fascination with flight the way many red-blooded nineteenth-century Americans got enthused about a topic of discovery or invention—by reading science magazines. It was an 1894 magazine article that first caught the interest of Wilbur, who then shared the information with Orville.[4] Throughout the late 1800s there were various emerging scientific communities devoted to the subject of aviation, which at that time included balloons, gliders, and the promise of powered flight. The Wrights' successful bicycle manufacturing and sales operation had proved them adept with the era's mechanical challenges. Why not plunge into the next technological fad?

The article provided detail on some of the experiments and flights then taking place in the new and growing field of aviation. The Wrights themselves got into the act in the 1890s, just as their bicycle business was starting to produce sales volume that could sustain their extracurricular pursuits. The business began in 1892 as a bike sales and repair operation. Just a few years later, the Wrights were manufacturing and selling their own brand. Building and repairing bicycles put the brothers on track to gain the mechanical and technical know-how they may not have acquired in printing. It also put them in constant contact with tools, machining equipment, and physical principles related to power, motion, balance, and control. Bicycle work also required a knack for troubleshooting, something that would serve the Wrights well as they experimented and tinkered with flying craft.

The pursuit of flight became a consuming passion for Orville and Wilbur. They alternately worked as one another's coach, leader, or understudy as circumstances or inspiration dictated. Their bicycle experience gave them an ability to design, develop, fabricate, improve, and tinker. And most of their real inventing occurred during the off-hours or off-seasons when the press of building and selling bikes had subsided.

The brothers were determined to discover and implement a manner of control for powered flying. Up to that point, airborne gliding was controlled solely by weight shifts and pilot body manipulations. The Wrights had come upon a theory of control called "wing warping" that would enable a craft to be turned while keeping it level. Legend has it that Wilbur happened upon the idea of warping by twisting a box that had contained a bicycle inner tube. This casual discovery aligned with the brothers' observations of birds, which they noted were able to turn in flight with slight tips and elevations of their wings. The twisted box concept could hopefully be replicated on a single wing, which supplied the principal means of gaining and holding loft.

In-flight turning was a feat that had confounded early aircraft developers. Until the Wrights' development of control methods, weight shifts were all that glider pilots had available. And the consequences of this limitation proved deadly. Germany's Otto Lilien-

FIGURE 11.1. The Wrights made extensive use of photography during their trips to Kitty Hawk. Here, Wilbur Wright pilots the 1902 Wright Glider. Courtesy of Special Collections and Archives, Wright State University.

thal, whose early glider flights appeared to be leading the worldwide race to heavier-than-air flight, was killed in an abrupt and unanticipated plunge of his glider, perhaps brought about by such a weight shift. The same fate came to British hang-glider pilot Percy Pilcher. Other early flight innovators met similar tragic endings.

But there were also inspiring successes to motivate the brothers. In 1896 Samuel Langley's unmanned model aircraft flew successfully, driven and held aloft by a steam-powered engine. Langley, for whom the DC-area Air Force base is named, was general secretary of the Smithsonian Institution and a major contributor to the worldwide aviation knowledge base. Plus there was the work of Chicago engineer Octave Chanute, who ultimately befriended and encouraged the Wrights in their efforts. Chanute had been successful at testing a variety of glider designs over the sand dunes along the shore of Lake Michigan.[5]

FOUR YEARS AT THE BEACH

By 1900 new means of transportation brought American states far closer to one another than they had been at the time of the nation's independence. Train tracks crisscrossed the country and speeds had improved dramatically. It was now only a day's journey or less between Dayton and many other midwestern and eastern destinations. Located between St. Louis and Chicago to the west and New York, Philadelphia, and Washington to the east, Ohio found itself smack in the middle of northern commercial energy. The telegraph had made long-distance communication instantaneous, and the phone would take communications even further. The Wrights had many resources at their disposal.

They stayed in close communication with the growing number of experimenters, inventors, and tinkerers in the US and Europe who had been avidly pursuing the dream of heavier-than-air flight. These included well-known inventors like Langley and Chanute as well as a wider community that had come to believe that flight was just a few discoveries away. And indeed it was.

Many more perfections would be required before heavier-than-air flight moved from the theoretical to the practical. This is the primary contribution of the Dayton printers turned aviation pioneers. Their efforts to master the physical properties of flight and control led to numerous experiments with loft, control, weight distribution, and power. Along with Charlie Taylor, a trusted mechanic from their bicycle shop, and a close-knit group of supporters, suppliers, advisors, and friends, the brothers pursued aerodynamic technology fervently—and virtually alone.

The Wrights merged known theories of the time with hands-on testing. Their work in early wind tunnels helped to iron out difficulties and prove their theories. But it was the windy dunes and beaches near Kitty Hawk, North Carolina, that would provide the ultimate proving ground.[6]

The brothers' North Carolina trips, first in 1900, and then in 1901, 1902, and 1903, subdivide a remarkable and systematic progression from gliding experiments to the world's first successful powered, manned flight. Their initial trip to Kitty Hawk occurred in the autumn of 1900, when they felt the demands of bicycle customers had sufficiently subsided for the winter season. Kitty Hawk offered an ideal wind environment for their testing. Headwinds were perfect for providing a natural lift to the wings of a glider or aircraft. Orville and Wilbur's goal was to conduct full testing of a glider. Actually more of a horizontal box kite in shape, their 17-foot-wide craft made numerous short flights off the dunes of nearby Kill Devil Hills, both unmanned and with Wilbur aboard in a lying-down, head-forward position.[7]

In 1901 they sought to improve loft and control with a larger, more "advanced" craft, but their experiments failed on both counts. Although the 1901 glider had a larger wingspan at 22 feet and significantly greater area, it failed to achieve the improvements the Wrights had expected based on a known lift-coefficient theory. It also proved disappointing in the effectiveness of its control, actually turning the opposite way of the intended direction.

The brothers were disappointed with their 1901 efforts, but thoughts of giving up on their pursuit soon gave way to another flurry of invention on their part. They embarked on a new journey of experimentation that had them challenging and improving on existing knowledge about loft and engaging in more wind-tunnel testing. They also built their reputation with the larger aviation community when Wilbur journeyed to Chicago to present a lantern slide show presentation of their tests to the Western Society of Engineers. He had been invited to the Windy City by Chanute.

For two vigorous and tireless experimenters, it really was nice to have a bicycle manufacturing business at their disposal. Proving grounds for what would become the 1902 glider were the increasingly paved streets and roads of Dayton. One of the brothers would feverishly pedal a bicycle tethered to a glider as they continued to test their theories about loft and aerodynamics. Ultimately, they recalculated old coefficient of lift figures, which had been developed decades earlier and had guided other experimenters.

The Wrights discovered that while wing warping would tend to turn the plane, the motion also created drag, which could counteract the maneuver. To solve this, they introduced the concept of a rear tail rudder, fixed at first and then movable. The rudder proved a significant control factor, enabling the craft to be controlled and aligned through each turn, and aiding in overall control for leveling off, coming out of turns, and counteracting wind disturbances.

Their work on the 1902 glider paid off. That year's journey to the beaches and dunes of North Carolina resulted in hundreds of successful, controlled glides. Improvising further got them to the point where their craft could stay aloft for more than 26 seconds and travel over 600 feet. The 1902 glider had all the key components in place except for a motor. Aviation historians frequently

FIGURE 11.2. This exacting display models the first military airplane. Wilbur Wright is shown providing instruction to military personnel. It is one of hundreds of exhibits and displays at the National Museum of the US Air Force, near Dayton.

cite 1902 (not 1903) and the glider experiments as the true birth of flight. Except for the powered component, the 1902 efforts brought together all the essentials that would enable successful turning and other elements of control. These included a forward "elevator" to control pitch and wing warping, which enabled controlled rolling essential to the turn of a fixed-wing craft. The rear rudder, noted above, kept the nose turning in the proper direction.

The next year the brothers' 40-foot craft would sport an aluminum block engine and propeller drive chains. The gravity-fed power plant was built in six weeks by bicycle mechanic Charlie Taylor, working closely with Wilbur and Orville.[8] Here again, the bike business proved its value. Proximity to midwestern manufacturing and immersion in a burgeoning industrial economy gave the Wrights important technical and material wherewithal. Their '03 flyer came together for under $1,000. This was at a time when the government-funded effort of Samuel Langley had consumed over

$50,000 before tumbling into the Potomac a week before the first engine-powered Kitty Hawk successes on December 17, 1903. These came in the form of four sustained, controlled flights on that December day. The longest, flown by Wilbur, lasted 59 seconds and covered 852 feet. For purposes of documentation and proof, the brothers had made certain to have cameras on hand and positioned in ideal locations along the beach, a practice they followed throughout their inventive years. And so powered flight was born in those short stints aloft, barely 10 feet off the ground.[9]

The world was not exactly waiting for the news with breathless anticipation. The casual request telegrammed to their father, Milton, that he "inform press" produced nothing but skepticism from even their hometown papers. Only a few scattered reports of the flight appeared in other papers. When they got back to Dayton, the Wrights issued a detailed account of their success in January of 1904, but the press and the public seemed little impressed. It would be a different story across the ocean, however.

THE WRIGHT INNOVATIONS

European flying enthusiasts and experimenters had been well aware of the Wrights. And while not all believed the written and photographic accounts that had emerged, the reports nonetheless garnered the attention of aviation pioneers in other areas of the US and Europe.

Orville and Wilbur had broken the aerodynamic necessities for flight down into three key components: something to provide lift in the nose (the elevator), a means of turning (wing warping), and a method of aligning the plane as it banked in and out of turns, or controlling yaw (the tail rudder). Although ailerons now control the first two components, the principles of powered heavier-than-air flight are the same in any modern aircraft. Ailerons are the hinged "mini wings" at the back edge of an aircraft wing. You will notice them when they are used to help stop the 787 you are riding in.

After their 1903 success at Kitty Hawk, it would be five years before the North Carolina community would see the Wright brothers again. Work in the years immediately following would take place in cow pastures near Dayton. By the end of 1904, they would master things such as flying complete circles and remaining aloft for longer than five minutes. By 1905 a Wright Flyer would be capable of soaring hundreds of feet above the ground and sustaining flight for more than 23 miles and 35 minutes.

These and other milestones would convince the brothers that heavier-than-air flight had commercial value. They soon decided to transition from being one of thousands of bicycle builders to being the world's first aircraft builder. Improvements in various areas of aerodynamics would see further evolved versions of the Wright Flyer. These would achieve ever-increasing milestones in loft, flying time, and commercial practicality.

By 1908 the brothers were fully into the airplane-building business. An enterprise that was originally known as the Wright Company changed to Wright-Martin but then merged in 1929 with the Curtiss Company of Buffalo, New York. Today, the Curtiss-Wright Company is still engaged in the manufacture and sale of aerospace and other high-tech components. A number of companies have some heritage in the Wright brothers' early operations. For example, General Electric's substantial Cincinnati presence can be traced to a decision to lease the old Wright Aeronautical piston-engine facility in the northern part of the city shortly after World War II.

The Curtiss name enters the Wright story very early. In fact, Glenn Curtiss stands nearly alongside the Wrights and Chanute on the rostrum of American aviation pioneers. But their standing with one another wasn't exactly friendly. There are some who believe that Curtiss's discoveries preceded the Wrights'. However, it is well known that Curtiss visited the Wrights on a fact-finding trip sometime in 1906. The Wrights had worked many years, thousands of hours, to unlock the secrets of controlled flight. Their three-way axis-control principles became the standard and accepted methods for controlling fixed-wing aircraft. While the development of new ideas involved a certain amount of collegiality among competitors, there were also commercial and ownership considerations in play. The Wright brothers had become fierce competitors with Glenn Curtiss, the French, and other early pioneers. Various disagreements led to years of legal battles between inventors, including the Wrights and their rivals.

But it was the French who gave the Wrights their first commercial breakthroughs. After nearly two years of travel back and forth across the Atlantic by Wilber, Orville, and even sister Katharine, they were able to secure hundreds of thousands of dollars in business in France. Their major sales and licensing agreements in the US and sales to the US government would come long after their European success.[10]

Still remaining in all the debates over invention were questions surrounding the commercial and military appeal of winged flight. The years following Kitty Hawk brought clarity. By 1914 the first planes carrying passengers were taking off for short flights in Florida. Less than a dozen years after Charlie Taylor's engine first powered the brothers' glider over the Kitty Hawk dunes, planes were being used for everything from carrying passengers to entertaining county-fair attendees to delivering mail.

By this point, airplane use was growing at a breathtaking rate. That's even more obvious when you consider that aircraft were essential to the Allied victory in World War I less than a decade after many Americans still publicly doubted the feasibility or reality of the Wrights' experiments.

CHAPTER 12

FROM DAYTON
TO THE MOON

It was 1963, maybe 1964, and I was six years old and immersed in life as a little kid in Tiffin, Ohio. And anyone who lived in Tiffin (named for Ohio's first governor, Edward Tiffin) during those years might remember a familiar weekend experience. A small plane would fly over the town, teasing people with a simple loudspeaker booming from the plane itself. "Airplane rides, airplane rides— penny a pound at the Tiffin Airport." After my mom explained that "penny a pound" meant simply that passengers for these short rides would cost a penny per pound of weight, I figured that my dad and I could probably fly for about $2.14.

The Tiffin Airport plane ride never happened. For me. And it was not until I was in my early twenties that I actually flew aboard any kind of aircraft. But those frequent weekend flying advertisements inspired plenty of curiosity on my part. Flight was beautiful! It was speed, power, mindboggling height, and freedom—all marked by the mysterious contrails left behind by jet aircraft. Those were just some of the elements that generated excitement among us kindergarteners and first-graders when we heard reports about Gordon Cooper, John Glenn, and those other of America's newest heroes. Everyone wanted to be a pilot or, even better, an astronaut.

There was also the lore surrounding the Wright brothers from Dayton. I had been to Dayton several times by then, and I knew that the story of America's first flying machines began in Ohio. To me, everything did. The state's aeronautic greatness is naturally marked in history by the Wright brothers. It also includes early flying legends like Eddie Rickenbacker and astronauts John Glenn and Neil Armstrong. Some might argue that Ohio was simply in the right place at the right time. It hit full stride as a manufacturing center just as America was discovering the wonders of the automobile and the airplane. Through the invention of the Wright brothers and the adventurous life of Eddie Rickenbacker, Ohio not only discovered flying but also showed the world how it could be used for both combat and commerce. Another such person was Paul Tibbetts, a retired major general and president of a Columbus executive air taxi service, who was best known for his fateful flight over Hiroshima, Japan, on August 6, 1945.

HISTORY WRITTEN IN THE NAMES OF AIRFIELDS

When it comes to peaceful pursuits and international treaties, most people think of places like London, Oslo, Paris, or Versailles, where World War I was brought to its official closing. Dayton, Ohio, is not usually at the top of most peacemakers' lists. Yet, one of the twentieth century's final treaty accomplishments was forever etched in diplomatic history as the Dayton Accords. Wright-Patterson Air Force Base was chosen as the primary negotiation site for warring Bosnian factions and other interested nations because it was ideal for keeping an interested world out. The base offered the security and the media-free zone required to keep participants negotiating in person rather than in the press.

Some of the world's best-known statesmen of the time, like Warren Christopher, Richard Holbrooke, Wesley Clark, and Russia's Igor Ivanov, plied their statecraft and produced a document that was ultimately signed by US President Bill Clinton along with leaders from France, Germany, Russia, and the warring factions.[1] Though the treaty was ultimately signed in Paris, the real work was done in Dayton. This was done primarily because negotiations could be protected from the desire of media and politicians to work out the treaty on the pages of newspapers and via evening newscasts. Wright-Patterson has always been a beacon in political and aviation innovation, both for Ohio and for the country as a whole. It is the second-largest US Air Force base in the country, renowned for research, innovation, and a long history of training and sharpening the country's best flyers.

Founded originally as McCook Field and then Wright Field, Wright-Patterson is also the home of the National Museum of the US Air Force, the oldest, largest, and best-known military aviation museum. The museum features more than 400 planes and missiles. It dates back to 1923 and is one of Ohio's most frequently visited tourist destinations, drawing more than a million people annually.[2]

The base is far more focused on the needs of today and the future of aviation. It maintains a presence throughout the world via 27,000 active-duty military personnel, civilian employees, and contractors who work there. It is the center of a vast worldwide logistics system and is the US Air Force's premier acquisition and development center. Its mission also includes research and development, advanced education, heavy airlift flight operations, and intelligence. The size of a small city, Wright-Patterson is Ohio's largest single-site employer. This is where America's military aircraft of the future are conceived, designed, built, and tested. It seems altogether fitting that the base is next to the renowned Huffman Prairie field where Orville and Wilbur Wright say they "really learned to fly."

The base anchors a permanent, regional focus on flight. Along with "Wright-Pat," as its name is affectionately shortened, the base is just one of many southwest Ohio attractions for aviation enthusiasts. Others include the National Aviation Hall of Fame. All of southwestern Ohio's aviation fame begins with or is derived from the Wright brothers, but Ohioans and the state as a whole have done a good job of picking up where the Wrights left off.

Just 80 miles to the east, the Rickenbacker Air National Guard Base extends the Ohio aviation legend in other ways. First known as the Lockbourne Air Force Base, the facility has served in numerous roles for the Air Force and National Guard since its beginning. These include being a well-known pilot training and testing center and the home for the Women's Air Corp during and after World War II. The Rickenbacker base was named for Eddie Rickenbacker, automobile test driver, Indianapolis 500 race car driver, top World

War I flying ace, president of Eastern Airlines, and noted authority on matters relating to aviation, politics, and world affairs. Rickenbacker's high-flying career began under hardscrabble circumstances in Columbus. Yet by the time he was 15, he would be well established in his automotive career.

It stretches the mind to think that a kid in his early teens could be immersed in an automobile career, especially when most people see today's kids so immersed in video games. The early twentieth century was a different era. Rickenbacker's challenging young career was not enough for the spirited lad of German-Swiss decent. With the US entering World War I, Eddie was eager to prove the competence of race drivers as pilots, and eventually he got the chance to excel. During a two-month period in 1918, he bested more than 29 German opponents, which made him the top US ace for the entire war.

After the war, Rickenbacker was no less spectacular. Productive and successful stints with General Motors and several other firms led up to a long career at what was once one of the country's largest airlines, Eastern. Rickenbacker joined Eastern, then a unit of General Motors, in the 1930s. After GM announced plans to sell it, he quickly raised enough money to purchase controlling interest in the firm himself. By that point, air travel was already becoming a passenger business, with more and more Americans taking to the skies for vacation and business purposes.

Eastern was innovative from the get-go. It was first to deploy the latest advances from manufacturers such as Douglas and Lockheed. It was also aggressive in its pursuit of mail and other government contracts. The airline worked hard to promote from within, creating a loyal employee base. It was for a time the country's most profitable airline. Rickenbacker would remain with the company until 1963, when he stepped down from the position of chairman at the age of 73.

To say that Rickenbacker did it all with Eastern is not an overstatement. His work with the company nearly killed him when a Douglas 3 crashed near Atlanta in 1941. Soaked with fuel and trapped, Rickenbacker is said to have provided advice and encouragement to the injured and dying even as he lay immobilized. After the crash Rickenbacker nearly died when his oxygen tent malfunctioned while his medical attendant was sound asleep. Only his wife

Adelaide's alert attention to the matter saved the flying ace, airline president, and crash survivor from an untimely departure from the planet.

Rickenbacker's career included serving as a military advisor during World War II. He also penned a popular cartoon strip in the '30s, known as *Ace Drummond,* based on the adventures of a fighter pilot. Eddie Rickenbacker and opportunity came together at quite the right time. His penchant for daring and his love for both risk and business made him perfect for the industries that were overtaking both his native state and the nation. He left a mark on both the automotive and airline industries, with his strongest and most lasting impression perhaps still that of the daring flying ace. That is how he will be known and remembered through generations.[3]

He should also be thought of as the man whose inclinations and aptitudes went a long way toward making the Wright brothers' discoveries both popular and practical in war and commerce. Together the lives of the Wrights and of Rickenbacker were essential to taking our travel imagination from the confines of rail and ship to one where we are truly a nation aloft.

After Charles Lindbergh's famous New York–Paris flight, Americans' interest in aviation was at an all-time high. Ohio companies, events, and people were key in establishing and maintaining this enthusiasm. Cleveland was an important center for a number of aircraft innovators and manufacturers. Its airport was considered the nation's largest and most innovative at the time.

Another phenomenon was the National Air Races, which made their Cleveland debut in August 1929 with floats and fanfare rivaling the Tournament of Roses parade. They drew attention, participants, and onlookers from across the country. Features included cross-country events in which racers would take off from locations like Portland, Oregon, or Los Angeles, California, and timed so that the big finish would occur before crowds numbering in the hundreds of thousands. Amelia Earhart was a contestant in the Santa Monica, California-to-Cleveland Women's Air Derby in the 1929 show. Cleveland's large number of aircraft-related manufacturers helped foster an alliance between the city and the show's organizers. As a result, Cleveland was selected as the host site for most of the next 20 years until the show was suspended after a crash in

FIGURE 12.1. A mechanic preparing the capsule of an early, unmanned Mercury flight at NASA Lewis Research Center. Photo courtesy of NASA/Glenn Research Center.

1949.[4] The National Air Races were reborn in 1964 as two separate events: the Reno National Air Races and the Cleveland National Air Show. These events continue to this day, with the Cleveland show occurring each Labor Day weekend.

The NASA Glenn Research Center has been known by various other names (including NASA Lewis) since it first opened in the early 1940s. But it has made vital contributions to flying, in the air travel sense, and to space and deep space exploration. The center's milestones include development of the jet engine in the 1940s. It proved the potential for liquid hydrogen as a reliable rocket fuel during the 1950s. And it has remained critical throughout the space exploration years, managing the Centaur rocket program, developing the International Space Station's electric power system, and ion propulsion systems for NASA's Deep Space I and Dawn missions. And if your plane ever needs de-icing on a cold January morning, you can thank the folks at Glenn for that service, too.[5]

HIGHER HEIGHTS

As Orville and Wilbur Wright painstakingly prepared for their extended trip to Kitty Hawk for the first time in 1900, it is doubtful that any of them could imagine that babies being born in the last year of the nineteenth century stood a good chance of living to see a man walk on the moon. But a scant 70 years later—a nanosecond in human history—Neil Armstrong from nearby Wapakoneta, Ohio, would become the first human to do just that.

Armstrong is but one of 28 Ohio astronauts. By most counts, the Buckeye State leads the rest of the country in astronaut production:

Kenneth Cameron, born and raised in Cleveland, was educated at Michigan State and MIT.

Mansfield native *Michael Gernhardt* has a doctorate in bioengineering from the University of Pennsylvania plus extensive experience with deep-sea diving and space-walking.

Nancy Jane Currie grew up in Troy, Ohio, attended Ohio State, and had a 23-year career with the US Army.

Carl Walz went to high school in Lyndhurst, Ohio, before earning a B.S. in applied science from Kent State University and an M.S. in solid state physics from John Carroll University. His career included analysis of radioactive samples.

James Lovell's remarkable life began in Cleveland and includes one of the country's greatest rescue missions—Apollo 13.

Donald Thomas was born in Cleveland and attended Case Western Reserve before a career that included work for AT&T and teaching physics.

Michael Foreman was born in Columbus but grew up in Wadsworth, near Cleveland. His career has included naval aviation and aerospace engineering.

Donn Eisele attended Columbus West High School before his college education. He has logged more than 4,200 hours as a test pilot.

Charles Bassett, an Air Force captain with over 3,600 flight hours, was born in Dayton. He attended both Ohio State and Texas Tech.

Thomas Hennen was raised in central Ohio, attended Urbana College, and spent 24 years in the US Army imagery intelligence field.

Judy Resnick, one of the country's first female astronauts, was born in Akron, where she graduated from Firestone High School. She earned a B.S. at Carnegie Mellon University and a doctorate from the University of Maryland en route to careers at the electronics and broadcasting company RCA and the National Institutes of Health.

Gregory Harbaugh grew up in Willoughby, Ohio. He holds a B.S. degree in aeronautical and astronautical engineering from Purdue University and an M.S. in physical science from the University of Houston.

Euclid, Ohio–born *Sunita Williams* has degrees from both the US Naval Academy and the Florida Institute of Technology.

Michael Good grew up in Broadview Heights, Ohio, and went on to receive B.S. and M.S. degrees in aerospace engineering from the University of Notre Dame. He had a long career in the US Air Force as a test engineer and test pilot.

Mary Ellen Weber earned advanced degrees from Southern Methodist University and Cal Berkley before careers at Texas Instruments and in health care administration.

G. David Low of Cleveland earned degrees at Washington and Lee University, Cornell, and Stanford University.

Robert Overmyer was raised in Westlake, Ohio, and earned a B.S. in physics from Baldwin Wallace University and an M.S. in aeronautics from the US Naval Postgraduate School. His long, distinguished career included service as marine pilot.

Robert Springer grew up in Ashland, Ohio. He earned degrees from the US Naval Postgraduate School and flew numerous training and combat missions over Vietnam. He later went on to become an executive in a unit of Boeing.

Cleveland native *Ronald Sega* earned a B.S. degree in mathematics and physics from the US Air Force Academy, an M.S. from Ohio State, and a doctorate in physics from the University of Colorado. This preceded his career in education and service as an undersecretary of the US Air Force.

Warren's *Ronald Parise* earned degrees from Youngstown State University and the University of Florida before a career that included work for Operations Research, Inc.

Terence Henricks was raised in Woodville, Ohio. He earned degrees from the Air Force Academy and Golden Gate University before a career as a fighter pilot, test pilot, and parachute jumper.

Cincinnatian *Karl Henize* earned degrees from the University of Virginia and the University of Michigan in 1954. He then worked as an educator and in the field of astronomy at the university level.

Guion S. Bluford Jr. holds both master's and doctoral degrees from the Air Force Institute of Technology at Wright-Patterson Air Force Base. In a 1983 Space Shuttle mission, he became the first African American to fly in space.

As a pilot, *Mark N. Brown* logged over 3,000 flight hours in five different aircraft. In addition, he flew two Space Shuttle missions, in 1989 and 1991. He holds an M.S. in astronautical engineering from the Air Force Institute of Technology at Wright-Patterson Air Force Base.

Born in England, *Gregory Johnson* has long called Fairborn, Ohio, his home. He has extensive experience as an Air Force pilot and has flown two shuttle missions, logging over 755 hours in space. He holds master's degrees in business administration and flight structures engineering.

A resident of Ohio for many years, *Kathryn D. Sullivan* has degrees from the University of California and Dalhousie University. She became America's first space-walking woman during a 1984 shuttle mission. She has 582 hours in space.

We're not done yet. No one can forget Ohio's second-most famous astronaut: John Glenn Jr. was born in Cambridge, Ohio, and earned a B.S. in engineering from Muskingum College before a distinguished lifetime career that included the Navy and six terms in the US Senate.[6] Glenn learned to pilot aircraft in a government-sponsored program while still a student at Muskingum College. "I was sold on flying as soon as I got a taste for it," he said.[7] Little did he know how far it would take him. I had the starry-eyed good luck to meet Astronaut Glenn during his first run for Senate. He was

112 · CHAPTER 12

engaged in an unsuccessful primary challenge to incumbent Howard Metzenbaum, and I was with my buddies at the Ottawa Park
Ice Skating Rink in Toledo, where he was making a brief campaign
appearance. I cannot recall a single word of the conversation, but I
remember thinking that this hero was most famous person I'd ever
met at that point in my life. He still may be, even at this late date.

Glenn and Armstrong. They were All-Americans at a time when
that was an ideal. Ohio's other astronauts fit that bill as well. But
what is it about Ohio that produced the nation's most—and most
famous—astronauts? That's impossible to say. But some people at
the NASA Glenn Research Center opine that it is perhaps the early
inspiration provided by these space pioneers and the fact that Ohio
was the birthplace of flight and the nucleus for early aerospace
development. For example, Neil Armstrong's career began when he
went to work as a research pilot at the NASA center.[8] Ohio schools
and the midwestern work ethic are also mentioned as motivating
forces.

The simple one- or two-sentence descriptions of Ohio's astronauts
above hardly do justice to their remarkable lives and achievements.
Separate those from their time in service to the space program and
you still have incredible résumés. Judy Resnick was one of these
people. Akron, where I lived in the 1980s, was rightfully proud of
its native daughter. The town felt it knew her. On my way to work,
I drove by the temple where she and her parents worshiped. Akron
shared the joy and the pride of her first space mission in 1984. The
radio talked about her incessantly before and during her mission.
Everyone knew she was the only one to earn a perfect SAT score
while attending Firestone High in the mid-'60s. And everyone felt
they had lost a neighbor when Resnick perished in the 1986 Challenger disaster. Both the triumphs and the tragedies of the space
program hit close to home for Ohioans.

Ohio seems to have a sense of itself as an airborne, aloft state.
Apart from the Wright brothers, the astronauts, and the innovations, over 450 Ohio manufacturers and suppliers serve or supply
aviation and aerospace. Ohio's economy seems bound to the sky
and to space. Wright-Patterson AFB goes far beyond merely landing planes, as home to one of Ohio's two large federal aerospace
laboratories. The other is NASA's Glenn Research Center in Cleve-

land. Ohio's portfolio includes 10 leading universities with doctoral programs in disciplines and fields related to aerospace. The state leads the nation in advanced propulsion and power technology. Its most shining example is GE Aviation, headquartered in the Cincinnati suburb of Evandale. GE Aviation is the world leader in providing commercial and military jet engines and components as well as avionics, electric power, and mechanical systems for aircrafts. It is both a commercial and a strategic asset to the US, supplying defense and commercial aircraft makers worldwide. While the General Electric Company has struggled in areas like broadcasting and entertainment, it has become a Goliath in the worldwide aircraft engine market.[9]

In fact, GE dwarfs competitors Rolls-Royce and Pratt & Whitney and maintains the lion's share of significant world markets. Jet propulsion is an engineering phenomenon that fits naturally with GE's history in steam propulsion, turbocharging, and other technologies that maximize power output. The company has been hard at work in those areas since the early twentieth century. It was the first company to build and then successfully mass-produce jet engines. According to recent figures, GE Aviation employs 7,400 people in Ohio and northern Kentucky. This workforce is largely drawn from Ohio's aerospace-related education programs. You could say that GE has significantly elevated the art first practiced by Wright brothers employee Charlie Taylor. But in a nod to the early twentieth-century aviation pioneers, the company calls its newsletter simply "Bike Shop."

Even some of the state's earthiest industries have had a major hand in aerospace. Apollo 11 and all of the other Apollo missions were transported to their launch pads via one of two enormous crawler-transporters that inched the vehicle to the launch site at a speed of just one mile per hour. That transporter, the largest self-propelled land vehicle in the world, was built by Ohio's Marion Power Shovel.[10] The company has been defunct since 1997, but its crawler-transporters continue to creep along. They have even been updated as recently as 2012.

CHAPTER 13

THE INTERNAL
MELTING POT

Ohioans, like people in the rest of the US, are products of traditions that go as far back as civilization itself. The most modern recognizable influences begin in Western Europe, particularly England,
400 to 500 years ago. The American colonies were the handiwork
of those English people with a high sense of adventure (or feeling of desperation) and desire to improve whatever life they may
have foreseen for themselves in their old farms of Lancashire or the
wretchedness of London rookeries.

But they also hoped to keep many of their old ways. In the
founding of Maryland, English Catholics hoped to preserve both
their Englishness and their Catholicism. Before their culture was
subsumed by English ways, Dutch colonists had hoped to recreate
their old lives in a "New Amsterdam." Puritans wanted to be Englishmen but free from being Anglican. For those who settled the
east coast of the New World, the American Revolution abruptly
and finally removed any notion of being subjects of a faraway ruler
and culture.

American history notes the importance of the Revolutionary
War. We all know about Paul Revere's ride, the "shot heard round
the world," the treachery of Benedict Arnold, and Cornwallis's surrender at Yorktown. The Revolutionary War can also be seen as a
consequence of an earlier conflict, the French and Indian War. Not

only did this approximately nine-year (1755–1864) series of battles between the English and French colonies (and their "parent" countries) pave the way for a largely English-speaking North America, it helped clear a frontier for what would eventually become the state of Ohio just to the west of where the conflicts began at the confluence of the Allegheny and Monongahela Rivers.[1] The war would rage up and down a territory that spanned from this area and western Virginia territory all the way up through eastern Quebec and Nova Scotia. Eventually everything ended with battle victories by the British and British colonists on the Plains of Abraham, near Quebec City, and a few years later with the Battle of Signal Hill in Newfoundland. These battles determined the future for the Ohio Valley and most unsettled land east of the Mississippi. The Ohio River, which begins near Fort Duquesne, both pointed the way west and provided a key waterway for westward migration.[2]

Legal traditions, established and Americanized from the English, had been adapted by individual eastern states like Massachusetts, Rhode Island, and others. The same goes for basic systems of organizing townships and other municipalities, setting up state legislatures and local governments. A new economic system had been well established in the East and would move west, adopted by each new state to join the union.

But any notion that America would be a new version of England had to be modified with the first waves of non-English immigrants from Ireland and Germany. The Anglo-inspired culture that would move westward was just as likely to be carried by people named McConnell and Mueller as by Smiths or Adamses. Yet the spirit of Yankee enterprise came with them all. Families that had been fishermen in New England, blacksmiths in Virginia, or shopkeepers in New York during the eighteenth century produced children and grandchildren who would take those trades to Ohio in the nineteenth century. There it was just as likely that they would enter a field that was entirely new to the family, like farming, surveying, or equipment manufacturing.

It turns out that what mattered was not their trades but their instinct for self-support and self-determination. Notions of class or viewing work as lowly were remnants of an old European postfeudal culture that had been largely bred out of migrating Americans, especially those in Yankee climates.

For its first 57 years as a state, Ohio was the major artery of American expansion. As the only "Free" state between Kentucky and Canada, it was both a destination and a pathway for a country moving west. Many with Northern free-labor sentiments from an expanse between New Jersey and Pennsylvania all the way up to Maine and Massachusetts decided they wanted to go west into territory compatible with their worldviews. You could say that Ohio was a "first exit" in a multigeneration transcontinental trip of people, ideas, and tradition. For many, Ohio was a permanent stop.

FLEEING FOR OHIO

The state found itself a magnet for the distinctly American culture that had formed in the Northeast and for the huge surge of immigrants that would settle the country and redefine its cultural landscape in the mid-1800s. Ohio was an open opportunity, waiting for whoever wanted to make a go at a better life. It was without the slaveholding baggage of the South. It was a key "line" on the Underground Railroad. Today, the National Park Service lists more Ohio locations for freedom's railroad than for any other state.[3] And it eclipsed the Northeast as a lure to enterprising families and individuals because of its available land, increasingly centralized location, and constantly expanding business climate. Later in the 1800s, most of my own ancestors came from Switzerland or the various Austro-Hungarian and German duchies that composed central Europe at the time. They arrived for all the reasons we read about in grade school, most settling in Ohio straight off the boat. Almost all came to farm, attracted by fertile land at fair prices.

As the geographic gateway for northern states' residents moving west, Ohio brought together a wide cross-section of easterners and created a new kind of American. It was a logical enough journey for adventurous young people along the Eastern Seaboard seeking riches, adventure, or just a little distance between themselves and their old family traditions. My great-grandmother, who had been born to privilege in Bohemia but whose family lost its wealth after her father fell out of favor with Vienna, came to escape that disappointment and the fact that her father had "taken up with a servant girl after her mother's death" (my mother's words). She came as the new bride of my great-grandfather, who hoped his artistic talents

FIGURE 13.1. Four-generation photo circa 1925. A smiling toddler held by her grandfather with her mother at left. Also pictured are her great-grandfather and great-grandmother, who immigrated to Fremont, Ohio, from Switzerland 50 years earlier.

would find an eager market in the burgeoning pottery industry of southeastern Ohio. Later in life, my great-grandfather, who had spent decades with Weller Pottery[4] in Zanesville, Ohio, was heard to lament (or joke) that "we came over here to get rich and all we got were kids" (eight of them).[5]

Families who stopped in Ohio, if only for a generation, were no longer immigrants or people who saw themselves as transplanted Englishmen. Nor were they Vermonters, Pennsylvanians, or Massachusettsans. As columnist, commentator, and baseball aficionado George Will once wrote, the people of Ohio were "the first thoroughly American Americans."[6] The northern half of the state in particular condensed the attitudes and cultures of everywhere from Maine to New Jersey and Delaware. The southern half drew primarily from southern locations, westward migrants from Maryland, Virginia, and West Virginia. Later southern immigration would come from economic migrants arriving from Kentucky, Tennessee, and the Deep South.

Others didn't come far at all. William Holmes McGuffey moved with his parents less than 100 miles from Claysville, Pennsylvania, to Youngstown in 1802. McGuffey began teaching at age 14 in a one-room schoolhouse in Calcutta, Ohio, before going on to an even more distinguished education career at colleges throughout Ohio. He is best known for his *McGuffey Readers,* which were essential to education at schoolhouses across the country for over 100 years. They are still in use in private and home school settings.[7]

Then there were those who came but did not stay for long. Joseph Smith brought the headquarters for his new religion, the Church of Latter Day Saints, from upstate New York to Kirtland, Ohio, in the 1830s. After just a few years, financial failures and violence against some members caused Smith to abandon Ohio for Missouri, taking many members with him. Though some believers would remain in northeast Ohio, the core of Mormonism would continue moving west until it rooted itself in Utah.[8]

During the period 1820–40, the state was also undergoing an explosion in canal building at a pace even more energetic than in New York and other Northeast states. There was no location in the state that wasn't within 200 miles of either Lake Erie or the Ohio River. Canals were connecting the two bodies and many points in between. This flurry of canal building required all varieties of skilled and unskilled labor, provided by the large numbers of German and Irish immigrants flooding in to work on projects like the Ohio & Erie Canal.[9]

It is also possible that some of those recent European immigrants were fleeing the emerging resistance to them in the Northeast during the 1840s and '50s. Many, especially the American Party, which became known simply as the "Know Nothings," promulgated this anti-immigrant feeling. That nickname came from the fact that organized extreme elements of the movement were to say that they did in fact "know nothing" about the existence of their organization or any nefarious or illegal activities.[10]

What resulted from this surging eastern influx helped to build a core American demographic for the next 100 years. These were people who could trace some ancestors to the Mayflower while also pointing to a parent or grandparent who had a deep German or Hungarian accent.

DID OHIO USED TO BE IN NEW YORK?

It might surprise some to know that the *first* Ohi-yo refers to an area between Olean and Jamestown, New York, and to the Allegheny River, which runs through that area and is the headwaters of the Ohio River. A drive on New York's Southern Tier Expressway (I-86) takes you along and then over the river known as the Allegheny to the white man and Ohi-yo to the Native Americans who predated his arrival. It is odd that the European settlers wait until it joins the Monongahela in Pittsburgh before they begin calling it "Ohio."[11]

The Native American history and presence is strong in Ohio. Although there are no federally recognized Indian reservations in Ohio, it bears a Native American name and numerous towns, counties, and other landmarks recognizing the influence of the Seneca, Miami, Huron, Ottawa, and Wyandotte. Human residents have been occupying Ohio since about 13,000 BC.

Early peoples in what came to be known as Ohio included the Erie, Kickapoo, and Shawnee. It also included the legendary mound builders who literally left a mark on the landscape. These settlers are known today as the Hopewell and Adena (although that is not what they called themselves). They inhabited the region that would become southern Ohio from a period that began approximately 3,000 BC until about 1,600 BC. Their legacy includes more than 70 earthen monuments, including some that rise more than 100 feet. They built mounds that seem to approximate the look of grass-covered pyramids and others that snake back and forth for hundreds of yards, appearing to represent gigantic serpents.

The Native Americans who first inhabited the mound-building regions have been judged to be rather sophisticated. Evidence shows that rather than subsisting as nomadic hunter-gatherers, they built sustainable villages complete with established agricultural systems. Much later, around 1650, the Iroquois Confederacy moved into the region, driving indigenous tribes out and claiming it as their own hunting and trapping territory. The Iroquois are credited with carrying the "Ohi-yo" name with them. Later, those that had been pushed out of eastern states by white settlers, including the Delaware and the Shawnee, moved into Ohio. Others like the Seneca (part of the New York Iroquois Confederacy) came in the 1800s, when some of them were driven out of New York. Despite leaving their legacies in the names of Ohio towns and counties, these groups remained in the area for only a generation or two. In 1831 they were pushed further west, ultimately to Kansas and Oklahoma, under US Indian Removal policy.

There were important battles fought in Ohio, pitting the armies of Tecumseh against the forces of the newly emerged US under General Anthony ("Mad Anthony") Wayne. The 1795 battle of Fallen Timbers, near where Toledo would emerge, was a decisive defeat that would lead to the establishment of the Greenville Treaty Line. Native Americans were driven even farther from an area that one people or another had occupied for millennia.[12] It seems that a forced "stirring" was imposed on some in this "melting pot," forcing Ohio's original inhabitants out. Counties and rivers carrying names like Muskingum, Huron, and Ottawa are about all that remain of their legacy.

OHIO ACCENT

While the Ohio landscape and state can be seen as a kind of funnel for northern culture—both European and Native American from east to west—the state can also be seen as a kind of fan that propelled an emerging American accent from east to west.

According to some, Ohio is the starting point for the accents that are cited as "standard." These include the Midland (North and South) as well as the Inland North Accent, which some call the Chicago accent. This particular accent is believed to follow the south coasts of the Great Lakes all the way from Chicago east to Rochester, New York. The very south of Ohio has speakers sounding as "southern" as one might find in Virginia, Kentucky, and Tennessee. The two Midland accents begin in Ohio and spread directly west.

So, within the 200 miles that separate two great bodies of water lie several key speech or accent types that are reflected in a huge percentage of the rest of the American population. Midland seems initially to follow Ohio's northern and southern border parallels. Some call this the "midwestern" accent, but that is a bit of a misnomer given that such vast areas of the Midwest speak with similar but distinctly different accents. Those in Wisconsin, the upper peninsula of Michigan, Minnesota, and the Dakotas have their own linguistic styles with a sound that seems to be influenced both by migration from Scandinavia and by Canadian English. Farther south, in places like Iowa, Nebraska, and Kansas, you will find accent characteristics that could easily be mistaken for accents that you'd find in northern, central, and southern areas of Ohio.[13]

A reporter for London's *Guardian* newspaper researched an assertion that Steubenville, Ohio, is where real "American English" is spoken. It is a story that is proven correct if one accepts "North Midland" as the standard.[14] Cleveland-born and raised Phil Donahue exemplifies the pleasantly neutral speaking style, which he used to become one of the best-known television personalities of the late twentieth century. Newscasters still use this accent, and viewers across the country listen to it day in and day out. So, it is not hard to see how this particular method and sound of speech may become even more predominant over coming generations. And it could be argued that the Midland speech band has begun to broaden a bit, extending all the way to the West Coast. Long ago, I noticed that accents that I judged to be coming from West Coast states like California or Washington seemed to sound pretty close to my own. In junior high I developed friendships with several kids who had moved from these areas to Toledo because of their fathers' progression up the Owens-Illinois or Owens-Corning corporate ladders. No one would have ever thought of them as having accents any different from ours, something we could not have said about other recent new classmates arriving from New Jersey, north Florida, or Texas.

One thing that modern linguists overlook is Ohio's role in decimating a once common style of American English where internal or terminal *r*'s were not clearly pronounced. This "*r*-less" style of speaking is different from the current and thriving Boston accent and was based in southern New England and downstate New York. It was a cultivated and practiced accent that was most common in upper-class speakers of those areas. And it may have extended further west at one time in our history. This speaking style had many elements of British English, which, among its many distinct characteristics, also drops internal *r* sounds, except when they occur after the first consonant as in "Franklin," for example. This brings us to Franklin D. Roosevelt, who was the last well-known presidential speaker of the *r*-less variety of English, which has been referred to as "Westport Lockjaw" but is more properly known as the Mid-Atlantic accent. Remember FDR saying "We have nothing to feahhh but feahhh itself." You can hear this same pattern in the preserved recorded voices of other speakers like William F. Buckley, Katherine Hepburn, and Douglas Fairbanks Jr., but it is largely gone from the American linguistic landscape.[15]

THE MELTING-AWAY OF OLD SPEECH STYLES

I maintain that the "cultivated" eastern speech style (Mid-Atlantic) actually began to die out in the late nineteenth and early twentieth centuries when Ohio presidents who pronounced their internal *r*'s began to have their voices transmitted, first by virtue of Edison's wax cylinder, then by phonograph recordings, and then, ultimately, via radio. These were the first presidents—the *first people* actually—to have their voices heard by Americans in remote regions. Benjamin Harrison was the first president preserved in audio (1889), and other Ohio presidents would follow over the next 30 years. Harrison's is the oldest known recorded voice, and it can be heard today via the magic of YouTube.[16] McKinley was the only Ohio president recorded without the internal *r* sound in his pronunciations. He can be heard with an accent that sounds distinctly "Westport"—odd for a guy born in Niles, Ohio. He may have been a "poser" or simply one who accepted the notion of prestige associated with pronunciation which had been present in New England, downstate New York, and the Old South. However, listen to Taft and Harding and you hear crisp pronunciation of the internal *r* just as with Benjamin Harrison.

Perhaps the best known "news voice," especially in the first half of the twentieth century, was that of Lowell Thomas. His radio broadcasts and newsreel narration made him and his baritone voice an American staple. Thomas was born and spent the first eight years of his life in Darke County, Ohio, where he too learned to pronounce the *r*.

All of this indicates a shift in standards. Whereas the natural *r*-pronouncing speakers of the nineteenth century may have believed that adopting the *r*-less pronunciation centered in the East and South would prove a career enhancement, there came a point where the situation would reverse. In 1960 people who watched the debate between John F. Kennedy and Richard Nixon on television seemed to believe, according to polls, that Kennedy had won. However, those listening on radio thought that Nixon had won. Perhaps that is because those who listened rather than watched didn't experience Kennedy's handsomeness or Nixon's on-camera sweating. They only heard voices. One of these voices was the standard, accepted r-full pronunciation of the Californian Nixon. Kennedy, in contrast, spoke with r-less pronunciation that may by then have struck American eardrums as a bit foreign compared with the everyday speaking styles to which they had become accustomed. Nixon carried Ohio in 1960, perhaps because he sounded like he was from Ohio.[17]

The death of the Mid-Atlantic accent and declining usage of r-less pronunciation—dying out with Katherine Hepburn, Franklin Roosevelt, and William F. Buckley—probably resulted from declining prestige. I personally have a hard time remaining neutral on this subject. You will understand why when you take a second look at my last name. The r's are there to be pronounced.

CHAPTER 14

WHERE SPORTS
FIRST MET MONEY

One gift of the market economics system under which we all live is leisure time, plus the money to fill that time. For many of us, free time is filled with sports. When people are not sleeping, working, or engaged in other essential activities, they are involved somehow in sports. Ours is a nation of weekly golf outings, cycling tours, tennis clubs, tai chi classes, kids' soccer tournaments, Vermont skiing, and trips to watch our favorite teams play on weekends.

We Americans fill our lives with movement. If our late ancestors from, say, 150 or 200 years ago could return to mortal earth for a couple of days, they would be amazed (or maybe appalled) that modern humanity can spend so much of its time at play. These, after all, were people who almost universally toiled from dawn to dusk to scrape out their most meager livings.

Perhaps the only thing that eclipses our enjoyment of sports participation is seeing others engaged in them. Watching as superior athletes try to outrun, out-hit, outmaneuver, and outscore one another on the competitive field does several things. For one, it enables vicarious participation and achievement. How many times have you heard a fellow fan or friend say "We won!" even though neither of you were playing in the game? Sports foster common cause or a sense of community among people with otherwise dissimilar backgrounds or interests. He might be a Republican and I might be a Democrat, but if we're both Green Bay Packers fans on Sunday, then all is right with the world. Right?

Not only do we watch our favorite teams, we wear them in the billions of dollars of apparel for sale, ranging from socks and sweatbands to full-replica uniforms. We put Stephen Curry posters on our walls. Pittsburgh Steelers flags fly in front of our homes. We extinguish our cigars in Kansas City Royals ashtrays. So pervasive have the various sports teams become that entire industries have evolved around them. Others have figured out ways to monetize the power of others' athletic talent. Fantasy gaming sites like Fan-Duel and DraftKings are unique mergers of the concepts of professional football, gambling, and sports fanaticism.

But where did it all begin? What started this economic colossus worth billions or even trillions of dollars in economic value? The answer, if you have read to this point in the book, will not surprise you.

THOMAS JEFFERSON WAS NOT
A WASHINGTON NATIONALS FAN

Thomas Jefferson was the first US president to serve the country from Washington, DC, a newly conceived and freshly built city on the Maryland side of the Potomac River. He first took residency there in 1801 after growing up and spending much of his early adult life on nearby Virginia plantations. We've all heard of Monticello.

So, if he'd been a modern president, it would be perfectly logical for a man like Jefferson to be a Washington Redskins football fan. Or to eagerly throw out the first pitch at Washington Nationals home openers each spring. But it would be well over a century before either team existed. A few important developments had to occur along the way. First, the games of baseball and football had to be invented. Market economics had to team with industrialization to create greater individual wealth and leisure time. And athletes and other interested parties had to adapt to the general notion that anything worth doing is worth doing for money.

This takes us to a couple of interesting developments that occurred in Cincinnati and Canton, Ohio, during a half-century (mid-1800s to early 1900s) that also saw the invention of baseball (descended from the British game of cricket and a colonial game called "rounders") and football (derived from rugby and soccer). These were our first major professional team sports. And in these games, individuals could invest leisure time, civic pride, and even self-esteem. These sports set the stage for professional teams in basketball, soccer, hockey, and other forms of play. Today, professional athletics consume major amounts of America's time and money.

OHIO'S OTHER WRIGHT BROTHERS

In October 1975 the Boston Red Sox and Cincinnati Reds were matched in a memorable World Series that featured the era's biggest names. Plays from that series are still shown regularly on television (Carlton Fisk's Game 6, 12th-inning homerun, for example). Although these teams were in different leagues throughout their existence, they share a common history reflected in their names. It all goes back to the 1869 Cincinnati Red Stockings.[1]

Before that year, baseball had only recently begun as the sport familiar to us today. It was the product of ball-and-stick games that had been popular since colonial-era boys played them. Depending on the town you lived in, games varied and had different names. Rules and the number of bases even varied. The stick used for hitting could hardly be identified as a modern bat. Balls were often rocks, wrapped walnuts, or some other round creation. Playing ball drew the energies of boys and young men when they were away from their toils in shops, factories, or farms.

In the early 1840s a club in New York began to bring a new kind of order to the game, establishing something close to the modern game and placing it on the diamond-shaped field we know today. As baseball evolved over the next 20 years, it spread across the country, surviving the Civil War and expanding its popularity. Still, except for the stadium owners who charged admission or bettors who gambled on the sport, it was entirely an amateur pursuit. Just for fun.

Then came Harry Wright, a British-born Cincinnati businessman. Wright grew up playing cricket, the ball-and-stick game of his father. He had even coached the sport as a very young man after he and his family came from England to settle first in Harlem. This was at a time when a new game was beginning to gain traction in the streets and fields of New York. Before long, Wright got hooked on baseball.

Eventually Harry and his brother George found themselves living in Cincinnati. Baseball had found a home in the river town as well. Wright watched the sport gain popularity year after year—not only with increasing numbers of players but with growing crowds of spectators. People enjoyed watching as much as they did playing. Wright concluded that if people were willing to pay to watch actors perform onstage, why wouldn't they pay to watch athletes perform on the field? And so, professional baseball was born with Wright's Cincinnati Red Stockings. Wright was a player, manager, and the financial brains behind the team.[2]

The professional Red Stockings had a glorious beginning. They traveled from city to city, coast to coast, playing local amateur club teams. At home, they drew huge crowds. They fittingly mustered a 69–0 record in the year of 1869 and played before an estimated 200,000 fans in total. The money that people were paying to watch the games was enough for Wright to pay salaries to his players. The centennial of Wright's Red Stockings was celebrated by Major League Baseball in 1969.

But the good times were short-lived. The team began losing in 1870, and the crowds began to shrink. At the end of the season, baseball's first professional team disbanded.

The next year, Harry and George Wright (the team superstar) decided to move east to Boston, taking their equipment and the Red Stockings name with them. Within a few years, they were winning impressively again and the Boston Red Stockings were capturing National Association pennants. Cincinnati's Red Stockings would reappear in 1876 as members of the American Association. They would play in this league until being invited to join the stronger, more prestigious National League in 1890, which is about the time they shortened their name to simply the Reds. Because the Cincinnati team was seen as the first Red Stockings, the Boston organization later changed its name to the Red Caps and eventually settled on the name Braves. That is the same team that later moved to Milwaukee and eventually Atlanta, where they still play as the Atlanta Braves. In the early 1900s a new Boston Red Sox team joined the new American League, their name serving to memorialize the old Red Stockings.

The early periods were not always easy. In 1879 a *Cincinnati Gazette* editorial proclaimed the end of the sport: "The baseball mania has run its course. It has no future as a professional endeavor."[3] But reports of the game's demise were greatly exaggerated. And more than once, the game of baseball put Cincinnati into the national headlines. The most famous edition of the team was perhaps the "Big Red Machine" of the 1970s—a veritable all-star team in itself featuring Pete Rose, Joe Morgan, Johnny Bench, Ken Griffey Sr., and Dave Concepción.

Major League Baseball has two distinct leagues—National and American. The National League is the older of the two, having formed out of the National Association in the mid-1870s. The American League is the younger of the leagues, having been organized by Byron "Ban" Johnson, a Norwalk, Ohio, native and product of Marietta College. Johnson formed the league out of a once struggling minor league, the Western League, promising a "clean" alternative to the rowdy, gambling-infested National League.[4] Ironically, Johnson fell victim to the infamous Chicago Black Sox game-fixing scandal. He lost his position as American League President in the early 1920s when a federal judge for the Northern District of Illinois became baseball's first commissioner with authority over both leagues. Kenesaw [*sic*] Mountain Landis, born in Millville, Ohio, received his unique name after Kennesaw Mountain, Georgia, where his surgeon father was wounded during Civil War service in the 35th Ohio Volunteer Infantry.[5]

Since those early Cincinnati and then Boston Red Stockings, professional baseball has built a presence in every state, through the "majors" and the minor leagues, which extend from the rookie leagues to Double A and Triple A clubs. No one should discount the minor leagues, either. For a number of major American cities, like Buffalo, Indianapolis, Nashville, Columbus, Memphis, Charlotte, Las Vegas, and New Orleans, Triple A ball is the biggest game in town.

Baseball is, by far, the most attended of the professional sports, owing partly to a long, leisurely season. In 2015 regular-season attendance was over 73 million, equivalent to nearly a quarter of the US population. Add television viewership and minor league attendance and numbers get even higher. Since 1975 the Reds, Braves, and Red Sox have combined to appear in 13 World Series, winning seven of them. What Harry Wright began in Cincinnati seems to have worked out pretty well. Football may be what arouses America's passions, but baseball is still its pastime, in the truest sense of the word.

HUDDLING WITH HUPMOBILES

Professional sports have existed in some form or another for centuries. In horse racing, jockeys were paid and money was wagered. Boxers and wrestlers were often paid depending on the locale. In the new sport of football, certain players and, in some cases, entire teams received payment for their efforts as early as the 1890s. Football had been seen as a college game and strictly amateur until enthusiasts in the new industrial heart of the country—from western New York and western Pennsylvania all the way through Indiana and Illinois—began playing an independent version of the game. This was important in an era when colleges monopolized the game, because not every city had a college. Unlike college games, which usually were played on Saturdays, this version of football was generally played on Sunday—virtually the only free day for both players and fans. More and more, players began receiving some kind of monetary compensation for playing the independent game.

The game of football was still creating itself in those days. There was a time when field goals were worth five points and touchdowns only four. Many teams were associated with athletic clubs that would pay one or two of their top players or use the promise of money to lure a star player away from a competitor. In Philadelphia, Phillies and Athletics baseball players would take up the sport of football in the fall after baseball season ended. They once formed a three-team league with a club team in Pittsburgh. The emerging "professional" football of that era was entirely ad hoc. Leagues, if they existed at all, were informal. Some teams played only two or three games per year. But by the early 1900s, the best professional football was taking place in Ohio among teams that would eventually become known as the Ohio League.

FIGURE 14.1. The Pro Football Hall of Fame's museum in Canton remains the centerpiece of a $600 million theme destination. The professional version of the game began in Canton 100 years ago.

In November 1915 Jim Thorpe signed a contract to play for the Canton Bulldogs for $250 per game. Football was still only partially professional. Clubs would play amateur teams and continue to employ amateur players. There was continuous controversy over teams that might be hiring college players despite collegiate prohibitions against professionalism. It was thought that college players would sneak away for the Sunday games and play professionally, using aliases.

Yet there remained a notion among team owners in places like Decatur, Illinois, Rochester, New York, and Dayton, Ohio, that professional football could be as popular and successful as baseball. They were optimistic even though the game was still viewed as an amateur sport, and Sunday play seemed to be at odds with American culture, which still largely regarded Sunday as a day of worship and rest.

Many felt football needed to be professionalized and have a bit more organization and structure before it would really take off.

That was the purpose of two meetings that took place in the late summer of 1920. In the first, on August 20, Ralph Hay, owner of the Canton Bulldogs, hosted the owners of the Akron Pros, Cleveland Indians (football team), and Dayton Triangles. The group agreed to form the American Professional Football Association. They also agreed that they needed more competition, so they wrote to other well-known clubs in the region. A second and larger organizing meeting took place September 17, 1920, in Hay's auto showroom. Other team owners and representatives in attendance were from Rochester, New York; Chicago, Rock Island, and Decatur in Illinois; and Muncie and Hammond in Indiana. It was said to be so crowded in the Hay showroom that attendees had to sit on the running boards of the cars on display.[6]

Hay had been using the Canton Bulldogs primarily as a marketing tool for his car dealership. The brands of cars sold by Hay were the Hupmobile and the Jordan. The Jordan name disappeared in the early 1930s, and the Hupmobile brand ended with the 1940 model year. But the sports brand that began in a car dealership would evolve to become one of the biggest sports marketing forces on the planet. Within two years, the American Professional Football Association would change its official name to the National Football League, even though it was hardly yet nationwide in scope.

You might expect that a league just staging its organizing meeting might need a year or two to begin fielding games. The young league, however, was off and running, even as teams continued to join during the 1920 season. The first teams are listed in Table 1. Teams came and went in those days and were mostly located in Ohio, Illinois, Indiana, and New York. Team names, host cities, and rosters were in constant flux. They could play nonleague teams, too.[7] One consequence of the fluidity was that the 1920 season had no clear winner. League management awarded the 1920 title to the Akron Pros, but not until April 1922. During the 1922 season, Ohio had three teams called the Indians: the Cleveland Indians, the Akron Indians, and the Oorang Indians. That last team was based in tiny La Rue, Ohio, and was strictly a traveling team playing 22 games over two years, all on the road. The only exception may be a game played in nearby Marion (also frequently credited as being the team's hometown). This team had the distinction of being composed solely of Native Americans. The roster included player-coach

TABLE 1. First NFL Teams—1920 League Standings

TEAM	W	L	T	PCT
Akron Pros	8	0	3	1
Decatur Staleys	10	1	2	0.909
Buffalo All-Americans	9	1	1	0.9
Chicago Cardinals	6	2	2	0.75
Rock Island Independents	6	2	2	0.75
Dayton Triangles	5	2	2	0.714
Rochester Jeffersons	6	3	2	0.667
Canton Bulldogs	7	4	2	0.636
Detroit Heralds	2	3	3	0.4
Cleveland Tigers	2	4	2	0.333
Chicago Tigers	2	5	1	0.286
Hammond Pros	2	5	0	0.286
Columbus Panhandles	2	6	2	0.25
Muncie Flyers	0	1	0	0

(Source: NFL.com)

Jim Thorpe, who was also the NFL's first president. Just imagine Roger Goodell suiting up for a game, today. La Rue, Ohio, maintains the distinction of being the smallest community ever to have an NFL team. The Oorang name belonged to a local dog kennel, where the Airedale was the breed of specialty.[8]

By 1922 teams from places such as Duluth, Minnesota, and Pottsville, Pennsylvania, came on board. There were teams familiar to today's NFL aficionado as well, including the Chicago Bears, New York Giants, and Chicago Cardinals (now the Arizona Cardinals, via St. Louis). The Green Bay Packers came and went a couple of times during the league's early years. The team had been started in 1919 by Curly Lambeau, a Green Bay football standout who had played for Notre Dame under Knute Rocke. Lambeau convinced the meatpacking company he worked for to back the team and was initially a player-captain, then later head coach. Early on, the Packers team suffered financially and withdrew but then shortly came back as a community-owned organization, similar to the unique way it is constituted today. Its founder's name lives on in the Packers' current home, Lambeau Field.

The Canton Bulldogs and Chicago Staleys, who soon became the Bears, were dominant early teams. Cleveland won its first NFL championship in 1925, delivered by the Cleveland Bulldogs (related to the old Canton franchise). Family names like Mara and Halas would first appear in NFL ownership positions and remain dominant for decades. As the 1920s waned, the league began shedding some of its small-town teams, dramatically cutting the number of clubs. This move was made to concentrate talent in larger markets. By 1930 Ohio had just one team in the league—the Portsmouth Spartans—even as NFL headquarters remained in Columbus.

The league in 1920 had begun as a way to bring order to the chaos of professional football. Not only had the NFL clarified issues related to employment of college players and the sudden exit of players for teams offering a bit more money, it had drafted a constitution, developed a system of standings, and offered territorial rights to teams. These were important steps in bringing the league toward the modern era. Still to be settled, of course, were many other issues. Some of these were not even imagined at the time, like revenue sharing, relationships with television and radio broadcasting, and the all-important question of exactly who could play the game.

CHANGING THE FACE OF SPORT

Racial barriers stood almost everywhere in the early twentieth century. The sports world was no exception. Early efforts at baseball integration had been attempted as early as the late 1800s, but they ultimately failed, and the sport adapted a separate and unequal system that led to the formation of the Negro Leagues. These teams employed some of the country's most talented players and became quite successful, drawing crowds that often rivaled the white major leagues and helping their usually black owners to prosper.

It appeared that the NFL was taking a more diverse approach to its game and its market. Its ranks included a Native American president, a coach and at least three players who were African American, and one team composed completely of people with

Native American heritage. One seldom-noted fact is that the first championship team, the 1920 Akron Pros, had two black players, Fritz Pollard and Paul Robeson. Paul Robeson would go on to become an attorney, an activist, and a well-known musical artist and actor. And Pollard had already broken a number of color barriers at the college level with Brown University. But one of the most significant breakthroughs came when he was appointed the Akron Pros' head coach for the 1921 season. He would compile an 8–3–1 record that year. When Art Shell became coach of the Oakland Raiders in 1989, it was widely perceived that he was the first African American NFL coach, but many sportscasters were careful to clarify that Shell was the first in the "modern NFL era." One thing that may have made such choices possible in a segregated era was that northern states like Ohio, although far from perfect, tended to be less segregated than southern states. It is also worth mentioning that there were no southern NFL teams in those years, due a southern commitment to "maintaining the Sabbath."

Pro football was not the major spectator sport that it is today. College football was far more important. The other major sports of that era included boxing, horse racing, and, of course, baseball. Comparatively, pro football fields seemed a more tolerant venue.

Even with that, being a pioneer was not always easy for Fritz Pollard.

Players who didn't want to see blacks on the field employed sometimes brutal discrimination techniques, such as two opposing players hitting him high and low simultaneously. Pollard even clashed with Jim Thorpe (who, like Pollard, had a Native American mother), but Pollard was resilient, something he no doubt began to incorporate into his internal strength during difficult years playing for Brown University. Pollard once told NFL Films, "I didn't get mad at them and want to fight them. I would just look at them and grin, and in the next minute run for an 80-yard touchdown."[9]

Then came a period of real segregation in the league. It began about 1933 and is said to have been the secretive handiwork of early NFL pioneer owners like George Halas of Chicago, Tim Mara of New York, Art Rooney of Pittsburgh, and George Marshall of the newly admitted Washington Redskins. Although there was no written, codified race-barring policy, it is believed to have been informally and uniformly practiced throughout the league for about 13 years.[10] By then the NFL was playing games in a wider geography that included southern states and border regions like Missouri and Washington, DC. Fortunately, pro football's period of segregation was much shorter than baseball's. And it may be argued that the NFL helped pave the way for integration in Major League Baseball.

Fast-forwarding to the late 1940s, America had undergone rapid change and was about to accelerate further in areas like civil rights. The economy was beginning to boom. Another world war had been won, with black and white troops often fighting alongside one another. Harry Truman officially ended segregation in the armed forces. In 1946 four black players signed NFL contracts, effectively ending the "gentlemen's" agreement on segregation. Cleveland factors into all four signings.

Cleveland's Rams had just moved to Los Angeles after winning the NFL championship, taking star quarterback Paul Waterfield and his Hollywood superstar and pinup-idol wife, Jane Russell, with them. The Rams had a young, forward-thinking owner, Daniel Reeves, who essentially fled Cleveland. His reason was that the new Cleveland Browns of the All American Football Conference (AAFC) would be arriving for the '46 season, coached by Ohioan Paul Brown. Native to New York but an Ohioan for much of the past 10 years, Reeves knew Brown's popularity as a player, coach, and articulate, well-known football innovator.

Brown had first made his football coaching reputation with the Massillon Washington Tigers, a dominant Ohio high school team. Then came Ohio State, where he recruited and played a number of African American players. Brown was coming off two years of military service at the Great Lakes Naval Training Station and was aggressively recruiting players he had either coached or coached against. These included Otto Graham, the legend of the Northwestern Wildcats, whom Brown's Ohio State Buckeyes had opposed; Marion Motley, whom he'd coached at the Naval Training Station; and Bill Willis, defensive tackle and pass defender, whom Brown had once coached at Ohio State. Paul Brown was stacking his new team in every way he could.[11] Both Motley and Willis were black, meaning that the new AAFC would again introduce integration to the professional game a full year before Jackie Robinson took the field for the Brooklyn Dodgers. Willis, who would have a successful career with the Browns and later go on to serve for 24 years as director of the Ohio Youth Commission, credits Brown with taking important first steps in changing the social fabric of the country through his "unwavering attitude that the best players should play on his team regardless of any other factors."[12] Reeves and the now *Los Angeles* Rams followed suit, signing two black players: Kenny Washington and Woody Strode.[13]

MONTREAL TO BROOKLYN

Ohioans would play a pivotal role in the integration of professional baseball as well. Social forces were already well at work in that direction during the mid- to late 1940s, and personality and personal history, as they so often do, played a big part in changing the game. Such was the case with the story of Jackie Robinson and Brooklyn Dodgers Owner Branch Rickey.

The Jackie Robinson story is one of physical talent and perseverance. And as is shown vividly in the movie *42*, Robinson's breakthrough had an important sponsor in Rickey. Born and raised in the small southeastern Ohio town of Stockdale, Rickey discovered the wider world during his years of study at Ohio Wesleyan University, a Methodist institution in Delaware.

Rickey arrived at the school in the early 1900s a poor young man of moderate athletic ability. He played baseball for Ohio Wesleyan and later coached. It was in that role that he came face to face with the impact of racism on young black athletes. On one occasion, Rickey's Ohio Wesleyan teammates were checking into their hotel before a game against Notre Dame, and one of his players, Charles Thomas, was refused a room simply because he was black. After some discussion and Rickey's threat to remove the whole team, hotel management acquiesced to Thomas's staying in Rickey's room. When Rickey returned there after an evening "bed check," he found Thomas sobbing, tearing at his face and openly deploring the color of his own skin. The image stayed with Rickey for the next 40-plus years until he signed Robinson to the Brooklyn Dodger organization in 1945, calling him up from minor league Montreal for his history-making Major League Baseball debut in 1947.[14]

Another black player broke other baseball color lines just a few months later. Larry Doby played his first game for the Cleveland Indians, thereby beginning the process of integrating the American League. Owing to his own talents and to the quality of the team he joined, he was also the first black player to play in or hit a home run in the World Series, when the 1948 Indians took down the Boston Braves in four games. Doby would be a seven-time all-star and was also the first black player to lead the league in home runs. Larry Doby and Jackie Robinson broke significant barriers and opened up opportunities for people like Willie Mays, Henry Aaron, Bob Gibson, Joe Morgan, and Frank Robinson.[15] In 1975 Robinson broke another barrier when he became Major League Baseball's first African American manager with the Cleveland Indians.

It is hard to measure the impact of sports on overall civil rights advancement. But through the 1950s and '60s, as young kids throughout the country tore open their baseball card and bubble gum packages, more and more of those cards contained the pictures and statistics of African American players. The game was changing for sports and for the larger society.

GAME CHANGERS

An ability to defy conventions and escape established paradigms doesn't always lead to greatness, but it is often your best shot. The ability to "think beyond" could be a personality trait that leads one to take chances in matters of race or in the play of the game. Paul Brown and Branch Rickey certainly were key innovators in their respective sports. Brown is often given credit for creating the modern, tactical, disciplined game that football has become. He was the first to scout opposing teams using film. Brown also professionalized assistant coaching, making it a full-time, year-round job.

Other Brown inventions included testing players on the team playbook and using guards to run plays in so that plays could be called from the sidelines (by him). Brown brought so much change to the game that his teams were nearly unbeatable for his first 10 years of coaching in the pro ranks. Between the AAFC and the NFL, the Cleveland Browns appeared in 10 straight league championship games. He innovated everywhere on the field. He created the draw play and realigned basic offensive strategy. Off the field, Brown developed the facemask and relentlessly schooled his team on every play in the playbook. To Brown, intelligence in a player was just as important as athletic talent.[16]

Those who have studied the full story of Paul Brown also know that his later coaching years were not nearly as productive. He was fired by the new Browns owner, Art Modell, in 1963. He later became owner and the first head coach of the new Cincinnati Bengals. Other teams had by that time fully employed his innovations to up their games to Brown's level. After leaving the team that bore his name, Brown never won another NFL championship. And the Cleveland Browns have won only one championship without him, and that was the 1964 team coached by Brown protégé Blanton Collier.

Brown is the only person with an NFL team named after him. The Cleveland Browns, despite their hard times, are still one of the most visible NFL brands and have one of the largest "backers" organizations in the country. He is also memorialized through the founding of his namesake's in-state archenemy, the Bengals, who play their games in the appropriately named Paul Brown Stadium.

By the prime of his life, Branch Rickey had become a successful sports businessman and owner. His innovations in baseball took forms different from those achieved by Brown in football. As an executive for the St. Louis Cardinals, he began to buy up nearby teams in other minor leagues in order to feed his own team with quality players. This action led ultimately to the modern "farm system," wherein a multitiered system of leagues further refines and nurtures young talent. As owner of the Brooklyn Dodgers, Rickey wanted to give his team a valuable head start on each new season, so he single-handedly created the concept of spring training, sending his team to Florida many weeks before the start of the season. Like Brown, Rickey always tried to protect his players and insure his investments. That is no doubt among the motivations that led to his introduction of the batting helmet.[17]

Both Brown and Rickey were born in Ohio. Unlike Rickey, whose achievements were spread between his time in Ohio, Missouri, and New York, Brown forged his coaching, management, and ownership career entirely within the state of Ohio—from Massillon to Ohio State to Cleveland to Cincinnati. Both changed their games in ways that were revolutionary for the time but ultimately proved fundamental to today's professional baseball and football games.

HELL NO, MODELL!

At the beginning of the 1995 World Series featuring the Cleveland Indians and Atlanta Braves, I remember a promotional spot that stood out. It reminded viewers of Cleveland's last appearance in a World Series, saying something like "back in 1954, Cleveland, Ohio, was the capital of sports." It was a jarring reminder of how far the city had fallen through the '60s, '70s, and '80s. Yet, on what seemed the verge of triumph, little did any Cleveland sports fan know that civic sports pride had still farther to tumble.

The Indians lost to the Braves in six games. A few weeks later, the beloved Cleveland Browns announced that they would be moving to Baltimore. There was inescapable irony in this story. Baltimore itself had been a "jilted lover" when the Colts were abruptly moved to Indianapolis. Now it seemed that Baltimore was doing the same thing to Cleveland. In the end, Cleveland owner Art Modell was allowed to take his team but was required to leave the Browns name and trademark assets behind.

A new Browns team would re-form and resume play in 1999. The replacement of one Cleveland Browns team with another is hard to imagine in any other locale. But this was Cleveland, ground zero for a twentieth-century sports phenomenon. The NFL knew its roots. And it knew better than to forsake a past which had done so much for the game.

CALDRON OF COACHES

The Ohio story always connects to football. Sports broadcasters have always enjoyed referring to Ohio as the "cradle of coaches." Sometimes you hear the name applied specifically to Miami University. Miami certainly has its ties to the game's history. It was a training ground for Woody Hayes, who coached there early in his career. And it gave the game a new offensive orientation, making the passing game far more important than it had been. Sid Gillman coached the University of Cincinnati and Miami University before going on to coach the L.A. Rams and then becoming general manager of the San Diego Chargers. His approach stretched the field, minimized blitzes, and provided numerous options to a quarterback even after the ball was snapped.[18] He and Paul Brown were the first to make extensive use of film study to scout teams and analyze team performance. Gillman's ideas led many to call him the father of the *West Coast Offense.* Ironically, that was a term coined well after Gillman passed away. Maybe it should really be called the *Ohio River Offense.*

The football innovation history goes even further back. Legendary Notre Dame player and then coach Knute Rockne not only met his wife in Sandusky, he perfected the forward pass on the nearby Lake Erie beaches at Cedar Point in 1913 along with teammate Gus Dorais. Both had been working there as lifeguards. Passing had not been common, as football was mostly a running and kicking game in that era. The two friends' efforts to turn the pass into an offensive weapon helped propel Notre Dame to a major upset victory over Army that November and led to changes in the very nature of the sport.[19]

Cradle of coaches. The term is alliterative. And it speaks to the state's uncanny ability to create college and professional football coaches. But on second thought, it might be worth refining that description to *caldron of coaches* and bring in notions of fire, the melding of elements and industries like steel and rubber. It is a perfect way to describe the gritty, blue-collar culture that also defines the state. And it is a fact that anyone who achieves success in Ohio does so by enduring a kind of trial by fire in some of the most challenging football environments anywhere.

It has been noted that Ohio has only 4 percent of the country's population but delivers a full 15 percent of its major college and pro coaches. The statistics get even more impressive when you consider the number of winning coaches. In the highest levels of football, it seems that you have to be born in Ohio or forged by the football experience there. Sid Gillman was, as were Woody Hayes and Paul Brown.

Hayes and Brown were important not just as teachers of the game but as molders of men. Hayes's early life as a teacher and passionate enthusiast for history and literature fed his insistence on players achieving in class as well as on the field. Dr. Donald Steinberg—father of my longtime friend and college roommate, Dan—played three war-interrupted years at Ohio State (1941, 1942, and 1945), the first two for Brown. This includes the school's first national championship team in 1942. In his 1992 book *Expanding Your Horizons,* Steinberg makes clear that Brown's efforts were just as important in creating highly successful attorneys, CEOs, educators, and doctors as they were in feeding talent into the professional football ranks.[20] Jim Tressel, coach of the 2002 National Champion Buckeyes, required all his players to read Steinberg's book.

Before you dismiss people like Hayes, Brown, Gillman, and even Rockne as football antiquity, consider the present-day landscape of top-level NCAA and professional coaches: the Harbaugh brothers (Jim and John), Pete Carroll, Mark Dantonio, Nick Saban, Urban Meyer, Jim Tressel (now president of Youngstown State University), Bo Pelini, Les Miles, and Bob Stoops. Even Bill Belichick of the New England Patriots had to be "tried and tempered" in a period of service to the Cleveland Browns. This is especially notable, as the Browns were the favorite team of his boyhood. Don Shula (with the Browns) and Bill Walsh (with the Bengals) were longtime disciples of Paul Brown. Between 2002 and 2017, 12 out of 15 Division I college champions were led by coaches either who were born in Ohio or who spent formative parts of their careers coaching in the state.[21]

The Buckeye State has given its legendary South Bend, Indiana, neighbor, Notre Dame, standout sideline generals like Lou Holtz and Ara Parseghian. It has also produced coaches who have broken Ohioans' hearts in effective service to teams like the Michigan Wolverines (Bo Schembechler) or the Pittsburgh Steelers (Chuck Noll). Bill Walsh, a Cincinnati assistant, who had hoped to be named the Bengals' head coach, ultimately went on to defeat his former team in the 1981 and 1988 season Super Bowls as coach of the San Francisco 49ers.[22]

CHAPTER 15

MORE THAN A GAME

November 25, 1950, may not stand out in national memory. The day occurred in an era when the country was recovering from World War II, gearing up for the Korean conflict, and discovering the new entertainment phenomenon of television. On the home front, the economy was accelerating, while President Harry Truman's popularity was plummeting. That Saturday after Thanksgiving was just like any other day. Unless you were either a meteorologist or a football fan in Central Ohio.

That day was the 47th meeting of the Ohio State and Michigan football teams. At that point, the rivalry had had more than half a century to develop. Together the schools dominated the Big Ten Conference, so there was no way that high winds and the snow that had fallen thus far in the Columbus area would stop the game. Cancellation was suggested but roundly rejected. Michigan players and fans had already made the trip, and calling the game off would mean a win for Ohio State according to the rules of the day.

It was impossible for Ohio State officials to deny this contest to Columbus and the legions of fans descending on Ohio Stadium— "The Horseshoe." Kickoff occurred almost as scheduled despite the five inches of wind-driven snow that had already fallen with blizzardlike ferocity. Plenty more would come in the Columbus area's worst snowstorm in nearly 30 years.

Tactically, the Snow Bowl, or "Blizzard Bowl," was one of the strangest games ever played or witnessed. Both teams seemed to employ a strategy of running two plays and then punting on third down. The idea was to have a second chance if the punter fumbled and recovered. Sometimes the teams punted on first down in the hopes of catching the opposing team by surprise and being aided by a ball that skidded down the icy turf close to the end zone. Countless punts resulted in fumbles by the receiving team. It was almost better to be on defense.[1]

Dr. James Lipson, a noted Rochester, New York, cancer physician, Michigan grad, and life-loyal Wolverines fan, is one of many people who told me of "being there." My late father-in-law, Donald Kielmeyer, said he was there as well. When I lived in Columbus in the early '80s, I met dozens of people who claimed to have been part of the fabled Snow Bowl of 1950.[2] I grew up thinking that my dad had been there too, until he finally told me that by "being there" he meant he was in Columbus and on campus but not in the stands. YouTube videos of the event show fans sitting on bleachers as snow piled up on the empty seats beside them. The video seems to make liars of the million or so people who say they were at the game.

Ohio State's Vic Janowicz's 27-yard field goal into hard-driving wind and snow is thought by many to be the single greatest feat by a Buckeye player. Janowicz, who punted and kicked, also played running back, scoring 16 touchdowns in 1950. He also won the Heisman Trophy that year.[3] By the end of the Snow Bowl, Michigan emerged victorious, winning 9–3 despite the fact that they had never made a single first down. The Wolverines scored on a safety and made a touchdown after recovering a blocked Ohio State punt in the end zone.

This was one of the most fabled contests in the long-standing, seldom dull pigskin war between Ohio State and Michigan. Some say this war is a continuation of the "Toledo War" waged in the 1830s. Watch an Ohio State–Michigan football game some year, and you will likely see the network share a clip from the 1950 "Snow Bowl."[4]

A SURROGATE FOR WAR

The story of Ohio State and Michigan is well known in college sports. Every year a host of publications and websites post listings of top college rivalries. And Ohio State versus Michigan is almost always ranked number one. But the notion of regional loyalties and animus toward neighbors reaches far beyond the sporting world.

Like the people that compose them, American states are partially defined by those they hang around with. In Ohio's case, Michigan has been kind of like the kid next door. He's the one you sometimes want to punch but often find yourself in league with, particularly when it comes to fending off gangs from the next street over. The two states have been geographic neighbors, economic partners, and sporting rivals ever since the "Toledo War" in the 1830s. The 1950 Snow Bowl was just one highlight. And Ohio State has always done its part to contribute to the rivalry.

Of the four undergraduate and graduate degrees earned by my parents, the one that really counted was my father's bachelor of engineering degree from Ohio State. In my childhood mind, it conferred some kind of lifelong Buckeye status, of patrilineal descent. My dad grew up in Fremont, Ohio, as the third of five kids. He became an engineer, as did his brothers, one of whom also went to Ohio State. His two sisters married brothers who were also engineers but who left with their brides to pursue careers and raise families in what was then America's hottest city—Detroit.

Cleveland may have been a boomtown in the 1950s, but it was nowhere on the scale of Detroit with its Big Four automakers in full production and American faith in the continued promise of cars. And as those cars grew longer, lower, wider, and more powerful each year, Detroit became the place for engineers. As a kid visiting my relatives in suburban Royal Oak, Michigan, I was subjected to the teasing of my cousins and their friends. They were more than willing to suggest that things weren't nearly as good in Ohio as they were in Michigan. They couldn't even imagine that the Baskin & Robbins in Ohio actually had 31 flavors just as they did in the Detroit suburbs.

My Michigan cousins were all "Chrysler Kids," their dads having taken various engineering assignments with the company back when Chrysler was still strong and vibrant. My dad always teased my uncles about the company and the brand. And just to revolt appropriately against his Michigan family members, our branch always showed up for family events in a Ford or General Motors product. The Ohio–Michigan line wasn't the only thing that divided our extended family.

As an industrial engineer, my dad's job was to make sure things *got made*. He engineered the processes of production for Sylvania Electric and American Standard in the '50s and '60s before a long career with Johns-Manville (of asbestos lawsuit litigation fame). It was his career in the Fiberglass Manufacturing Unit of Manville that took us to the Toledo area, where all things glass were produced. He was one of tens of thousands of engineers graduated by Ohio State, whose science, engineering, and architecture graduates compose a veritable *Who's Who* of American invention.[5]

One of the automotive industry's early leaders and most prolific inventors, Charles Kettering, studied electrical engineering during his time at Ohio State. He went on to work at Dayton's National Cash Register Company before founding Delco (Dayton Electric Company) and moving on to a career as vice president for research for General Motors.

Ohio State may not have graduated Ohio's native son Thomas Edison, but it did produce the country's number two in terms of patents. Melvin De Groote was a remarkably accomplished chemist whose 925 patents[6] give him the second greatest number of US patents after Edison (1,097).[7] Another Buckeye, Roy Plunkett, received his Ohio State Ph.D. in 1936 and went on to invent Polytetrafluoroethylene, better known as Teflon.[8]

Ohio State graduates in the sciences have flown space missions, headed product development at giant manufacturing corporations like Westinghouse, and led the Canadian Astronomical Society and the Korean Society for Energy Research. They have taken the state's passion for "growing things and making things" to the highest possible levels. They are at work in tens of thousands of businesses and public organizations, solving problems ranging from how to build more efficient gas turbines to finding ways to sharpen the effectiveness of radar. They are experts at nano- and microfluid technologies. Ohio State grads are master builders of great things like shopping malls and small marvels like engineered molecules.

They've founded numerous consumer tech enterprises, too, including Wikipedia.[9]

Ohio State's contributions to the NFL are impressive in any era, from greats Paul Brown, Howard "Hopalong" Cassidy, and Paul Warfield of the 1940s, '50s, and '60s to Jack Tatum and Archie Griffin in the '70s and '80s and later graduates like Mike Vrabel and Joey Galloway. Football is not the only game that has distinguished the Buckeyes. It has produced NBA notables like John Havlicek, Jerry Lucas, and Clark Kellogg. No one can forget golf's legendary Jack Nicklaus, winner of a record 18 major tournaments and hundreds of other PGA titles. Nicklaus earned his Ohio State degree while distinguishing his game at the collegiate level.

Jesse Owens is the most famous Buckeye Olympic gold medalist, winning four in the 1936 Berlin games. George Steinbrenner, the industrialist, shipbuilder, and sports entrepreneur, once served as graduate assistant to Woody Hayes while pursuing a master's degree.[10] He was later known to host Ohio State versus Michigan football parties in Yankee Stadium facilities.

BIG

That The Ohio State University is *big* is something perfectly in keeping with what has long been the state's unique combination of patriotism and populism. The seed for the university (or the "germinated buckeye" if you will) was planted early in the administration of Abraham Lincoln. Most associate the era of Lincoln with the national catastrophe that was the Civil War, but the country had to look to its future interests in a world becoming increasingly industrialized. Europe, England in particular, had developed from agricultural to industrial economies. In the US, the dual challenges of attracting and feeding a growing population joined the need to foster scientific discovery and mechanical ingenuity. Despite the war, or because of it, the number of patent applications continued to increase, only to be followed by an explosion in patents after the conflict was over.

Lincoln was a believer in science and technology, as were many in the northern congressional delegations. America's first Republican president, like most in this new political organization, was committed to the ideals of the Whigs, the GOP's recently defunct forerunner. The Whigs believed that government had an important responsibility to foster an ideal climate for business and economic growth. A class of people who were well educated in the higher arts of agriculture and manufacturing was essential to this philosophy. The Morrill Act of 1862 was an effort to provide for the nation's future educational needs by granting federal land to states for constructing and operating what became known as land-grant colleges. "Donating public lands to the several states and territories which may provide colleges for the benefit of agriculture and the mechanic arts" resulted in universities that would become key to the northern Midwest cities in which they were placed. The act was passed in late 1861 and signed by President Lincoln on July 2, 1862. It would be another eight years before the Ohio General Assembly established the Ohio Agricultural and Mechanical College in Columbus. Just imagine it: "Ohio A&M"!

Its birth as a land-grant college is something else that differentiates Ohio State from the University of Michigan and puts it somewhat in league with U of M's other big rival: Michigan State University. The founding of the University of Michigan predates Ohio State, Michigan State, the Morrill Act, and even the existence of Michigan as a US state. Founded in 1817 as the Catholepistemiad of Detroit (and moving to Ann Arbor 20 years later), the University of Michigan has gained a reputation as "a public Ivy" and is known as one of the top research universities in the world. U of M's motto, *Artes, Scientia, Veritas,* means simply "arts, science and truth."

Ohio State's early aspirations were a little more down-to-earth. As a land-grant university, even Ohio State's motto, *Disciplina in Civitatem,* "education for citizenship," perfectly articulates what a Buckeye State resident valued most about higher education—the ability to cultivate, create, and make a better life for him- or herself in the process. As the initial "A&M" name of the university indicates, the Ohio culture of the time balanced perfectly the notions of those things agricultural and mechanical. The state's ultimate objective of "growing things and making things" was also central to the mission of the college, which was rechristened The Ohio State University in 1878.

Many in Ohio, including then governor Rutherford B. Hayes, thought the university should have a wider and more far-reaching objective than merely serving as an A&M "tech school." Hayes is known to have had a rather heavy hand in steering the university's initial board of trustees and manipulating the university's location toward the goal of making it a more well-rounded institution.[11]

THE DEFINITE ARTICLE

Every college or university can lay claim to success when it witnesses the achievements of its graduates. Ohio State is no different, except that the sheer size of its graduating classes assures that it will achieve proportionally more successes in all areas. Ohio State has come to be a badge of honor among graduates wherever they roam. Listen to any of the legions of Ohio State stars that graduate to the NFL and you will hear them announce themselves with pride as being from *The* Ohio State University. Curiously, the inclusion of the article "The" is something that has been part of Ohio State's official name ever since it gave up the "Ohio Agricultural and Mechanical College" identity in the late 1870s, but it was only in the late twentieth century that the "The" (with a long "e") was proudly stressed. Part of that was the result of marketing and positioning efforts by university officials in the 1980s, ostensibly to differentiate the school from Ohio's other state universities and from other "OSUs" around the country, including Oklahoma State, Oregon State, and Oswego State (New York).

Ohio State's 500,000 living alumni around the world have done much to perpetuate the image of the university as a strong, proud, and contentious institution. Who knows: perhaps the decades of derision by Michigan fans as the "lesser of the two schools" academically has been an underlying motivation to increasing academic standards in recent years. In just the world of sports alone, Woody Hayes earned his master's degree at Ohio State before embarking on a fabled teaching and coaching career. Ohio State also launched many of its best-known rivals. Hayes' protégé turned adversary Michigan coach Bo Schembechler was also an Ohio State alum as well as a coach. Bobby Knight, an Orville, Ohio, native, played three basketball seasons for Ohio State, including one as

FIGURE 15.1. Approaching from the north end of the Ohio State campus is a fragment of the 110,000 Buckeye fans likely to file in to Ohio Stadium (the "Horseshoe") on any fall Saturday.

the "sixth man" on its national championship team. He went on to beat the Buckeyes many times as the fiery and temperamental coach of Indiana's famous championship-winning basketball teams.

The well-known rivalry between the University of Michigan and The Ohio State University is a prime example of rivals relying on each other's resources. This is something that plays out both in "the real world" and in sports. The two universities cooperate on a number of initiatives related to medicine, manufacturing, materials science, and initiatives to bolster the midwestern economy. In 1932 the University of Michigan band was the first to perform a version of what Ohio State turned into its famous "Script Ohio" formation by the Ohio State's "Best Damn Band in the Land." In the case of football teams, both have recruited from the other's state.[12] However, Ohio has provided more players for Michigan than Michigan has delivered to Ohio State. If you can't play for The Ohio State University, then Michigan is probably the next best thing.

HANGING WITH SLOOPY

I cannot remember the sportscaster who said "there two kinds of college football fans: those who hate Ohio State and those who went there." The greater point is that the school has, by various methods, made itself larger than its physical dimensions, its endowment, its annual enrollment, or its alumni corps. Ohio is one of the few states where the largest university's sports team name matches state's informal demonym (Indiana and Illinois are others). So, everyone from Ohio is a *Buckeye*—even those from the Toledo area who root for what Woody Hayes referred to as "that team up north."

Name yourself after a mildly toxic nut and you can be whatever you want to be. That's what Ohioans have done since before the first President Harrison embraced the term in his 1840 campaign songs. Ohio State has made the term *Buckeye* something to be feared, admired, cherished, revered, envied, loved, and loathed, but generally applauded.

This brings us to the curious adoption of the Buckeyes' informal theme song, something I saw evolve when I was a kid. The R&B song "Hang On Sloopy," known best by the version covered by the McCoys, romanticizes a downtrodden girl of the street, urged to keep going despite the odds against her. I always mocked the song. Why simply hang on? To me, the official Ohio State rendering of "Fight the Team across the Field" was more appropriately jingoistic and inspiring. But the 2014 Buckeye football season may have proved Sloopy's merit. After an embarrassing loss to Virginia Tech in an early game, Ohio State's football season appeared ruined. The team had already lost their starting quarterback and were destined to lose his replacement. Yet they *hung on* impressively throughout the season and found themselves in the Big Ten Conference championship game. And, as they were in the process of beating Wisconsin 59–0, their band could be heard playing "Hang On Sloopy." Next, they hung on to stun Alabama in the national semifinal and then to handily win the first "playoff era" national championship over Oregon.

Given that, perhaps the song is not so bad. And maybe the 2014 football team's success despite all indications to the contrary is a proper metaphor for the Buckeye State as it continues to emerge from a generation of declining industrial production, economic malaise, and population flight. "Hanging on" does not sound very heroic, but it is often the first step toward glorious conquest.

This is something that Michigan and Ohio have realized many times since the "Toledo War" of 1835. It has played out in frequent Ohio State–Michigan contests where the comeback games are often the most glorified. "Hanging on" is reflected in the way the two states have challenged and reinforced one another through the years. We are united as one country. But we remain and thrive as separate (and competing) states.

CHAPTER 16

BEING CLEVELAND

In 2014 Cleveland was selected to host the 2016 Republican National Convention, beating out hipper locations like Dallas and Las Vegas. It was good news for Clevelanders of all political stripes. After all, if you run a bar or a multi-million-dollar hotel you really don't care whether the money coming in to your town comes out of red or blue wallets.

It is not always good news that comes from Ohio's second-largest but arguably most famous city. The convention award came just a year after Arial Castro horrified the nation with the kidnapping and decades-long imprisonment and torture of three young women. Five years earlier, dark notoriety came in the discovery of 11 bodies—some dead for years—inside a duplex in the ironically named Mount Pleasant neighborhood.[1]

Cleveland has always been a city of highs and lows. It gave the world some of its greatest industrialists and is home to what many consider the country's leading health care facilities and one of the world's top symphony orchestras. But it is also known nationally as the place where the river caught fire.

This happened in the summer of 1969, during the height of anti-Vietnam sentiment, civil rights anxiety, and tensions arising from the city's own financial decline. On the morning of June 22, the Cuyahoga River, an oozing cocktail of oil, industrial discard,

FIGURE 16.1. Progressive Field in downtown Cleveland is one of three popular sports venues that draw fans for games and other special events.

and floating debris, suddenly and unexpectedly caught fire. The fire was quickly extinguished and received little attention from the local media.[2] In fact, the fire that became a legend was so short that no photographs are known to exist. That did not stop *Time* magazine from headlining the event to the nation in an issue devoted to environmental concerns. For its cover story, the publication needed a good photo, so it went to its archives and retrieved a 1952 photo of the Cuyahoga consumed by huge clouds of black smoke and flames. Yes, the Cuyahoga had caught fire in the past—the first incident going back to 1868. River fires had also occurred in Buffalo, Baltimore, Philadelphia, and other cities over the previous hundred years.

Yet for some reason the 1969 Cuyahoga River fire is the only river fire anyone seems to know about. It became a flashpoint in a movement that spawned volumes of clean-water laws and other environmental regulation. It may not have been the first American river fire, but the 1969 flare-up that inspired songs, microbrewery beer brands, and countless late-night jokes has thus far been our last.[3]

Being Cleveland means the equivalent of serving as a metropolitan and social roller coaster. There are lots of ups and downs. Being *from* Cleveland means that you are in for the ride, whatever it is, and that you endure it with part anticipation, part exhilaration, and part anticlimactic letdown. The plight of its sports teams offers the perfect metaphor for the entirety of a Clevelander's experience. In 1945 the Cleveland Rams won the NFL championship, and then ownership promptly moved the team to Los Angeles. Then came the roller coaster ride that was the Cleveland Browns, who won numerous championships in the 1940s and '50s and then again in 1964. They got close on several occasions in later years but then packed up and moved to Baltimore in 1996, where they became known as the Ravens before being replaced by an expansion team also named the Browns in 1999. Then there are the Cleveland Indians, who, in 1997, were two outs away from defeating the Florida Marlins for the World Series championship. Instead of winning 2–1, they lost 3–2 thanks to struggles on the part of their usually reliable closer and a routine ground ball that rolled past the glove of second-baseman Tony Fernandez.

A steady playoff contender for nearly a decade, basketball's Cleveland Cavaliers had every reason to believe they could bring an NBA championship to Cleveland. They missed out again in their second trip to the championship series in 2010. Then came the one of sports' most tortured moments. While shopping the free agent market, the Cavs star player and Ohio native, LeBron James, planned a nationwide broadcast announcement of his decision on ESPN. Despite the fact that James was lobbied heavily by the Chicago Bulls, Miami Heat, and other teams, he was expected to remain with Cleveland. He'd grown up in Akron, less than an hour away from the Cavs' home at Quicken Loans Arena; the Cavs were his hometown team. But before a national audience and in the community-minded setting of the Boys Club, James jilted his native northeast Ohio with the words "I'm taking my talents to South Beach." And so, the local hero and pride of Akron St. Vincent-St. Mary High School dashed the sports fantasies of those who shared his home soil. James's departure for South Beach assured that the Miami Heat would be a leading NBA title contender for the years he played there, and they won two titles during his four years with the Heat.[4] James later redeemed himself with Cavaliers fans, returning to Cleveland in 2015 and leading the team to its first NBA championship in 2016.

MOSES' PROMISED LAND

The first person to leave Cleveland behind was its founder. Moses Cleaveland, a successful Revolutionary War general and attorney, was a native Connecticuter during the time when northeast Ohio was being called "New Connecticut." Cleaveland was high-energy and highly likable—traits that no doubt served him well during a career that included stints in the Connecticut Assembly and the ratifying convention for the US Constitution.[5] They also served him well in business. Cleaveland was a founder and major investor in the Connecticut Land Company. This company purchased the New Connecticut lands from the original state of Connecticut with plans to begin exploring and settling the area which was then becoming known as Connecticut's Western Reserve.

Any big plans for settling and civilizing this New Connecticut would require a survey and a certain amount of civic planning. And the other owners and directors of the Connecticut Land Company thought Cleaveland was the perfect man for the job. So, with about 50 men and a few boats, his expedition set out from Schenectady, New York. They followed an aquatic course that would include the Mohawk and Oswego rivers in upstate New York along with Lake Ontario, the Niagara River, and Lake Erie. And there would be plenty of portaging to get around impassable waters, such as Niagara Falls.

The party came prepared to do the necessary work of surveying, and Moses Cleaveland came prepared to deal. Well aware that native peoples had their own claims on the territory, the company provided the means, financial and otherwise, for Cleaveland to cut the necessary deals. And he used these resources like a fixer at a horse track. First, he paid off local inhabitants trying to halt the party near Buffalo. At least one more time before he made it to the mouth of the Cuyahoga River, the site of the city that would later bear his name, Cleaveland's party won permission to proceed by plying those who stood in his path with beads, whiskey, and various other goods.[6]

After weeks of sailing, rowing, and portaging, Cleaveland's expedition party found itself in a flat, highly habitable area rich in forest and other resources needed to build and sustain a town.

The party surveyed the Western Reserve, mapping out the various townships and planning the layout of Cleveland. Then they went home, leaving a new city of just four inhabitants. By 1820 Cleveland would still have only 120 residents. The city also lost the "a" in Cleaveland's name, but how that happened is a matter of debate. Some blame a misspelling on an earlier map, while others say that a Cleveland newspaper dropped the letter to save space. Neither explains how or why Grover Cleveland, a distant relative of Moses Cleaveland and a New Yorker, also dropped the "a" from his name.

CLEVELAND CATCHES FIRE (FIGURATIVELY)

To this point, we've discussed river fires, blown sports glory, and a founder who didn't care enough to stick around for even a few months. But Cleveland deserves a lot of attention as one of the country's first interior boomtowns. By 1840 the population had grown to over 6,000, nearly six times its 1830 population. The city had become the nation's 45th largest owing to its strategic location as a port city and growing rail center. Then the industrial age provided an opportunity for Cleveland to teach the country a thing or two about growth. By 1900 it was the seventh largest US city and would remain either the fifth or sixth largest through the 1940s. By the 2010 census, however, Cleveland found itself back where it was in 1840. It was the nation's 45th largest city. If things go up for Cleveland, they must come down.

Here are just a few of the things that happened during those 170 years when Cleveland ranked considerably higher than 45th. For one, it grew into the centerpiece of a sprawling metropolitan area that aprons the southern midsection of Lake Erie, from about Huron to well past Mentor. It requires an hour of driving on an easy traffic day to make it through the approximately 65 miles on Interstate 90 that constitute greater Cleveland. Perhaps because Lake Erie forces such east–west sprawl, the city and greater Cleveland area loom large for any auto or truck traveling along the country's longest and northernmost interstate, I-90, which stretches from Boston to Seattle.

Cleveland was the hub for three of the country's most essential industries during the late nineteenth and early twentieth centuries—steel, oil, and shipping. Companies like Republic Steel and Standard Oil drew billions in capital and financed a population that enjoyed seemingly limitless growth for at least 100 years. Cleveland's factories were an obvious draw to legions from Ireland, England, France, and Italy along with Central and Eastern European countries like Poland, Ukraine, Turkey and many of the countries that made up the Austro-Hungarian Empire. Internal immigrants such as the parents of John D. Rockefeller came, too, bringing a spirit of Yankee mercantilism that would enable themselves and their children to thrive in the trading atmosphere of the young city. They paved the way for development of entirely new industries related to chemicals, automobiles, and manufacturing during the time of their grandchildren.

The industries that built Cleveland remain, but their share of the area's employment has declined. This is in part because they have spread to other cities and states and because of the general deindustrialization of the country. A more serious problem is that the city may be slowly vanishing. On average, Cleveland has been losing 43 people a day since 1970. That fact alone took it from 10th in US population rankings in 1970 to its 45th position in the 2010 census. In 2014 Cuyahoga County experienced the second-largest population drop in the country.[7]

It is not lost on Ohioans that the three largest cities / metro areas seem to be in a perpetual race for leadership and Buckeye bragging rights. Cleveland is still the largest metro area but finds Cincinnati close on its heels, due more to Cleveland's population loss than to Cincinnati's gains. While Columbus has been able to claim status as the largest city, it falls behind both Cleveland and Cincinnati in terms of metropolitan area (but remember that Cincinnati's metro includes portions of Kentucky and Indiana). Of course, there are many who might welcome less population in urban areas, imagining less congestion, more green space, and reductions in the pollution that humans typically bring.

But there is a significant downside to population loss. First, loss of population means fewer taxpayers. Fewer taxpayers means fewer individuals to support the facilities, infrastructure, and service organizations that grew to support a city that was once thriving. It means abandoned buildings, shuttered enterprises, closed schools, and boarded-up churches. It is a betrayal of dreams, a squandering of promise.[8] What has befallen the Cleveland area in the last half-century may account for its topping *Forbes Magazine*'s "20 Most Miserable Cities" list in 2010.[9] However, just further down the list are four other Ohio cities, several in California, and iconic cities like Chicago, New York, and Miami.

Yearning for renaissance, Cleveland won its bid for the 2016 Republican National Convention precisely when it was unveiling a number of improvement initiatives, including one of the most ambitious in the city's history. The lakefront project seeks to develop hundreds of lake and riverfront acres that stand today as underused remnants of the city's bygone industrial and shipping heydays. Further, the lakefront project will better integrate these lands with the nearby Rock & Roll Hall of Fame and First Energy Stadium, home of the Cleveland Browns. New roadways and bridges will unite the area with the greater part of downtown Cleveland.[10]

Few states meet the water as gracefully as does Ohio. Mostly flat terrain introduces itself to the shallowest of the Great Lakes through sandy beaches backed up by verdant forest or grasslands, except for those areas where cities or suburbia intercede. This is largely the case from Toledo to Cleveland to Buffalo. Cleveland was known as the Forest City in its younger years, a nice contrast to being known as the city where the river caught fire. It is quite possible that Cleveland's successful lakefront project will marry the assets of Cleveland's past with the promise of its future. It really needs to.

WHERE THE CLEVELAND "BRAND" IS STRONGEST

From its native son Bob Hope to modern late-night comics and TV producers, Cleveland has been a famous but predictable punch line for many years. The television show *Hot in Cleveland,* which ran from 2010–15, mocked the city beginning with a title that seemingly ridicules the mere possibility of being both an *attractive* female and from *Cleveland.* Other comedies, such as *The Drew Carey Show* (1995–2004), paid a working man's homage to the city Carey grew up in, but did so with characters that epitomized misguidedness, a quality ascribed to Cleveland itself.

But ask anyone in the world of classical music about Cleveland, and you'll hear nothing but superlatives. A long-standing "top five" American orchestra, the Cleveland Orchestra is frequently touted as one of the best in the world, ranking alongside London and Berlin. Ever since conductor George Szell (1946–70) fortified it from the struggling orchestra it had been in the postwar years to one known for a warm, vibrant "European" sound, the orchestra has been Cleveland and Ohio's premier cultural ambassador. An ambitious touring schedule includes extended residencies in the European locations of Vienna and Lucerne as well as New York and Miami. Miami-Dade County has become a third home for the Cleveland Orchestra, along with its historic and beautiful Severance Hall in Cleveland and one of America's most beloved outdoor venues, the Blossom Music Center, near Akron.[11]

Classical music is considered one of the most beautiful and lofty of humankind's artistic pursuits. Its practitioners are dedicated and passionate. Classical often forms the universe, gravity, and oxygen of musical education, key even to those who ultimately achieve in areas like folk, blues, or other genres. Even those who don't regularly listen to classical music often wish they did. But they actually do when you consider that classical music is as ubiquitous as rock and roll in forming the soundtrack of our lives in movies, television shows, and even cartoons.

The rarified air that Cleveland occupies in the world of classical music is a sharp contrast to the common view of Cleveland as a dowdy, declining midwestern city. There's nothing dowdy about Cleveland in the frequent reviews of the Cleveland Orchestra (and symphonic music in general) in the European press. A classical music reviewer for the *London Telegraph* referred to the Cleveland Orchestra as the aristocrat among American orchestras. Contrasting the Cleveland sound with the Continent's, he added:

> Everything about them bespeaks a fine old tradition; the silvery hair of many of its players, their dignified mien, and of course Franz Welser-Möst, their music director. He leads the orchestra with fastidious and understated grace. There is also that famously precise sound. When the Berlin Philharmonic plays a chord, it's together but somehow soft. When the Cleveland Orchestra plays a chord, it's as sharp-edged as a skyscraper.[12]

The skyscraper simile is fitting as Cleveland finds its reputation in the arts towering above the rest of the nation. Culture redeems the city that has made so many "miserable" lists. In 2017 Cleveland's allure got the city named to *National Geographic*'s "Best of the World" travel destinations, one of only three US locations to make the list.[13]

THE ARTISTRY OF HEALING

Biomedical manufacturing is something that people have a hard time getting their heads around. The two parts of that term seem contradictory: one reinforces images of sophisticated science, biology, and medical practices and research. The other calls to mind an era when Cleveland was best known for steel, petroleum, and equipment assembly. The sensors, fluid handling, robotics, lasers, and countless other manufacturing talents that are part of the city's past are a lucrative part of Cleveland's future.

Strengthened by a long manufacturing history and the intellectual capital and resources of schools like Case Western Reserve University, Cleveland has seen the biomedical manufacturing industry grow to account for nearly 3 percent of local economic activity. Today, northeast Ohio is a leading location nationally for the field, which forecasts strong future growth.[14]

It also helps any medically related business to be located close to the Cleveland Clinic. Cleveland is a great place to be if you have an acute heart condition or any number of cancers. And while that may seem a strange and backhanded tribute, it is really an illumination of the clinic's prominence in the medical world. The clinic was founded in 1921 and has since pursued a simple mission: "Better care of the sick, investigation into their problems and further education of those who serve."[15]

A few of its most significant medical miracles, going as far back as the 1940s, are the following:

Major steps toward treatment of hypertension through the first isolation of serotonin, a key factor in the disease

First coronary angiography
Development and refinement of coronary bypass surgery
First minimally invasive aortic heart surgery
Discovery of first gene linked to coronary artery disease
Pioneering success in deep brain stimulation for psychiatric disor-
    ders and minimally conscious state
Nation's first near-total face transplant
First through-the-navel kidney surgery
World's first heart/liver transplant in patient with total artificial
    heart

Known as one of the country's top five hospitals and often cited
as *the* best, the Cleveland Clinic drew 24,000 patients in 2014 for
heart care alone. Since the 1990s it has consistently held the top spot
for cardiac care and surgery. The primary location has 12 buildings
spread over 100 acres. And though Cleveland does not have the size
or cachet of places like New York, Los Angeles, or London, it brings
in patients from every location on earth: princes and kings, captains
of industry, and those with conditions that just can't be fixed anywhere else in the world.[16]

Administrators of the institution founded in 1921 had grand
and glorious visions, but few could envision the day when the
clinic, along with University Hospital (also highly rated), would
form a corridor of medical solutions significant enough to add lus-
ter to the city's reputation. Within recent years, it has been frequently asked whether the healthcare field could save the life of
Cleveland itself. While that question may take a number of years
to answer, the Cleveland Clinic continues to expand its brand into
new health fields and locations including Las Vegas, Toronto, and
London.

And, like the Cleveland Orchestra, the Cleveland Clinic has a
presence in Florida, where it delivers 35 medical specialties at locations in Weston, West Palm Beach, Palm Beach Gardens, and Park-
land.[17] Ohio has a long history in Florida's development. Henry M.
Flagler, John D. Rockefeller's partner in building the Standard Oil
empire, went on to develop south Florida. After falling in love with

St. Augustine, he was instrumental in the growth and development of locations like Palm Beach, Miami, and the Keys.[18]

The many arts of Cleveland touch the rest of the country in numerous ways—from medicine to steel and classical music to rock and roll. Despite many challenges, the city reflects the best of the nation it grew up with.

CHAPTER 17

KILLING MARILYN
AND SAM

Columnist, commentator, and author Bill O'Reilly continues to expand his series of books on the assassinations of famous people. They are simply titled *Killing Kennedy, Killing Lincoln, Killing Patton,* and so on. They are about assassinations that brought down big people, producing huge consequences.[1] The story of Sam and Marilyn Sheppard is not about the death of famous, larger-than-life people, but the consequences were enormous for the nation and the world.

The Sheppards' story began in the 1950s, an era that was seen as Cleveland, Ohio's, heyday. Its steel and manufacturing sectors were producing at full tilt. Chemical and polymer-based businesses were capturing market share that would make Cleveland's paint companies and nearby Akron's rubber companies the undisputed leaders in their industries.

Cleveland was also "the sports capital of the world," with the Browns as perennial champions and the Indians on the way to a record-breaking 111 regular season wins. Disc jockey "Moondog" Alan Freed was several years into characterizing his R&B programming as "rock and roll," a term gaining usage all over the country. In 1954 Cleveland was America's sixth largest city. Its metropolitan area sprawled 65 miles along Lake Erie from Lorain to Painesville. It was, as one old newsreel announcer called it, "Queen of the inland waters . . . thriving terminal of trade and transportation."[2]

Cleveland suburbs were a mural of the American dream. One of these was Bay Village, where Marylyn Sheppard, mother of a seven-year-old son, enjoyed a spacious house by the lake. Her husband, Sam, was an osteopathic physician working with his father and brothers running Bay View Hospital. Marilyn was living the "American dream."

Until it ended at the hands of a killer.

SAYING "GOODNIGHT" TO THE AHERNS

The Sheppard tragedy began early on the morning of Sunday, July 4, 1954. It was so early that the Sheppards and their dinner guests, Don and Nancy Ahern, had still not closed out July 3. They spent a long, lingering evening enjoying dinner and drinks. Side chatter between Marilyn and Nancy may have included the fact that there were marital difficulties in the Sheppard household. Both Sheppards had discussed such difficulties with friends and family members in the past. But, if anything, their relationship appeared steadier than it had been in some time.

At half past midnight, midway through a long holiday weekend, Marilyn said goodnight to the Aherns and headed to bed. The guests departed shortly thereafter. Sam, wearing his corduroy dinner jacket, fell asleep during the late movie they had all begun watching, *Strange Holiday* (1945). The evening must have left Dr. Sam tired enough to stay put on the downstairs daybed, where his sleep was later shattered by his wife's piercing screams and desperate calling of his name. At first he thought the screams might be related to her pregnancy. As he entered the bedroom, he saw what he described as "a form" (clinical doctor's vocabulary). Then he was struck from behind and fell to the floor unconscious.

Sheppard said that when he came to, he chased the intruder down to the water in front of his property, where he was again struck. He awoke again, stunned and partially in the water, and rushed back to the house, where he found his wife badly beaten, no pulse, lifeless. His first reaction was to call neighbors and family friends Esther and Spencer Houk. Spencer was also the mayor and safety director of Bay Village. His words were simply "I think they've killed Marilyn."

THE "CRIME" AT THE CRIME SCENE

By 6 a.m. on Independence Day the Sheppard home was a full-fledged circus. Neighbors gathered in the front yard and in the living room. Law enforcement swarmed. Teenagers snuck up and down the stairway to peek at Marilyn's legs, which still dangled over the edge of the bed. As Sam, his father, and brothers struggled to understand what had happened, evidence was seriously compromised. Seven-year-old Sam Reese Sheppard—or "Chip," as he was known—was abruptly wakened and hustled past his mother's bedroom, down the stairs and out of his house forever. He would live to adulthood with his uncle Steve and be forever haunted by that weekend.

No commonsense rules of evidence-handling were followed. Clothing from the murder room was piled up downstairs. A lady's watch was picked up and casually handled, which destroyed any possibility of pulling prints from it. With all the police, fire, and medical workers on hand, no one thought to close off and closely inspect the murder room or victim. A bag containing the couple's valuables was found by teenage boys, who eagerly pawed through its contents. Only in late July did police return for a close crime-scene inspection.

Police procedures have long called for careful, systematic, and thorough gathering of evidence within a sealed crime scene. Normal practice, then and now, demands that police investigators quickly speak with as many people as possible, as soon as possible. Friends, neighbors, relatives, hired hands—anyone who had been in contact with the Sheppards during the period—should have been contacted and interviewed. Such procedures give police the greatest chance of identifying a perpetrator.[3]

There were no less than six legal authorities investigating the case—Bay Village Police, the Cuyahoga County Sherriff's Department, the Cleveland Police Department, the Office of the Cuyahoga Coroner, and the Cuyahoga County Prosecutor's Office. If there is irony in the situation, it is that the Bay Village Police Depart-

ment—completely inexperienced with murder investigations—
was the only governmental investigating body that took a careful,
deliberate approach.

Rather than initiating an investigation, authorities almost immediately looked at the case with prosecutorial eyes. Nearly every one
of those eyes focused on Sheppard. By midday on July 4, Sam Sheppard was in the hospital being treated for head and neck injuries.
That is when a police officer leaned over him and said, "I think
you killed your wife."[4] From that point on, the murder of Marilyn
Sheppard would be less about investigation and more about building a case against her husband.

TRIAL BY THE CLEVELAND PRESS

Cleveland was a town of contentious politics and a very aggressive,
advocacy-oriented press. Whether this stems from the multigroup
ethnic melting pot it had become or from the city's position as both
a labor and a commercial center isn't known. But in 1954 Cleveland had three thriving, highly competitive daily newspapers and
numerous radio stations. The city also had its share of television
stations, with several network-owned outlets.

Events at the Sheppard home occurred too late to make the
Sunday issue of the *Cleveland Plain Dealer*. When the *Plain Dealer,
Cleveland Press,* and *Cleveland News* came out on Monday, the
news was reported objectively. Early editions reported it as resulting from a possible robbery related to drugs. Then, as now, the
desire to steal drugs was viewed as a likely motive when a medical
professional's home was invaded. But it didn't take long for the
headlines to change. This became a ferocious murder of a pretty
wife and mother. The Cleveland media wanted someone to pay.
Loaded, incendiary headlines continued for months. The *Cleveland
Press* headline writers were particularly strident.

STATE PREPARES CHARGE AGAINST BAY MURDERER
NEW SEARCH IS ORDERED FOR CLUES
TESTIFY NOW IN DEATH, BAY DOCTOR IS ORDERED
DOCTOR RE-ENACTS STORY OF MURDER; REJECTS LIE
    TEST
CHARGES SAM FAKED INJURIES

BUT WHO WILL SPEAK FOR MARILYN
SUSAN SAYS SAM LOVED HER, WANTED TO DIVORCE
MARILYN

Perhaps the worst was a *Cleveland Press* front-page editorial entitled:

THE FINGER OF SUSPICION

And then there was:

GETTING AWAY WITH MURDER

While the Sheppards had enjoyed the lives of successful but relatively anonymous Clevelanders, they also provided rich subject matter for a populace obsessed with wealth and class. The *Cleveland Press* (then the strongest of the city's three dailies) believed in standing for the underdog, the common man or woman.[5] They could identify editorially with the murder victim. It was easy for them to adopt the idea bandied about kitchen tables throughout the city and nation—*Gee, she's murdered at home and no one broke in? Of course the husband did it.* There were elements of class resentment infusing the story, too. The family could be called "nouveau riche."

Cleveland print and broadcast media also found themselves in the enviable position of being an information hub for a nation and world that was obsessed with the story. Whether in Lorain, Ohio, Atlanta, Georgia, or Nice, France, people hated what had happened to Marilyn Sheppard. The circus atmosphere was fed by a kangaroo-court-style coroner's inquest at the hands of the politically ambitious Dr. Sam Gerber. Astonishingly, his coroner's verdict contained zero science. Rather, his conclusion was based on three points that would seem completely laughable to a modern attorney or judge. He found that Sam Sheppard had to have killed Marilyn Sheppard because

1. he was home at the time of Marilyn's murder,
2. he hired an attorney to defend himself, and
3. his story was, according to Gerber, simply "unbelievable."

Sam Sheppard was *guilty by coroner's hunch,* you might say. The ambitious Gerber provided just enough emotional momentum for a revenge-starved media and community anxious for justice to believe his conclusion.[6]

Next came the grand jury. Again the media, particularly the *Press,* held nothing back. Names and addresses of grand jurors were published. There were constant exhortations for them to do the "right thing." Ultimately, Sheppard was bound over for trial. Throughout the five-month pretrial period, law enforcement, the media, and others influencing the legal system all sharpened their focus on Sheppard, armed with only the most conventional of conventional wisdom. The system seemed to follow Gerber's primitive logic. If Marilyn Sheppard was murdered and Sam Sheppard was home when the crime occurred, then Sam had to be guilty.

"Guilty" was the verdict rendered by the trial jury after all the testimony and deliberation. Being found guilty of second-degree murder meant that Sheppard was spared the possibility of the death penalty but would face life in prison.[7] In just months Sam Sheppard had gone from successful young doctor to national pariah. And the strange, sad journey cost him dearly. He had lost his wife. His seven-year-old son would live his formative years without his surviving parent. A month after the verdict, Sam Sheppard's mother, Ethel, would put his brother's pistol to her head in a suicide driven by the gravity and severity of her loss. Sam's father, Richard, would die shortly after of gastrointestinal cancer. Sam Sheppard would grieve the loss of his parents from behind prison bars. His long, depressing days were broken only by letters and occasional visits from family members, especially the ones from his son, Chip. His skills as a doctor were put to reasonably good use as he assisted prison medical staff. He also took part in cancer research experiments.

Between December 1954 and 1961 there was very little to bring optimism to Sheppard's life. His lawyer, William J. Corrigan, convinced famed criminologist Paul Kirk to become involved. Shortly after the trial was complete, Kirk was allowed to examine evidence that still remained in the Sheppards' lakeside home. Kirk's work was truly groundbreaking, making full use of available technology in blood typing as well as his voluminous work on the physical properties of blood as it relates to drying, splattering, and other characteristics.[8] Although his involvement in the case would not help much in the short term, it would prove valuable years down the road.

F. LEE

In the summer of 1961 Sheppard's attorney, William Corrigan, died. This opened a new chapter in the saga with the hiring of F. Lee Bailey, an ambitious, young, media-savvy defender from Boston. Bailey approached the case aggressively, almost immediately working to convince Sheppard to take a lie detector test and the state to accept it. He even approached *Cleveland Press* editor Louis B. Seltzer about the matter. When Seltzer refused to endorse the test, Bailey promised he would "beat them." Strong words for an attorney taking on a powerful newspaper and city that wanted the case to go away.

Bailey filed a *habeas corpus* motion on Sheppard's behalf. The core of his argument centered on the media circus atmosphere that had overwhelmed the Sheppard side. And there was more. Bailey's people had uncovered a remarkable but previously unreported tale revealed by famous columnist Dorothy Kilgallen. According to an affidavit provided by Kilgallen, Judge Edward Blythin told her during the 1954 trial that it was "an open and shut case." When she pressed him further, Blythin, who had died in 1958, said simply, "Well, he is guilty as hell. There is no question about it."

The emergence of Bailey proved a godsend for the Sheppard family. And for Sam, the adoration of a German admirer, Ariane Tebbenjohans, proved a marvelous tonic to a broken heart and shattered life. Tebbenjohans, a wealthy divorcee, had been captivated by the story and had corresponded with Sheppard beginning in the late '50s. She also began to send money to Bailey for Sheppard's defense.

In the summer of 1964, a district judge in Dayton ordered Sheppard's release in response to Bailey's *habeas corpus* appeal. The judge included excoriating remarks about press coverage. In particular, he cited the *Cleveland Press* as chief offender and prime example of the problems associated with "trial by the press."

Although the ruling that released him from prison was soon overturned, Sheppard remained free on bail, and the case ended

FIGURE 17.1. Sam Sheppard confers with attorney F. Lee Bailey while his new wife, Ariane Sheppard, looks on. Photo was taken after concluding arguments in his second trial in 1966. The Cleveland Press Collection, Michael Schwartz Library, Cleveland State University.

up in the US Supreme Court. On June 6, 1966, the Supreme Court cited a litany of judicial misconduct in its finding for Sheppard, saying, "the massive, pervasive and prejudicial publicity attending petitioner's prosecution prevented him from receiving a fair trial consistent with the Due Process Clause of the 14th Amendment."[9]

It wasn't over yet. The ruling merely discarded the results of the 1954 trial. Sheppard was still under the indictment issued in 1954 by the grand jury. After several months of dithering on the matter, the Cuyahoga County Prosecutor's Office proceeded toward a second trial, and Sheppard was again arrested. This time the trial judge took extraordinary steps to avoid the contaminating influences that had degraded the process in the original trial. Media seats were limited. In all, there were only 42 seats for spectators. Today similar precautions are routinely practiced, particularly in high-visibility or sensational murder trials.

This time the verdict went Sheppard's way. He was a free man, released to his new wife and son and able, presumably, to retake his place in society. But his life would remain in shambles. His marriage to Ariane would disintegrate, and his relationship with Chip would be difficult. The death of a patient in his care would end his medical career.

Sheppard was out of prison but now hopelessly adrift. He moved in with friends in Columbus, taking up with and marrying their 20-year-old daughter and embarking on a short but well-publicized pro wrestling career. At 31 Sheppard had been a respected young doctor and a member of one of the most prominent families on Cleveland's west side. At 46 he was a failed alcoholic. And that is where it ended for Samuel Holmes Sheppard. He died on May 6, 1970, as much a victim of July 4, 1954, as his wife had been.

YOUNG SAM AND THE WINDOW WASHER

The third person deeply affected by the tragedy of July 4, 1954, was the younger Sam Sheppard. Thanks to his uncle Steve, Chip grew up in as normal a fashion as one could have hoped, given the circumstances. However, he would always have to contend with whispers, stares, averted eye contact, and the other slights that go with a presumed family shame.

After his dad's prison release, the happy reunion that the two Sam Sheppards envisioned never really took place. There were times when they did live together, but the older Sheppard's relationships and unstable career prospects made that difficult. Young Sam even lived for a time with F. Lee Bailey in Boston as he studied to become a dental assistant. And it is that career that helped him achieve anonymity through young adulthood. Unfortunately, when he was about the age his parents were in 1954, the case worked its way back into Chip's life.

Sheppard's renewed interest paralleled his growing activism in the anti-death-penalty movement. The little boy who had slept through his mother's hellish murder, one room over, was now a man opening files and other long-closed repositories of information about the case. Sheppard's curiosity would become a passion to clear his father's name. Inevitably, it would bring him into contact with the man many now believe to be his mother's killer— Richard George Eberling.

Eberling was the Sheppards' window washer in 1953 and 1954. Known as having both a jealous disdain for Sam and a lingering desire for Marilyn, he received scant attention in 1954 and 1955. It was not until he was caught in possession of Marilyn Sheppard's ring in 1959 that anyone began to consider the possibility of his involvement. But nothing stuck to Eberling regarding Marilyn's murder. However, there were other suspicious deaths.

Shortly after the Sheppard trial, Eberling began a relationship with Barbara Kinzel, who had been a nurse in the Sheppards' Bay View Hospital. She had treated Sam on July 4, 1854. Her testimony related that Sheppard was severely injured from the attack that night. In 1956 Kinzel died in an automobile accident in Michigan, where she and Eberling were traveling for a weekend getaway and hit the side of a parked car. Eberling was driving Kinzel's convertible at the time and was unhurt. Kinzel was not thrown from the car but was found crumpled on the floor, in front of the passenger seat. The death appeared suspicious.

There were more deaths to come. Myrtle Irene Fray was found brutally beaten in a style not dissimilar to Marilyn Sheppard. Fray was the sister of Ethel May Durkin, a widow whom Eberling had cared for and fleeced for more than two decades. Fray had expressed deep reservations about her sister's dependency on Eberling, whom she described as a "crook" and a "creep." No one was ever arrested for the Fray murder. And Eberling himself said that she "got her face beaten in just like Marilyn Sheppard." The next suspicious death was that of Ethel May Durkin herself. It was Durkin's murder that ultimately put Eberling in the Ohio Penitentiary.[10]

DNA testing done in 1997 on the exhumed body of Sam Sheppard showed that blood presumed to be his or Marilyn's actually belonged to neither. Eberling's blood could not be ruled out, however.[11] Eberling and young Sam Sheppard had a few conversations later in Eberling's life, prompted by a letter the younger Sheppard received from Eberling professing to know the inside story of his mother's death. Ultimately, the surviving Sheppard theorized that it was Eberling who had committed the murders, based on long-known inconsistencies, blood, blood spattering, and other evidence. One example of additional incrimination is that a former Eberling employee said that he had cleaned the windows at the Sheppard home two days before the murder (not Eberling, as he had long claimed). Eberling died in 1998, and the matter has been put to rest, destined to remain forever unresolved.[12]

REINVENTING THE COURTROOM

Marilyn Sheppard's murder is a story with no winners. Even two of the Cleveland newspapers that profited mightily from their sensational coverage have gone out of business.

It may be difficult for Americans today to understand why a single murder in Cleveland was able to garner enduring national and international attention. As noted earlier, Cleveland in that era was a "happening" place, full of industry, commercial success, and the promise of suburban tranquility. Today, some believe that the beginning of the city's decline can be traced to the Sheppard matter.

In any case, America gained a morbid passion for mysterious murder cases, a fascination that would be sated over the decades with sensational stories on the Manson murders, Son of Sam killings, and John Wayne Gacy's gruesomeness. F. Lee Bailey became a legal hero and would loom as a significant presence in courtrooms and public dialogue from the time of his flamboyant appearance in the Sheppard case to his highly publicized performance in the O. J. Simpson trial. The Sheppard case also spawned, famously, the television series *The Fugitive* and movie in the 1960s.

The Sheppard case's biggest impact on America came in courtrooms large and small all across the country. The 1966 Supreme Court decision that overthrew Sheppard's conviction (*Sheppard v. Maxwell*) was a landmark in its finding that the press had a unique ability to *prevent* a fair trial. Judges everywhere now err on the side of protecting accused perpetrators. Jury sequestering, new media standards, and changes of venue are now commonplace in murder cases and other criminal matters. Rules of evidence-gathering now make extreme caution the first priority. Crime scenes are rigorously protected from compromise or tampering.[13]

From the point of the Sheppard murder case forward, the rights of the accused receive far more attention and protection than they ever did before 1954. But all of this would probably be small comfort to Sam Reese Sheppard and his long-deceased parents.

CHAPTER 18

ENDING THE '60s

It was May 5, 1970, just after school. Rather than springing into delivery of my afternoon paper route, I just sat and stared at the newspaper. I was going to get the facts, so the 63 or 64 subscribers would just have to wait. In the background, my mom's oversized kitchen radio was carrying news and breathy analysis of the same information that was then confronting my 11-year-old mind and delaying my usually prompt delivery of the *Toledo Blade*. There had been a shooting at Kent State the day before.

Kent State University was the alma mater of my mother, who also served the *Blade* as regular columnist when I was growing up. Kent was 145 miles from me and my newspaper route. It was like so many other American campuses of that era, caught up in protest—both peaceful and violent. The mixture of war fatigue, youthful idealism, and the effects of outside agitation had resulted in a loud but disorganized force of energy. Many feared that this force was becoming too powerful for its own good. Violence might escalate any day, resulting in injuries or deaths.

Add law enforcement and politics to the powder keg, and things had the potential to get very ugly. American campuses through the 1960s had been gradually losing their status as "temples," immune from the press of the real and sometimes violent world. The country had largely grown weary of the Vietnam conflict, which had

174

been both a simmering and a hot boiling quagmire, first for France and then for the US but always for the Vietnamese. Richard Nixon was elected president a year and a half earlier based partly on his pledge to end the conflict.

On April 30 Nixon announced what he felt was a major step in that direction. He would be taking the war to Cambodia. To be precise, Nixon was intent on committing ground troops and bombing the daylights out of the North Vietnamese and Viet Cong troops who had relocated to Cambodia. The enemy was using its neighbor to the east as a refuge from the intense US bombing of their forces inside both North and South Vietnam. In his announcement, Nixon said, "We take these actions not for the purpose of expanding the war into Cambodia, but for the purpose of ending the war in Vietnam, and winning the just peace we all desire."[1] However well-reasoned Nixon's case may have seemed, the remarks shattered any semblance of domestic peace at hundreds of American colleges and universities, including Kent State.

THE MOMENTUM OF A PROTEST ERA

The Kent State shootings are also known as the Kent State massacre, or, to people living in the Akron and Kent areas, merely as May 4th. The tragedy is typically attributed to the escalation of the war and more directly to Nixon's Cambodian expansion. In reality this landmark in history was preceded by 15 to 20 years of increasing angst among American youth. During the 1960s the nation was undergoing at least a half-dozen minirevolutions. The very first baby boomers were reaching their turbulent young adult years. As kids, they had watched *Father Knows Best* and *Ozzie and Harriet* on television. By the mid-'60s, they were, it was believed, the focal point of a much-talked-about "generation gap." To many it seemed that never before had the values of a new generation seemed so at odds with those of the previous one. The gap was reflected in long hair, wildly casual and far more colorful clothing, increased sexual permissiveness, and experimentation with marijuana and other drugs.

Some believe that the fuse for all of these eruptions was lit earlier in the decade with the assassination of President John F. Kennedy and the subsequent escalation of America's involvement in Vietnam. It may also have been a lost sense of idealism. Perhaps the sense of national unity that had held over from the Great Depression and World War II eras had fractured. Many see the era of unrest as having deeper roots in both the civil rights movement and simmering youthful angst reflected by the '50s' "beat generation." The popularity of cultural '50s icons like actor James Dean and writer Jack Kerouac reflected increasing unease or even discontent among the country's young people. Seeds were also germinating for a new era in civil rights. School desegregation rulings were enforced in places like Little Rock, Arkansas. In 1955 in Montgomery, Alabama, Rosa Parks refused to give up her bus seat to a white man.[2]

Feelings turned into action on February 1, 1960. That's when four African American students at North Carolina A&T University decided that they had had enough of racial segregation in local diners and restaurants. Their remedy was to seat themselves at whites-only lunch counters and await service. The tactic caught on. Within weeks, sit-ins spread throughout North Carolina and other areas of the South.[3] In many areas, these largely peaceful protests achieved some success in bending Jim Crow limitations that had affected the African American population for decades. Perhaps the most illustrious event in the era of peaceful protest occurred just three months before Kennedy's death, when 250,000 people marched on Washington, DC. This was the event marked by Martin Luther King Jr.'s "I Have a Dream" speech.[4]

The era of protest would not always be peaceful. Youth movements on college campuses saw student groups protesting everything from corporatism and imperialism to the makeup of their colleges' own leadership. Some of these activities were marred by violence ranging from minor vandalism to the breaking of windows and overturning of cars. America was not alone in the outbreak of violence among the college-aged. In France the protests were against the regime of President Charles de Gaulle. Japanese youth marched and rioted against the presence of American troops, not in Vietnam but on the Japanese island of Okinawa and in American airbases on the mainland. Venezuelan youth marshaled perhaps the most violent protests of all, inspired by pro-Castro sympathies.[5]

As the Vietnam War escalated, various US movements merged their previous passions with those who wanted American forces out of Indochina. Outside the campuses, urban areas were the setting for massive civil rights protests. There were the Watts Riots in 1965 and the famous march from Selma to Montgomery, Alabama. Detroit had violent and large-scale riots in 1967. Virtually every American city of any size experienced some kind of civil unrest after the King assassination on April 4, 1968. While riots were violent in many cities, including Washington and Baltimore, they were especially so in Chicago. There, more than 125 fires were started and more than 200 buildings damaged, many heavily. Sixty-seven hundred Illinois National Guard troops were called in, and they were bolstered by 5,000 regular military troops ordered to the Windy City by President Lyndon Johnson. In the end 39 people lost their lives.[6]

Chicago would get yet another opportunity for riot infamy later that summer, when the Democratic National Convention came to town. Joining the party were protest groups from far and wide who descended on Mayor Richard J. Daley's city to air grievances about Vietnam, poverty, corporatism, colonialism, and racial oppression. Groups had come ostensibly for a youth festival timed to coincide with the convention. The presence of the National Mobilization Committee to End the War in Vietnam (MOBE), Students for a Democratic Society (SDS), Youth International Party (aka "Yippies"), and other protest groups ensured that the festival would be more than a celebration. Not even 23,000 National Guardsmen and police mobilized by Daley could preserve order, and the streets came alive with protests.[7] Some of the above groups were later known to have a strong presence on the Kent State campus in 1970. The SDS's Bernadine Dohrn, Ohio-educated and a cofounder of the Weather Underground, was also a frequent visitor to Kent.[8]

Such disturbances continued throughout the summer and for the rest of 1968, but the election may have calmed things a bit. Protesting and rioting seemed to recede in 1969. The country had a new president who had promised to end the war. Congress had begun to act in response to what seemed to be a nationalized discontent. In addition, various state legislatures were taking their own steps by granting voting rates to 18-year-olds, lowering drinking ages, and removing various forms of codified discrimination based on race or sex.

Chronological purists always note that a decade doesn't really end until its tenth year is completed, as they did with the conclusion of the year 2000 (which ended, all at once, the 1990s, the twentieth century, and the second millennium). They might argue that the decade of the 1960s could not really conclude until 1970 was over. So it is that the events of 1970 seem to fit perfectly with that decade of protest—the '60s.

TIN SOLDIERS AND JIM RHODES COMING

Of the many songs about Ohio, sadly the most famous relates to what unfolded near Prentice and Taylor Halls and across from the burned-out ROTC building at Kent State just a little after noon on May 4. Many are familiar with the eerie refrain: "This summer I hear the drumming, four dead in Ohio".[9] The song, Crosby, Stills, Nash, & Young's *Ohio,* is one of the best-known anthems of twentieth-century angst and a constant reminder of what occurred at the crest of the anti-war movement.

It all began with Richard Nixon's April 30 announcement about the Cambodia incursion, which did anything but convince the anti-war movement that the war or America's involvement was coming to a close. With campuses erupting everywhere, Ohio's attention fixated quickly on Kent, where protesters had been active. Students and others began to amplify their discontent on Friday, May 1. The first major event of the day was relatively peaceful, a burying of the Constitution, which was said to have been "murdered" by Nixon on April 30. About 500 students participated as the document was interred in front of the Victory Bell on the campus commons. Later that night groups of students began to gather at local bars, many discussing the Cambodian incursion. There was a feeling that there were several enemies confronting the Kent idealists and agitators. One was the Nixon administration and the US war effort. The other was growing antipathy toward the Ohio National Guard. A group of mostly African American students had earlier held a small rally denouncing the guard's presence at Kent and other campuses. By 11 p.m. an outbreak of violence was occurring throughout the area of Kent known as the strip. Windows were shattered in several dozen buildings. In the early hours of Saturday, May 2, a state of emergency was declared. The relatively small law enforcement contingents from the Kent Police and Portage County Sheriff's Office had difficulty containing the crowds or stopping the violence. The mayor declared a state of emergency.

The morning of Saturday, May 2, found Kent in an unexpected state of calm. Students and townspeople joined in cleaning garbage, glass, and other debris from the streets. Things would escalate through the day, however. The mayor had alerted the National Guard to the problems on campus and in the town, and the guard was quick to reinforce its personnel in the area. By Saturday evening the National Guard and students were in open conflict. A small gathering had begun with speeches and chants and then escalated to a large-scale march through campus. It gained students and energy as it passed through dorm areas toward Kent's ancient ROTC building. By that time the guardsmen were in pursuit, many with bayonets affixed. By the end of the evening, the ROTC building was on fire, ultimately burning to the ground.

Other issues were at play here, too. Ohio Governor James A. Rhodes was nearing the end of his second term and was limited by the Ohio Constitution to serving two consecutive terms. His next hoped-for political act would be a seat in the US Senate. But first he had to win the Republican primary for the seat, which was scheduled for May 5. His overall pitch to voters had focused on his "law and order" approach to governing—something that seemed undermined for the time being by the protests in Kent. In Washington President Nixon had been watching the unfolding protests throughout the country and had been particularly concerned. In one comment he directed an aid to make sure "Rhodes esp. rides this."[10]

Rhodes did actually ride up to Kent on Sunday, May 3, but to little avail. By the time he got there things were about to get even worse. On arrival Rhodes gave a speech at Kent calling agitators who initiated the riots "the worst type of people we harbor in America, worse than the brown shirts and the communist element . . . we will use whatever force necessary to drive them out of Kent!" That statement may have pushed the situation beyond the point of no return, as the governor's statement, directed at outside groups like the Weather Underground and Students for a Demo-

FIGURE 18.1. Protesters running. One appears to be throwing some object. Used with permission from the May 4 Collection. Kent State University Libraries. Special Collections and Archives.

FIGURE 18.2. National Guardsmen with gas masks and rifles. A group of students can be seen in the distance. Used with permission from the May 4 Collection. Kent State University Libraries. Special Collections and Archives.

cratic Society (SDS), was taken as an attack on ordinary Kent students themselves. Some feel Rhodes's take-no-prisoners approach may have given the Guard tacit approval to go beyond standard or expected control measures. Kent State was now fully occupied by National Guard troops. Armored personnel carriers were stationed throughout the campus. At 8 p.m., hundreds of students had again gathered by the Victory Bell at the commons.

This time the guard was having none of it. Responding to the protests, the guard announced a new curfew and the Ohio Riot Act was read. Tear gas filled the air. Lighted helicopters hovering above added both drama and intimidation. Students were literally driven back toward their dorms by the armed guardsmen. Numerous bayonet wounds and other injuries were sustained that night, but no bullet wounds. An attempt at a peaceful rally in the downtown area was similarly thwarted.

MONDAY COMES

By 11 a.m. on Monday, May 4, several hundred students had again assembled on the commons. Their numbers would grow quickly. As more and more students—many of them merely spectators—faced the more than 100 guardsmen, it was clear that the conflict was nearing its crest. Guardsmen ordered them to disperse immediately but were met with chants, jeers, and rocks. Armed with M-1 rifles and tear gas, the guard troops formed a skirmish line and moved toward the protesters. They cleared the commons and pushed the growing crowd up and over what is known as Blanket Hill and a practice football field. They drove the most aggressive and vocal students into the parking lot of an academic building called Prentice Hall.

The exchange of rocks and tear gas canisters continued. At some point, guardsmen knelt and aimed their weapons directly at the students in the parking lot. Then, concluding that the crowd was dispersing, the guard troops began moving back up the hill toward the commons. Once they reached the top of the hill, for reasons still in dispute, approximately 12 guardsmen simultaneously turned 180 degrees and fired their weapons toward the parking lot. It is estimated that 67 shots were fired over 13 seconds. Four students, Allison Krause, Jeffrey Miller, Sandra Sheuer, and William Schroeder, were killed. Nine more were injured, including one who would remain permanently paralyzed.[11] An investigation that concluded in 1975 determined that a verbal order to "fire" was given, but to this day no one knows who gave that order.[12]

James Rhodes, Ohio's sitting governor, lost his primary race for Senate to Robert Taft Jr. by just 3,000 votes (out of 900,000) on May 5, the day after the Kent State tragedy.[13] Exactly 10 days after the Kent shootings, a similar but less well-known incident occurred at Jackson State College in Jackson, Mississippi. Together, the events horrified a nation that had become increasingly concerned that academic institutions had mutated from halls of learning to centers of unrest.

WHAT KENT MEANT

One of the most famous photographs of the twentieth century is the Pulitzer Prize–winning shot taken by Kent photojournalism student John Filo. The young photographer, who also served as a correspondent for a Pittsburgh suburban newspaper, captured the image of 14-year-old runaway Mary Ann Vecchio kneeling and screaming over the mortally wounded Jeffrey Miller, who was lying in the Prentice Hall parking lot. The image of her anguished face and outstretched arms was seen around the world within 24 hours in daily newspapers and broadcast news accounts of the shootings. Though it is not included in this book, today there are few other historical accounts of the events at Kent State that do not feature Filo's image of Miller and Vecchio.[14]

Kent State provided a national turning point that was not understood by my not-quite-12-year-old mind. I was smart enough and well-schooled enough to know the core issues of the day. I knew a few things for certain. I did not want to go to Vietnam like some of the older kids in my neighborhood had. I didn't like assassination, protest, or the riot police I was seeing on the national news. I was more enamored of the "good old days" presented in the afterschool reruns of *Leave It to Beaver, Ozzie and Harriet,* and *The Andy Griffith Show.* I wanted to go to college in six or seven years, but I knew I didn't want to be at risk of getting shot or pressed by the campus zeitgeist into becoming an angry activist.

Looking back on the era, it appears that the rest of the country was coming to similar conclusions. They saw two immovable, intractable forces that continued to accelerate in energy and rhetoric. The law-and-order-at-all-cost approach of Rhodes met the increasingly militant anger of protesters. Both sides were determined to win, but in the end everybody lost. The era of campus violence subsided quickly after 1970. By the time I went to college in 1976, the only noise came from overly loud concerts and sporting events.

America was in a different era by that time. Some believe it was brought about by what happened at Kent. Some would say that the demands of '60s-era protesters were answered by a variety of legislation. The aforementioned reductions in drinking age and voting age were occurring throughout the country. The reduction in voting age became a national measure in 1971. On March 23 of that year, both houses of Congress passed a proposed amendment to the Constitution granting voting rights to all citizens 18 years of age or older. It became the 26th Amendment to the US Constitution, and it was ratified by the states in just three months. This fact makes it the most quickly passed and implemented amendment in history.[15] Other effects included a removal of the draft, hated and viewed as unnecessary by many on both sides of the Vietnam War issue. For a time, there was not even a requirement for 18-year-old males to register. An amendment with the stated goal of assuring "equal rights for women" (the ERA) was also submitted to the states, though it was never enacted. Congress moved quickly to cut funding for the war effort, ultimately cutting it to a point that forced the American withdrawal from Vietnam five years later. Numerous civil rights and environmental programs were approved by Congress and signed into law by presidents Nixon, Ford, and Carter.

There were also dark consequences of the Kent State episode and the protest era that preceded it. President Nixon's chief of staff, H. R. "Bob" Haldeman, indicated that his boss was deeply disturbed by the shooting and deaths at Kent. He was concerned that his actions had set them off. Haldeman, in his 1978 book *The Ends of Power,* asserts that the shootings began a downward slide in the president which may have ultimately led to the Watergate Hotel break-in and ensuing scandal.[16]

One challenging era ends and a new one begins.

CHAPTER 19

THE ELECTORAL
COLLAGE

A guy named James Blaine did it in 1884. Benjamin Harrison did it eight years later in 1892. Thomas Dewey repeated the feat 52 years later in 1944. Richard Nixon was the last to do it, his achievement occurring in 1960, eight years before he was elected president of the US.

These are men who won the electoral votes of Ohio without winning their runs for the US presidency. And there have only been four of them since 1860. Note that 1860 is significant only because that is the point from which one could trace the modern breakdown of political parties—Democrat and Republican. That was the year Abraham Lincoln won his first election, also a first for the relatively newly formed Republican Party (Republican candidate John Charles Fremont lost to James Buchanan in 1856).

Blaine, Harrison, Dewey, and Nixon may have won Ohio in their respective losing efforts, but a whole slew of GOP candidates (14 since 1860) have won with the help of Ohio or because of Ohio. The Ohio statistics get even more interesting when you consider that Democratic Party candidates since 1860 have always won the election when they've won Ohio. That linkage is something that would have been almost statistically impossible at the beginning of the Democrat versus Republican political era just before the Civil War, but it's indisputable according to the electoral records. Ohio is also the only state to have picked the winner every election since 1964 (13 times in a row). If you win Ohio, you almost always win the whole show.[1]

In addition to voting for the election winner the most times since 1860 (35 of 39 times), Ohio has one of the best records as a bellwether state since the Lower 48 were first all in place and voting in 1912, picking 25 of 27 winners, tying Nevada in that measure during the 2016 election. New Mexico has also been accurate at mirroring the electoral opinion of the entire country. And there have been other states to have picked consecutive winners more than Ohio's 14 in a row.

Because of the Electoral College, presidential elections have to be looked at a little differently than any other type of election. Unlike the other contests—from local school board to US Senate or governor—the concept of "one person, one vote" doesn't apply. People voting for president have to look at themselves as making a tiny fragment of a larger statewide decision. There are 51 such decisions made each presidential election year—the 50 states plus the District of Columbia. This fact produces some pretty interesting considerations, too. First, the sheer magnitude of California's population and the significance of its 55 electoral votes don't translate into much power for individual California voters who, based on population, have 690,000 citizens per electoral vote. California does get visits during election years, but these are usually accompanied by fund-raising efforts.

Ohioans fare little better in this measure, with 640,000 per vote. The states that do really well on a population-per-vote basis are the smaller states. Wyoming has just three electoral votes. But a population of fewer than 600,000 means that there are fewer than 200,000 Wyoming voters per electoral vote. Somehow it is doubtful that Wyoming voters feel more attended-to than those in Ohio or the other swing states. Attention paid by both media and candidates goes to those states that can offer the highest number of votes and the highest degree of unpredictability. In 2012 Florida outperformed Ohio on both scores, but in a number of previous elections it has generally tended to be more reliably Republican and less contested by Democrats.[2]

So why is Ohio more significant than Nevada? Or New Mexico? One could easily answer that question by looking at the state's

FIGURE 19.1. Ohio has seen vigorous campaigning from presidential hopefuls for well over 100 years.

long history as not only a harbinger of outcome but a nice prize in terms of electoral votes. Although its population percentage has dropped relative to other, faster-growing states, Ohio's nearly 11.7 million people still make it the seventh-most populous state in the country (at one time it was third). This means that for well over 150 years, Ohio has been an important electoral objective. New Mexico, Nevada, and other bellwether states have tiny populations and many fewer electoral votes than Ohio. At one point in US history, Maine was said to be an ultimate prognosticator of presidential election outcome. "As Maine goes, so goes the nation," was the saying. But Maine, which has only four electoral votes today, has always been small in terms of population.[3]

Although any state could view itself as being determinant during a close election, states carrying the allure of a large population (and many electoral votes) plus the interest-generating effect of being a "toss up" are going to get a lot of focus from the presidential candidates and their parties.[4] Imagine if California with its 55 electoral votes was a state that parties thought could go either way.

States in the middle part of the country, the so-called border states (terminology held over from the Civil War era), including

Tennessee, Kentucky, and Missouri, had long runs as bellwether presidential electors until all became more consistently Republican in their voting patterns. They also did not offer nearly the number of electoral votes as Ohio. One state that has significant population and at one time bellwether status is Illinois. It correctly picked the ultimate presidential winner in every election between 1916 and 1976. Today it has become reliably Democratic in presidential elections. Even though the vast majority of Illinois counties are still "red," the huge population swell in the Chicago area has tipped the Land of Lincoln to the Democrats in most elections over the last 60 years. New York and Pennsylvania exhibit similar characteristics, with the overwhelming numbers in New York City and Philadelphia nearly always pulling those states to the side of the Democratic contenders.

Ohio also owes its Election Day significance to the fact that it is not party-loyal. Neither party can be counted out. But neither can take the state for granted. Over the last 70 years, Ohio voters have pinged back and forth between Democratic and Republican governors. Even the four terms of Republican James Rhodes were broken by the four-year term of Democrat John Gilligan. Ohio's political landscape is and usually has been a microcosm of what goes on throughout the country. Ohio's General Assembly and Senate are currently controlled by Republicans, mirroring the US Congress as of this writing. It has one US senator who is a Democrat and one who is a Republican. Its big-city mayors are mostly Democrats. Remember, "big city" in Ohio ranges from Columbus, with 850,000 inhabitants, to Lorain, with just 64,000. And that might be one of the points in Ohio's favor as an electoral indicator. There are no really huge cities dominating the state, its politics, or its representation.

TALES OF LOST ELECTIONS

In the autumn of 1968, Richard Nixon was campaigning furiously for the presidency in his race against Democrat Hubert Humphrey. This naturally required stops in Ohio, where Nixon saw a sign that read simply "Bring Us Together." It was in the hands of a Deshler, Ohio, teenager during Nixon's brief appearance in the small community. Throughout the rest of his campaign and into his presidency, Nixon would refer numerous times to the rally, the slogan, the Ohio town, and the circumstances that led to his adopting the girl's words as his own. It was part of an approach that would make him more ordinary, more of an "everyman." He was, after all, a poor-born person from Yorba Linda and Whittier, California, whom the nation had come to associate with influence and power (and a certain amount of political misfortune). In spite of a squandered and star-crossed political career that included the Watergate scandal, Richard Nixon is one of only two people to have won Ohio's electoral votes in three different presidential elections. Franklin D. Roosevelt is the other. Consider his two vice presidential wins on the Eisenhower ticket and he is Ohio's clear electoral college champion.

Nixon carried Ohio in his unsuccessful national campaign against John F. Kennedy. One might have expected him to feel confident of its votes in 1968, but it is also possible that Nixon remembered the plight of Thomas Dewey. Dewey campaigned against incumbent Harry Truman as a second-time Republican candidate. He lost the 1944 election to FDR but had won Ohio. Logically, he might have expected to take Ohio again when facing Truman in 1948, particularly given Truman's declining popularity. Throughout that summer, Dewey led in all of the national polls. He was expected by many to easily win over Truman, who had succeeded Franklin Roosevelt after his death, in 1945, and who had a difficult three and a half years in office. Further bolstering Dewey's confidence was the fact that, at the time, Ohio was one of the most Republican states in the country, with the party controlling the legislature and the governor's mansion. The Republicans also held a vast majority of Ohio's congressional delegation. Ohio also had two popular GOP Senators, John Bricker and Robert Taft (son of President and Supreme Court Chief Justice William H. Taft).

"Give 'em hell Harry" Truman marshaled a game attempt at re-election. This included a vigorous whistle-stop tour through the Midwest. Many destinations in the Buckeye State saw and listened to the president's rousing denunciations of Republican policies and Dewey in particular. He was particularly adept at tailoring messages depending on whether they were given to urban or rural audiences. Here are some remarks given off the rear platform of the

Presidential railcar, *Magellan,* in the small town of Ottawa, Ohio, on the afternoon of October 11, 1948:

> There is a great difference between the Democratic and the Republican Parties. One of the most important differences is in farm policies. Under the Republicans, the farmers don't count. The farmers are left to shift for themselves. The Republicans are interested in looking after the interests of the big manufacturers of the East. They are not very much interested in the welfare of the farmer. The Democratic leaders know that the farmers of this country are the foundation on which the welfare of the country is built, and that they must have fair prices for their products. That is the reason for the farm price support program which was carried forward by this administration.[5]
> (Source: Truman Library)

October 11 was one of the most memorable days in a highly improbable comeback by a man who had seemed to be an incumbent doomed to defeat. Truman made numerous stops in the state that day, starting in Cincinnati, where he emphasized traditionally "big city" Democratic Party themes such as education, classroom size, and Republican attacks on labor. He finished the day in friendly territory—heavily Democratic Akron. A recurring theme in every location was that voters should vote their self-interest. And he made sure that he was seen as the one with their self-interests in mind. Ultimately this approach hit home with Ohioans. On Election Day, November 2, 1948, the two candidates awaited results throughout the night and into the morning of Wednesday, November 3. When radios across the nation finally announced at 8:30 Wednesday morning that Ohio's 25 electoral votes had gone for Truman, he had the 270 electoral votes needed for victory. Illinois and California later went Truman's way as well.

Dewey had been so confident about winning Ohio that he did no personal campaigning there. At one Ohio stopover while traveling to other states, Dewey kept his train car curtains closed and didn't bother to step out to acknowledge potential supporters. Maybe the New York governor got what he deserved. Other candidates have discovered the unfortunate fact that once won over, Ohio can be a faithless mistress. Herbert Hoover won the state easily in 1928 but was trounced there by Franklin D. Roosevelt in 1932. Jimmy Carter carried Ohio in 1976 but was badly beaten by Ronald Reagan in 1980. George H. W. Bush easily won the state in 1988 but then lost it in his race against Bill Clinton and Ross Perot in 1992.

So, getting back to Nixon, it is clear that he was taking no chances that his 1960 electoral advantage in Ohio would repeat in '68. No recent candidate has taken that chance either. In 2012 President Obama and his challenger, Mitt Romney, visited the state 83 times. The previous three presidential election years, 2008, 2004, and 2000, saw similarly high rates of visitation by the contesting parties. Ohio is widely viewed as making the difference in the 2004 race between John Kerry and incumbent George W. Bush. Kerry had been viewed as the leader in the state at many points in the race. Even on Election Day, early exit polls showed Kerry winning Ohio, which would have put him in the White House. However, in the end, Bush carried the state, as he had done in 2000.

NORTH MEETS SOUTH. EAST MEETS WEST. CORPORATE MEETS COUNTRY.

Another way to look at Ohio from a presidential candidate's perspective is to see it as a sort of test market of ideas. That is one reason why both major political parties were eyeing the state as a convention location for 2016. It is also a reason why Cleveland was selected as the GOP's 2016 convention site as well as the host of the first Republican debates in 2015.

Events such as these garner significant attention not just from national media but from local reporters as well. A senator expressing an opinion on favorite local chili or rib places or, in the case of Cleveland, being seen with his kids at an Indians game is just good public relations. It also reflects the salesman's pitch on a large scale: "We really appreciate your business, Mr. and Mrs. Ohio." Test a rhetorical idea in Ohio and, if the approach moves the polls in your direction, play it nationally. Campaigning is marketing. Ohio is a terrific test market.[6] Ideas expressed at such events are also likely to get closer scrutiny by those in host cities and states.

Ohio and Ohioans have long been catalysts for how the nation mixes politics and social change. The career of Toledo native Gloria Steinem as a writer and social justice activist included decades as one of the country's best-known advocates for women's equality. In 1968—during a time of national unrest—Cleveland elected the nation's first African American mayor in Carl Stokes. Stokes's brother Louis began an epic 30-year congressional career during that period as well. As previously noted, Ohio gave rise to some of the country's most powerful and prominent unions as the nation wrestled with the emerging relationship between labor and capital early in the twentieth century.

The state is a great place for trying new ideas, too. Columbus is a premier test market for restaurant menu items and other consumer products. That's because it brings together a rich combination of Middle America, corporate culture, and worldwide demographics via Ohio State and a dozen other nearby colleges. This also makes Columbus and the state it anchors ideal for testing political appeal and candidate styles. With Ohio, political parties are reaching demographic groups that sample the larger nation.

There is plenty of suburbia that accompanies Columbus, Cincinnati, Cleveland, Toledo, and other cities. These often toggle between Republican and Democratic candidates depending on the year, issues, and economic considerations. Mining interests are strong in the east and south regions of the state. Northern cities like Youngstown, Akron, and Cleveland have major manufacturing and steel production operations along with labor unions like the United Auto Workers, Teamsters, and United Steelworkers.

Strong farming cultures throughout the state seemed to have turned numerous counties Republican red in many elections over the most recent decades. Small-town America is present throughout the state in towns like Belleview, Copley, Bucyrus, Mt. Gilead, Zanesville, Chillicothe, Mt. Vernon, and scores more. Most of these have residents who voice concerns about vanishing factories, declining opportunity, and reduced relevance. In these communities, one can still feel the presence of nineteenth-century America in beautiful classic Greek revival and Victorian architecture, but the interests of the residents are mostly of the twenty-first century.

Presidential and gubernatorial elections generally lead news organizations to publish red-county/blue-county maps of individual states. These color-rich collages are much like the national map that shows red and blue states. A look at an Ohio-by-county map will show blue clustered in or near urban areas like Toledo, Cleveland, Akron, and Youngstown. Southern Ohio is largely red except perhaps for Montgomery (Dayton) and Hamilton (Cincinnati) counties. As overall population density decreases, the possibility of the county tending to vote Republican increases (Truman's 1948 success notwithstanding).

It's worth asking why these phenomena so tidily represented by Ohio are reflected on a larger national scale. For decades, sociologists and political scientists have discussed a general tendency for people to cluster around like-minded people. This includes not only work and lifestyle habits but voting tendencies as well. A flight to suburbs by working and professional classes has left the most urban areas in the hands of a citizenry more heavily apt to support Democratic politicians, while those in suburban areas have a slight propensity to support Republican candidates. Rural areas tend to be as heavily Republican as urban areas are Democratic. But with smaller populations, it takes more rural counties to balance the effect of urban counties.

Another view is held by academics studying communications and "social judgment theory." This theory holds that people have latitudes of acceptance or rejection in which they continually evaluate new ideas based on their current attitudes and beliefs. It suggests that people are willing to make small, incremental steps toward another belief especially if they don't have high ego involvement in the question at hand. It is easy to see in either of the above scenarios that populations can easily shift views and values over time.[7] Whether people are willing to admit it, we are influenced by those closest to us.

This has happened in much of the industrial Northeast and a large portion of the Midwest. It has reached a point where states that at one time could go either way in presidential elections became solidly "blue." This included states like Pennsylvania and Illinois, mentioned earlier, along with neighboring Michigan. Demographically and culturally these states closely mirror the Buckeye State, but each of these three states has at least one huge urban city: Chicago, Philadelphia, and Detroit, although Metro Detroit is dwindling. More than half the entire Illinois population resides within the Chicago metropolitan area. The size and population density of these urban areas had been enough to pull these states into the Democratic column since at least the first election of Bill Clinton. It would be a powerful enough characteristic until his wife, Hillary Clinton, sought the office in 2016.

But what about Ohio's one-time population anchor, Cleveland? While many big cities of the Northeast and Midwest have experienced declining populations since 1970, the rate has been precipitous in Cleveland. For the cities of Chicago and Philadelphia, population decreased about 20 percent between 1970 and 2010. Cleveland, on the other hand, lost 48 percent, or nearly half. One has to imagine that if the Cleveland of 1970 had maintained a slower rate of decline, similar to that of Chicago, it would have about 200,000 more inhabitants than it does today. Columbus has seen its population increase in the period 1970–2010, bucking a general decline trend for cities in the region. This has not been enough to make up for Cleveland's decline nor for population losses in Cincinnati, Toledo, Akron, Dayton, and Youngstown.

In Ohio, you are looking at a state that has lost up to a half-million big-city residents over 40 years. Whether they move from Cleveland to nearby Medina or much further south to the Carolinas is unknown. But such urban flight has reduced the populations of areas that have a much greater tendency to vote for Democratic candidates, particularly during presidential election years. This urban–rural balance may be what keeps the colors of the Ohio "collage" balanced, making the state a highly competitive electoral challenge in contrast to some of its solid-blue neighbors. John Kerry might have appreciated having some of those vanishing Cleveland voters back in 2004.

CHAPTER 20

EIGHT
AVERAGE PRESIDENTS

Ohio as an election spectacle goes at least as far back as James A. Garfield's beloved front porch. The sprawling platform that bedecked his Mentor, Ohio, home just east of Cleveland is still there for everyone to see. And while the home is certainly large even by today's standards, it looms even larger as a landmark in the evolution of the American presidency.[1]

This particular porch was the launchpad for a new style of campaigning. Garfield, well known and regarded as a public speaker, broke a long-standing tradition among presidential candidates of having others do their talking: he spoke for himself. That is significant because there was once a time in our history when it was believed to be unseemly for presidents to actively campaign on their own behalf.

Potential public servants were supposed to be uninterested in pursuing higher office yet open to being called by their electorate. How genteel; yet how unrealistic. The notion that people are uninterested in higher office is absurd, especially those already in politics. And it is well established that the elder statesmen of this country's first century spent quite a bit of time scheming, lobbying, fraternizing, and otherwise seeking ways to make sure they would be "called to service." Garfield knew that there were few better at prepared or extemporaneous speaking than he. His porch oratory

FIGURE 20.1. The Mentor, Ohio, home and porch that launched the presidency of James A. Garfield.

on his own behalf won acclaim from reporters, supporters, and the simply curious, all of whom came by the trainload. Ultimately, it won him the presidency.[2]

The seven presidents born in Ohio are Ulysses S. Grant, Rutherford B. Hayes, James A. Garfield, Benjamin Harrison, William McKinley, William Howard Taft, and Warren G. Harding. In addition, William Henry Harrison (grandfather of Benjamin) considered himself a Buckeye and ran as an Ohioan even though he was born in Virginia. When you get down to president-producing bragging rights, more presidents were born in the state of Virginia. However, Virginia's claim to presidential leadership is less convincing in that three of the eight presidents born in Virginia—Harrison, along with Zachary Taylor and Woodrow Wilson—spent much of their lives and launched their political careers as citizens of other states.[3]

Ohio might have only 4 percent of the nation's population and just 1 percent of its landmass, but its presidential statistics are impressive. With eight Ohioans serving, the state can stake at least some claim to 18 percent of the nation's chief executives. With seven of those eight being Republicans (the first, Harrison, was a member of the Whig Party), Ohio can claim a whopping 37 percent of the country's Republican presidents. There are all kinds of interesting ways to slice the statistics, not all of them pleasant. For example, half of all assassinated presidents—Garfield and McKinley—were Ohioans.[4]

But it has been quite a long time since 1920, when the last Ohioan was elected president. In that race, it was Ohioan versus Ohioan at the top of both tickets as Marion's Warren G. Harding faced off against Ohio's sitting governor, James M. Cox. This was the only time a governor and senator from the same state faced each other in a race to become president.

Buckeye State candidates have certainly thrown their hat into the presidential ring on a number of occasions since. Senate Leader Robert Taft was Eisenhower's primary Republican challenger in the 1952 election. And Democratic senator and astronaut John Glenn made a much anticipated but strikingly unsuccessful bid for the Democratic nomination in 1984. Governor John Kasich made a quixotic run for the GOP nomination in 2016, winning only one state primary—Ohio.

Ohio's ability to produce presidencies in recent years may be diminished, but one thing is clear in wide view of the American experience: Ohio made presidents when it counted. The state's presence as a central northern locale before, during, and after the Civil War meant that it was the critical political pivot point between eastern and western northern states. It was not only the population center point during the time of the Civil War but also the third-largest state in terms of population. Today, it is still among the top 10 states in population and no less diminished as a presidential "must win."

Another reason why Ohio presidents had such an impact on the country is that many of them were the first generation of presidents to be seen and heard by such a wide swath of the American people. Until the end of the nineteenth century, presidents hardly ever traveled outside of Washington. That's when trains made them more mobile. Photography and daily newspapers made their images and daily musings accessible. The invention and perfection of audio-recording technologies by Ohio native Thomas Edison ensured that presidential voices were heard across the country. America was becoming more politically aware and intent on getting to know its presidents.

Garfield's front-porch oratory is just one example of how Ohio presidents changed the country slowly—decade by decade, presidency by presidency. No, Ohio did not produce a Washington, Jefferson, or Lincoln. But the unique qualities and characteristics of its eight presidents helped recreate presidential politics and reshape the American political and cultural landscape in many ways during the years when an Ohioan in the White House was more the rule than the exception.

THE BIRTH OF POPULIST CAMPAIGNING

It may be a less than flattering distinction, but while Ohio does claim fame as a producer of US presidents, only Grant served a full two terms. Two terms or eight years is seen today as the norm. For most of the nineteenth century, however, it was fairly rare for a president to seek a second term. William McKinley was elected to two terms, but his second was cut short on September 6, 1901, by an assassin's bullet in Buffalo, New York. Still, McKinley's service, second longest of the Ohio presidencies, contrasts with some really short ones, namely that of the aforementioned James Garfield and Ohio's first US president, William Henry Harrison.

Harrison was a Whig, the first member of his party to win the presidency. His victory over incumbent Martin Van Buren broke a long series of presidential wins by what had then become known simply as the Democratic Party. Harrison had been a large figure in nineteenth-century America, first winning fame as a general in the War of 1812 and the Indian wars that dominated life in the Ohio Valley in the late eighteenth and early nineteenth centuries. His performance in the Battle of Tippecanoe (located in what was to become Indiana) earned him the "Tippecanoe" nickname he would carry the rest his life. Harrison's election brought him to the capitol steps on March 4, 1841, where he took the oath of office and set about on a punishingly long inaugural address. He spoke for two hours, still a record for inaugural length. That speech is said to have been the catalyst for a devastatingly severe cold or flu, which took his life 32 days later.[5]

Harrison's presidential milestones are confined to unenviable personal statistics. He had the shortest term, was the first president to die in office, and was the oldest president ever elected prior to Ronald Reagan. Many people who had never heard of Harrison became familiar with his name throughout the 1980 campaign when the prudence of electing a man of Reagan's age was hotly debated.

With Harrison's administration quickly giving way to that of John Tyler, there is little for which Harrison is remembered except for how his campaign began to change the character of American presidential elections. It provides one of the first examples of the parties' and their candidates' personalizing campaigns. Harrison supporters held numerous parades and rallies (not to mention barbecues and hard cider giveaways). They employed posters and wrote songs to popularize their own candidate and to demonize the other party. It was personalized politics at its best. The Van Buren camp made fun of Harrison's frontier home and his folksy ways, but Harrison's people immediately turned these characteristics into virtues, ultimately winning the day. Populism was born.[6]

Because of their success, the 1840 Whigs helped to cement a two-party system in the country. Their party gathering in 1839 (for the 1840 election cycle) also established the party convention as a means for selecting a presidential candidate, rallying the faithful and framing and disseminating platforms and other campaign messages. Today we are all familiar with famous political campaigns that seemed to ride on a very short slogan: *Morning in America, Hope and Change, Nixon Now,* and *I Like Ike,* to name just a few. Harrison's campaign may have started the trend with the timeless line *Tippecanoe and Tyler, Too.* It's a safe bet that a significant number of even school-age kids today have the slogan committed to memory. It is almost as though it's a part of our political DNA.[7]

Harrison also led a westward march of the nation's political center. Before his election, only Andrew Jackson had been elected president from a non-original-founding state. Since Harrison's election, well over half of American presidents have hailed from states that were admitted to the Union after the US Constitution was ratified.

As discussed in chapter 5, Ohio-born presidents played important roles in the Civil War. Their experience was a defining one. No matter how their politics might have shifted, they would always have something in common with the largest, most powerful part of the American electorate—Civil War veterans—at a time when the country was getting over the conflict and getting on with business. Ohioans with substantial Civil War experience began a tradition of the country demanding or at the very least applauding the military credentials of presidents.

WHAT'S HE DRINKIN', ASKED LINCOLN

Like so many American presidents, Ulysses S. Grant (born Hiram Ulysses Grant) saw his general popularity decline during his two terms in office. That was the nature of Grant's life. Born dirt-poor in Point Pleasant, Ohio, Grant lived a consistent tug of war between the ups and downs of fate and fortune. His educational record at West Point, like his early business career, was anything but spectacular. He and his wife had to live with her parents in St. Louis for many years. In the controversial Mexican–American War, Grant earned just modest distinction.

His life mixed highs and lows like a bartender mixes cocktails. He was known as a hard-driving, hard-drinking commander during Union campaigns in the Mississippi Valley and Tennessee. But not everyone disapproved of the drinking. President Lincoln once asked a petitioner "to find out what brand of whiskey Grant drinks, because I want to send a barrel of it to each one of my generals." In the war, Grant succeeded where numerous other generals failed. And once Grant took complete command of Union forces, it was only a matter of time before the "rebellion" was crushed.[8]

Grant was enormously popular during his early presidency, even drawing converts to the Republican Party in the formerly adversarial South and carrying several southern states. Following a rocky, scandal-plagued second term, the former president was able to restore a fair amount of goodwill that scandals of his presidency destroyed. Yet, he was unable to re-earn his party's nomination during a try for a third term in 1880. One of Grant's lasting achievements was the publication of his two-volume memoirs, written entirely by himself, in which he provided a thorough account of his life, the Mexican–American and Civil wars, and his presidency. Completed just before his death in an effort to keep banks and other creditors at bay, the books are considered required reading for any scholar of the American Civil War or the political landscape in the years after.[9]

PARTYING AT THE HAYES HOME

When I was a kid, my family went to numerous family picnics and swimming events at what my cousins and I called "Hayeses." By that we meant Spiegel Grove, the Fremont home of Rutherford B. Hayes, the second consecutive Union general to serve as a US president. My great-uncle worked at the estate and was in charge of restorations, so we had easy access to the swimming pool on the property (the pool is no longer there).

Hayes had come to the presidency over Samuel Tilden in one of the most contested political elections since the election of John Quincy Adams, in 1824, and until the election of George W. Bush, in 2000. A review of the entire matter might lead some to think that the Bush-Gore controversy of 2000 was civil and orderly compared with the Hayes-Tildon election controversy in 1876, America's centennial year. This occurred just after the South was reintegrated into the Union and was in the midst of a difficult reconstruction period. It was the beginning of what would be called the Jim Crow era.

This period also began America's long period known as the temperance movement. Hayes's wife, Lucy, was an ardent opponent of alcoholic beverages who made the White House liquor-free during their years there. Immensely popular, "Lemonade Lucy's" support for temperance helped provide momentum for dialogue that would ultimately result in Prohibition in 1920.[10]

The Hayes presidency, considered along with Grant's, reintroduced the country to the kind of stability in which businesses could once again take root and thrive. Historians typically view the 1870s as the launchpad for the American industrial revolution. Numerous inventions that would become staples of business and home emerged.[11] Labor unions began to form. Urban sprawl began to dramatically affect New York, Boston, Baltimore, and other large cities, driving the first of what would be known as suburbs and spurring the young and adventurous to seek new opportunities out west. Baseball was beginning to gain traction as a national pastime. Early inventions by Edison and the chemists of Standard Oil, Proctor & Gamble, and numerous other manufacturers would reshape how the country went about its work and survived at home.

ANOTHER SHORT ONE

When Garfield took the oath of office on March 4, 1881, the country had just completed 100 years since its first national constitution (the Articles of Confederation) and now occupied a landmass 50 times greater than the original 13 colonies. It embodied states like Ohio not even imagined during the time of the revolution. The US population was 20 times larger, too, swelled by waves of immigrants from the countries of Western Europe and even more exotic areas including Poland, Hungary, the Middle East, and what was then known as the Far East. Garfield also continued a tradition of Union soldiers eventually ascending to the White House.

Garfield was a member of the Republican faction known as "Half-Breeds," committed to various issues related to America's increasing industrialization. His nomination included the time-honored practice of selecting a member of a rival faction as a party unity maneuver. His vice president, Chester Arthur, was part of the Stalwart faction, committed to continued caution and suspicion relative to the South. Unfortunately, party unification didn't work out so well for the young president from Mentor, Ohio. As he waited for a train on July 2, 1881, he was approached by Charles Guiteau, a frustrated patronage seeker. Guiteau fired two shots into Garfield, saying, "I am a Stalwart and Arthur shall be president." All of this occurred just less than four months after Garfield's inauguration. The wounded president appeared likely to recover for a time, but in the end he succumbed. The date was September 19, 1881. Garfield was 49 years old.[12]

One result of the assassination was a move to eliminate the patronage system for civil service employment. This had been a raging argument within the republic and divisive among the Ohio presidents during their era. Garfield and Hayes opposed patronage, while Grant favored it. Garfield, it would seem, paid the ultimate price for his opposition to patronage. Despite his short 199-day presidency, Garfield's name occasionally tumbles off the tongues of commentators and news anchors. This occurs whenever someone in the House of Representatives is said to be considering a presidential run. Garfield remains the only person to go directly from the "People's House" to the White House.[13]

BEATEN BY THE MAN HE BEAT

Following the three-and-a-half-year term of Chester Arthur and Grover Cleveland's first four-year term, it was Benjamin Harrison's turn to be president. He served from 1889 until he relinquished the office to Grover Cleveland's second term, in 1893. Harrison, raised and educated in Ohio, was the grandson of William Henry Harrison. Others in his notable ancestry included a signer of the death warrant for England's Charles I and a great-grandfather (also named Benjamin) who signed the Declaration of Independence. Like Grant, Hayes, and Garfield, Harrison was an Ohioan (also claimed by Indiana) who had distinguished himself during the Civil War.

Harrison's term is little noted but for some of the unusual statistics it provided. He was one of only a few presidents to win a majority in the Electoral College while falling short in the popular vote. He and Cleveland were the only two men to have defeated one another for the presidency (with Cleveland winning it back in 1892). Harrison was also the only grandson of a former president to become president himself (the Adamses and Bushes did the father-son trick). And during Harrison's term, the federal budget reached and exceeded a billion dollars for the first time.

A longtime goal was achieved for Harrison with the addition of six states to the union—the most in a presidential term. These were North Dakota, South Dakota, Montana, Washington, Idaho, and Wyoming. Democrats were concerned that the states would increase Republican representation and had largely opposed their admission. To this day, the Democrats' concerns remain realized, with all but Washington proving to be consistently "red."[14]

THE GUY WHO GOT US HAWAII

As Grover Cleveland's second term was coming to a close, the US experienced one of its most interesting and hard-fought political contests. It was between the well-known Democrat and populist William Jennings Bryan and the former Ohio governor William McKinley. The key issue of the race was the question of whether the US should abandon the gold standard for a looser, freer, silver standard advocated by Bryan. Other major issues were looming disputes between Spain and its Cuba colony. This carried portents of war between a declining world power and the emerging American military and naval presence. A solid citizen with a somewhat porky frame, McKinley sought the office at a time when America had been struggling economically. The nation's financial panic involved overspeculation, too much credit extension, and the failure of a large Argentinean bank—the stuff you find in almost any financial meltdown, right? Hundreds of financial institutions and thousands of businesses collapsed during a period that extended through the 1896 election.

McKinley faced off against the silver-tongued Bryan, known as a spellbinding orator and passionate advocate for free silver. Simply explained, the silver movement demanded that US Mint facilities accept individuals' silver bullion for conversion to coins (less a small fee) just as they did gold. The free silver people also advocated that the metal be pegged at a value equal to 1/16th that of gold, something most people thought would be inflationary. That such a move might be inflationary did have populist appeal because the panic had resulted in crippling deflation. And with inflation, indebted farms, businesses, and individuals would be able to pay off old debt with inflated or "less valuable" currency. Bryan logged tens of thousands of whistle-stop miles promoting the idea.

McKinley knew his limitations. Always acknowledging Bryan's oratorical advantages, he instead borrowed a page from Garfield and conducted almost 100 percent of his campaign from his front porch in Canton, Ohio. But while McKinley remained home, his message was carried across the country by numerous whistle-stopping surrogates like his friend, advisor, and financier, Ohio Senator Mark Hanna.

Hanna himself is something of a political wonder, embodying the financing weight of modern-day moguls like George Soros or Warren Buffet plus the political acumen of players like Terry McAuliffe, David Axelrod, and Karl Rove. He was key to the presidential aspirations of three fellow Ohioans: McKinley, John Sherman (never elected), and James Garfield. Hanna spent most of his life on his very successful business career until serving in the US Senate. Like many powerful individuals who gain a president's trust, Hanna was often portrayed as McKinley's puppet master.[15]

McKinley's sound money message and porch politicking carried the day. His victory over Bryan in 1896 was followed by dramatic improvement in the American economy and a relatively short, successful war that the US used to rid Cuba of what it saw as "Spanish oppression." The US also collected Puerto Rico, Guam, and the Philippines in the process. The country went extracontinental, in more peaceful ways, annexing Hawaii after the queen's overthrow by the Hawaiian populace. The islands would remain a territory for over 60 years, achieving statehood only in the late 1950s.[16]

America was forging its own kind of empire. Congress had firmly established the country on the "gold standard," and McKinley was riding high into the 1900s, when he again confronted the charismatic but politically hapless Bryan. It is noteworthy that Mark Hanna was opposed to McKinley's 1900 vice-presidential running mate. He said of Theodore Roosevelt, "There's only one life between that madman and the presidency."

Hanna was prophetic. After winning handily, McKinley would only serve six months of his second term. While attending the Pan American Exposition in Buffalo during September 1901, McKinley was stalked and ultimately shot by a disgruntled anarchist, Leon Czolgosz. Anarchists were part of a loose but growing movement in the era that had slain leaders of Italy and other countries. As with Garfield, McKinley was initially expected to survive the shooting. He was up talking to family and friends within a day, but his prognosis turned grave as gangrene set in. He died on September 14, 1901.[17]

McKinley was both the final president of the nineteenth century and the first of the twentieth. His bearing, character, and administration reflect the transition between the periods. Born poor in rural Niles, Ohio, he would die at the height of his popularity and power. As for his assassin, the wheels of justice turned quickly in those days. Leon Czolgosz followed McKinley into eternity just a month and a half later, via electric chair in Auburn, New York.[18]

HE FORGOT HIS OWN PRESIDENCY

William Howard Taft would have loved to live his life completely occupied with the family business—the practice of law. His father, Alphonso, had been both a lawyer and a respected judge in addition to serving in Grant's cabinet. The legal life would have suited the younger Taft just fine. As a young judge, Taft expressed his ultimate ambition as serving on the Supreme Court. Two things got in the way: his friend Theodore Roosevelt and Taft's own wife, Nellie.[19]

Roosevelt was just one of a number of important Republican figures who had come to respect the Cincinnatian. William McKinley knew of Taft's court ambition but selected him anyway to serve as governor-general of the newly acquired Philippines, a job that Taft performed ably and enthusiastically. He was so committed to the job that he turned down his first real Supreme Court offer from now president Theodore Roosevelt, who was seeking to make good on McKinley's promise to Taft. Taft later turned down a second offer. Inspired somewhat by Nellie's ambitions for him, he decided to continue in service to Roosevelt. And Roosevelt saw his old friend as the ideal replacement once his second term was complete. As Secretary of War from 1904 to 1908, Taft was both advisor to and protégé of the charismatic and popular president from New York.

By 1908 Roosevelt decided to observe the time-honored tradition of presidents who had limited themselves to two terms. The 22nd Amendment to the Constitution later made the two-term limitation law, but at that time it was a matter of honor. "TR" campaigned vigorously for his friend. He was convinced that Taft would continue in his progressive tradition, which included battling the power of huge corporations and trusts. Taft ran as a progressive, defeating William Jennings Bryan, who—having also been beaten twice by McKinley—holds the record for the number of times a major party nominee went down to defeat.

Election night 1908 was the height of Taft's presidential career. After shifting to a decidedly more conservative posture than Roosevelt's, Taft was seen by the progressive elements in the Republican Party as catering to big business and moneyed interests. Taft himself founded the US Chamber of Commerce as a counterbalance to the growing labor union movement and other forces that seemed to be lining up against the business world.

Shortly after his retirement in 1909, Roosevelt set off on a 15-month personal vacation. His adventure included an African safari and an extended trip through Europe, where he was treated like a king by numerous old-world monarchs. His return by steamship in September 1910 carried the air of a national holiday. Taft was one of many national, state, and local officials who ensured that Roosevelt's entrance into New York Harbor was a grand event. Taft sent word that he was eager to resume their friendship and to accept any counsel the former president had to offer.

But the two were soon at odds over Taft's less-than-progressive governance. While they had once been brothers in arms in the battle against trusts, Taft's antitrust actions against US Steel drew open anger from Roosevelt (who excepted the J. P. Morgan-owned operation as a "good trust"). By 1912 the men were battling one another for the Republican nomination. Despite his incredible popularity, Roosevelt was defeated by Taft, due perhaps to a split among progressive Republicans and Taft's quiet lobbying of conservative delegates. But Roosevelt wasn't through yet. He bolted from the Republican Party to form the American Progressive, or "Bull Moose," Party. The new party had a platform endorsing minimum-wage laws, full women's suffrage, Social Security, direct election of senators, an eight-hour workday, and a number of other reforms that were ultimately implemented by successive generations of congressional actions or constitutional amendments.

Taft was humiliated in the election, losing to both the victorious Democrat Woodrow Wilson and his old friend, Roosevelt. His only consolation might have been that in outmaneuvering Roosevelt for the GOP nomination he'd preserved the party's generally conservative and pro-business nature. The GOP might have evolved in a significantly different direction had the progressives held sway.[20]

While a landslide electoral defeat might humble some to the point of silent oblivion, Taft had a great post-presidency. First, he shed a great deal of weight (he had reportedly gotten stuck in a White House bathtub because of his corpulence). The weight loss boosted his vitality and got him more interested in long-forgotten outdoor pursuits. He served as president of the American Bar Association, lecturing and writing extensively. One of Taft's favorite causes was a vigorous and outspoken opposition to Prohibition. In this effort, the former president predicted many of the unanticipated consequences that occurred during the Prohibition Era.

In 1921 Taft's lifelong dream was realized when he was named the 10th chief justice of the US Supreme Court. Nominated by President Harding, Taft succeeded the late Edward Douglass White, whom he himself had nominated for elevation to chief justice. "This is the greatest day of my life," Taft said. Taft was an effective and highly regarded chief justice and enjoyed the job so much that he is said to have quipped on numerous occasions, "I've forgotten I've ever been president."

Taft served as chief justice during the height of Prohibition. Curiously, and despite his anti-prohibition writings, Taft actively and decisively enforced the 18th Amendment. His court also upheld most of the Volstead Act, which provided for Prohibition's enforcement. This might seem to counter Taft's once-public position, but a 1908 *New York Times* article meant to expose Taft's anti-Prohibition stance cites him as quoting and agreeing with a remark made years earlier by President Grant that "the best way to secure repeal of a bad law is to strictly enforce it." Perhaps that was something Will Taft had not forgotten.

PUTTING THE ROAR INTO THE 1920s

Grow up in Ohio and chances are quite good that you lived not too far from where an American president also was born, raised, or established a political career. Such is the case for many in my wife's hometown, Marion, Ohio, also the hometown of Warren Gamaliel Harding. It surprised me to learn that many Marion residents have never visited Harding's home, a national historic site.

I think that may be because Marionites harbor a collective guilt about Harding, most famous for dying in office before the full extent of the Teapot Dome scandal was known. To summarize the scandal in two sentences, Secretary of the Interior Albert Fall leased several oil fields, which had previously been under the con-

FIGURE 20.2. Final resting place of President Warren G. Harding, in Marion, Ohio.

trol of the Navy, to private oil investors. And it just so happened that these investors had made significant interest-free "loans" to Fall, who would eventually gain the distinction of becoming the first cabinet secretary to serve time behind bars.[21]

Harding had other problems. He consistently battled Congress (heavily in the control of his own Republican Party at the time) over the Bonus Act, designed to provide extra funds to World War I veterans or survivors of deceased servicemen. And his handling of a major rail strike in 1922 was largely viewed as ineffective. As a bit of irrelevant trivia, Harding also had the largest feet of any president, wearing size 14 shoes.[22]

I remember as a school kid in the 1960s and '70s that Harding was universally acknowledged as America's "worst president ever." So maybe that's why so many who live so close by in Marion never visit the Harding home.

Looking at things from the standpoint of economic turnarounds, Harding might be viewed as one of the country's best presidents. When he took over from the ailing Woodrow Wilson in

1921, the country that some call the "land of milk and honey" was pretty much just down to milk. And farmers were going broke on it. Crop and livestock prices were plunging. Demand for all varieties of mined, milled, and manufactured products was down sharply.

The economy was having a difficult time transitioning from war production to domestic production. Returning veterans swelled the ranks of the unemployed. Harding, who had campaigned on the promise of a "return to normalcy," took action and backed legislation that significantly reduced what were then increasing regulatory burdens. He cut taxes and imposed disciplined budget processes and emergency immigration quotas to stem the tide of desperate European immigrants, then approaching one million per year. Most of these measures worked to the advantage of the American people.[23] They were eager to get back to the "normalcy" that Harding had sold the country on from his own front porch during his presidential campaign.

Harding's period of disrepute did not occur until after his death, so it is a pretty safe bet that he never heard of himself referred to as "worst president ever." Before his death on a western trip in 1923, the economy improved measurably, and Harding was enjoying wide popularity. By the time his successor, Calvin Coolidge, was elected, the 1920s were fully roaring.

AVERAGE PRESIDENTS, EXCEPTIONAL COUNTRY

By the account of many historians, the most interesting things about the Ohioans' presidencies were the historical footnotes they provided—the first Harrison's record long inaugural and record short service, Grant's scandals, Hayes's disputed election, Garfield's and McKinley's assassinations, Taft's service *both* as president and as chief justice of the Supreme Court, and Harding's Teapot Dome and sudden, mysterious death. But collectively they made a big imprint on US culture just as it was expanding. To a man, they were proponents of industry and trade. They were careful in taxation and budget matters. The later Buckeye presidents (McKinley, Taft, and Harding) were inclined to worry about regulation and other threats to corporate interests, including the growing power of the labor union movement.

In 1924 New Englander Calvin Coolidge made one of his most famous remarks that "the chief business of the American people is business." Little quoted is his further clarification:

> They are profoundly concerned with producing, buying, selling, investing and prospering in the world. I am strongly of the opinion that the great majority of people will always find these are the moving impulses of our life.[24]

It should not escape anyone that President Coolidge said this after a 50-year swath of time that saw the invention of the automobile and airplane, the light bulb, the electrification of America, the creation of motion pictures, recorded sound and radios, and the advent of ticker tape on Wall Street. Eleven presidents served during this period of rapid industrialization and technological progress. Seven of them were from Ohio.

CHAPTER 21

YARD SIGNS
IN THE HEARTLAND

One of the things that makes human beings unique among the species is our obsession with eliminating uncertainty. The desire to know the future before it occurs has been the basis of religions, the inspiration of scientists, and the unachievable fantasy of everyone ranging from Michel de Nostradame to newly minted MBAs looking to make big things happen on Wall Street.

And there have been plenty of times when people looking for the future have thought they saw it in Ohio. The state has, for over a century and a half, served the country by indicating what the future could look like. Good or bad. Ohio helped light the country's way out of slavery in the mid-1800s. Later in the nineteenth century and into the twentieth, Ohio proved the value of market research, mass production, automation, and other tools of business efficiency. Ohioans invented America's way into electricity and demonstrated the power of petroleum.

In the early and mid-1800s, a vigorous commitment to canal building and railways put Ohioans closer together, from a time standpoint, than any nation or state's citizenry had ever been before. Young Rud Hayes, who would become the 19th US president, remarked in almost breathless writing to his girlfriend in 1851 that Dayton had become a suburb of Cincinnati because it could be reached in just two-and-a-half hours rather than the several days that the 50-mile trip used to require. In his exaltation to the future Lucy Hayes, he predicted the end of canal boats and other old transport modes: "The 'iron-horse' has taken away your occupation, to keep it until aerial ships take away his!"[1] Then just 29, Hayes clearly had a vision of the future that went beyond his enthusiasm for train travel. And little more than 50 years later, two young men from Dayton—that "suburb"—would introduce the world to the promise of aviation.

In recent years Ohio's reputation as a bellwether has made it an obsession for a different class of futurists—reporters, commentators, political scientists, and politicians. It is closely watched and bombarded with ad spending up to and through election years. Then it is scrutinized in off-years by political observers interested in potential shifts in the state legislatures or governor's mansion.

Ohio was leading the Midwest out of the recession during the later years of the Obama administration and John Kasich's term as governor.[2] It would continue to be a political barometer all the way to Election Day 2016. Both sides of the political argument could claim some of the state's statistical successes—lower unemployment, increasing economic activity, even reduced outmigration to other states. But in the early days of November 2016, an unusual thing happened in Ohio for a presidential year. Both campaigns "eased off the gas pedal" before Election Day. That is, the Hillary Clinton and Donald Trump campaigns drew down on their frenetic efforts in the Buckeye State. Normally, Ohio is visited by candidates and pounded by commercials all the way through Tuesday morning.[3]

Polls just after the summer convention period had Clinton up by several points in Ohio.[4] By mid-August, she was up by six. And it didn't help Trump that Ohio's sitting governor did not endorse him and never would. However, national statistics and personal realities don't always align. While the Clinton camp took comfort in the late-summer polls, the Trump campaign (like Bernie Sanders in the primary campaign) was drawing huge crowds in places like Canfield, Canton, Springfield, and Toledo. Signals remained mixed in both Ohio and the other 49 states. People would listen to reports of Clinton polling leads juxtaposed with TV footage showing Trump in front of huge, cheering gatherings of supporters.

Perhaps the most prescient observer was iconoclastic filmmaker Michael Moore. In July the vociferous Trump critic predicted the general election as it ultimately played out. Moore correctly predicted that Trump would win Ohio, Michigan, Pennsylvania, and Wisconsin.[5] Then, in October, a *New York Times* reporter made a cross-country motorcycle trip. In a story filed from Hudson, Ohio, he wrote that he stopped counting "Trump for President" signs when he got into the hundreds. But he added that, traveling east from Portland, Oregon, he got 2,500 miles before seeing his first Clinton sign. Those with Trump signs appeared more enthusiastic and inclined to add their own homemade touches. The largest, he noted, was that of a Celina, Ohio, small business owner who had spent $500 on a 22-foot-high custom sign in support of the GOP candidate.[6]

I was in my hometown, Toledo, 10 days before the election and observed two things. First, there were a lot of yard signs, far more than in the uncontested state of New York, where I now live. Second, the signage seemed to be split evenly between Clinton and Trump. This was significant, I thought, because Lucas County is a reliable "blue" area of the state.

Yard signs and crowd sizes, of course, offer little more than anecdotal evidence. They cannot serve as statistical predictors. Polling—actual quantitative data—is what really matters. Or so we are told. Yet for many an Ohioan (or Michigander or Wisconsinite), positive indicators in unemployment numbers are unreal if your own employer has just closed down. It's hard to trust in anything when the news you watch or read counters everything going on in your personal life. Imagine hearing a radio announcer saying your area is coming out of depression while you are driving your husband or daughter home from drug rehab.

In the end, it was the hundreds of pre-election polls that proved to be anecdotal. The six-point Ohio lead that Hillary Clinton had showed in August was now gone. The final *Columbus Dispatch* poll before November 8 indicated that Clinton had just a one-point lead. The benchmark RealClear Politics average of five Ohio polls showed Trump up 2.2 points.[7] The polling shift portended an affliction in the Clinton campaign that seemed to make it rush attention to other places in the national body. Pennsylvania. Michigan. Florida. Wisconsin. They did not like the immediate future that Ohio was showing them.

Early in the general election contest, advisors to the former Secretary of State had talked about the possibility that she would compete in traditionally Republican states like Georgia, Arizona, and Texas. Now Clinton and surrogates ranging from famous entertainers to President and Mrs. Obama, Vice President and Dr. Biden, and the candidate's husband, former president Bill Clinton, were feverishly working once reliably blue heartland states.

But the state that handily rejected Donald Trump in the GOP primary eight months earlier in favor of its own governor, John Kasich, went for the real estate magnate in a big way on Election Day. He took Ohio by 8.1 percentage points—more than 400,000 votes and a wider margin than either side had seen since the 1988 election of George H. W. Bush over Massachusetts governor Michael Dukakis. The tidal event in the Buckeye State was enough to wash into neighbors like Pennsylvania, Michigan, and Wisconsin. Just as filmmaker Moore predicted, Trump scored slim victories in those states which, at the presidential level, had been reliably Democratic since the 1980s. Taking the 46 electoral votes of those particular Ohio neighbors—by less than 80,000 votes in all—was what made Donald Trump president instead of Hillary Clinton.

ECONOMIC CARDIOLOGY

So, what led to Trump's toppling of the ultimate bellwether state? It was clearly an appeal to the state's rural and working-class voters, according to many postelection analyses. This is the state that has always prided itself on giving the world more of the things it grows and the products it builds. Ohio has always considered itself key to America's industrial and cultural heartland. For many years, the state used the slogan "Heart of It All" for tourism and other promotion efforts. But there is another term that counters the generally positive imagery of the word *heartland*. This term, *Rust Belt,* clichéd though it may be, describes an area that seems to follow the lower contours of the Great Lakes from Syracuse, New York, westward through Chicago and up Lake Michigan to places like Milwaukee and Green Bay, Wisconsin. Whether the country is looking at the heartland or the Rust Belt, Ohio tends to be a focal point.

Portions of America's heartland have been aching for change. Concerns like jobs and the economy were front and center in 2016, even considering numerous military and diplomatic issues around the world. Trump won rural counties—traditionally Republican-leaning—by larger margins than Mitt Romney had in his 2012 loss to Barack Obama. And he was able to "flip" a number of what some describe as working-class counties won by Obama, including Montgomery and Trumbull, which is home to a large GM assembly plant. Trump was also able to eat away at Democratic margins in Obama counties like Franklin, Hamilton, Lucas, and Lorain. Obama's Lorain County victory margin in 2012 was more than 20,000 votes. In 2016 Clinton held Lorain for the Democrats by just 131 votes. Ohio's experience illustrates the pain in places like Youngstown and Lordstown, where the ups and (mostly) downs of the auto and steel industries go all the way back to the 1960s. Sometimes the affliction is just dull irritation. Steadily declining real estate values have recently landed Ohio cities like Dayton, Akron, and Toledo on lists of places where you can get a lot of home (including beautiful, large Victorians) for "dirt cheap." These may be appealing headlines to some. But they are painful for those who invested in and cared for those homes for decades after subscribing to the all-American notion that "a home is your best investment."

The rural and working-class combination is broadly reflective of both the state and the nation as a whole. Ohio is not strictly a manufacturing state. Nor is it tied to maritime interests, corn growing, mining, finance, health care, high-tech, or autos. It is, rather, a bit of everything. Perhaps no other piece of geography sums up American interests, aptitudes, enthusiasms, or angsts better than the 17th state. In Ohio the sluggishness of manufacturing has been particularly injurious to smaller cities and towns. Marion, Ohio, is my wife's hometown and still where the majority of my extended in-law family reside. And while I consider Toledo to be my home, Marion has earned a place almost as dear in my heart. I first became familiar with Marion in the late 1970s and early 1980s. I was in my youth, and the town was in its heyday. It had a number of large manufacturing operations, including Marion Power Shovel, then a division of Dresser Industries, employing over 3,200 people. The "Shovel," as it was known by the locals, built huge power shovels and excavators, primarily for the mining industry. It also built the trawler that NASA used to transport Saturn 5 rockets and the Space Shuttle to its launchpad. The company is gone now, along with many other employers.

Marion, Ohio, is perhaps the only small town that can claim both a native as a US president and a former NFL team. It has seen better days. And it may be seeing its worst ones now as a city overcome by a drug epidemic in general and heroin in particular. In 2014 Marion County led the state's 88 counties in admissions to opiate treatment programs.[8] The state as a whole has put up some grim statistics related to drug abuse, too. For example, in 2016 one in nine Americans who died from a heroin overdose did so in Ohio.[9] It's a dubious distinction for a state that generally likes when it can be "first."

For some reason, people look to politicians to act as doctors for economic and social ills. During the 2016 election cycle, the two politicians best able to tap into the gnawing anxiety were Donald Trump and Bernie Sanders. Despite their clear political differences, Sanders and Trump shared many temperamental, philosophical, and rhetorical characteristics. Both are natives to the New York City area. Both were completely new to national political campaigning. And both appealed to the public with a high-decibel intensity that attacked establishment Washington and a "rigged system."[10] They went after entrenched interests that they could associate more closely with the opposing party but also took aim at common enemies. Though from different parties, both candidates opposed the Trans-Pacific Partnership (TPP) and voiced doubts about the North American Free Trade Agreement (NAFTA). Sanders vilified Wall Street, while Trump emphasized illegal immigration. Both in their way were making a play for Ohio's rural and working-class voters.[11] And one has to wonder how many former Sanders voters in counties like Lorain and Mahoning ended up voting for Trump once the campaign was between him and Clinton.

Candidate Trump promised to get all kinds of jobs back for Ohio, including those in coal mining. Belmont County, generally a reliably Democratic area, went heavily for him in 2016. Yet the county and neighbors along the Ohio River still might not be seeing those coal jobs come back. Rather, the area has better hopes with a combination of a competing energy solutions, technology, and for-

FIGURE 21.1. "New economy" Columbus thrives on the strength of education, government, finance, insurance, and other service industries. It is, nevertheless, a historical "river city," formed on the banks of the Olentangy and the Scioto.

eign investment. Ohio has a significant new presence in alternative energy, particularly in the western counties of Paulding and Van Wert, where two large projects partially owned by Amazon use 350 enormous wind turbines. Thailand's PPT Global Chemical is investing heavily in a Belmont County facility for ethane cracking. This is the process of chemically breaking down a hydrocarbon-based fuel like the wet natural gas found in the Utica Shale into more useful energy products such as plastics.[12] Cracking is a molecular process you can trace back to chemists employed by John D. Rockefeller. This is, as Miami University economics professor James Brock suggests, a "back to the future" scenario for Ohio's economy.

WHAT IS PAST IS PROLOGUE

While the rulers of old rose and fell according to the outcomes of war and palace intrigue, economic concerns reflected at the ballot

218 · CHAPTER 21

box have determined government since the beginning of the American experiment. Ohio spoke loudly in 2016, even as things seemed to be heading in the right direction in the state. James Brock also thinks that Ohio may now be showing the Midwest and the rest of the country a way to shed both the imagery and reality of the Rust Belt metaphor. He says, "I grew up in communities out west that were heavily tied to things like cattle, oil, or coal. Ohio has incredible economic diversity that gives it a real advantage." He also believes that Ohio was well positioned for growth no matter who won in 2016. Brock points to the fertility of Ohio's land, the productivity of Ohio's manufacturing sector, and its leadership in health care technology and health services. "The rustbelt description might have applied 30 years ago, but that was an economic forest fire that has burned itself out. Now much of the 'rust' has been washed away."[13]

Resilience has always been a key to economic success. This has been evident in Ohio for decades, even as pockets of pain have persisted. Old line coal mining is giving way to opportunities begot by hydraulic fracturing or ethane production technologies. The sons and daughters of ironworkers and toolmakers now engage in the biosciences and biomedical manufacturing. The state attracts companies based not only on its ability to educate designers and developers but also on the resources to produce materials and assemble products. Pain inflicted by business closures in the counties of Marion and Fairfield can be mitigated by a fairly easy commute to Columbus for jobs in insurance, higher education, finance, and pharmaceuticals. Columbus, incidentally, has exhibited remarkable growth over the past several decades and is now the second-largest city in the Midwest after Chicago. Another Ohio economics professor, Ohio State's Bill White, says, "Any person's view of Ohio is just going to greatly depend on whether you're sitting in Columbus or Youngstown." He points out, however, that even the Mahoning Valley may have reason to cheer, as demand for steel pipelines has led to the rehiring of workers.

How Ohio solves problems like opioid and opiate abuse is another matter. Its government has attacked the problem with a variety of new regulations, including shortening prescription periods to just seven days.[14] Ohioans have shown the country and world solutions to pressing social issues in the past. This was demonstrated in 1935 in Akron, where Bill Wilson and Bob Smith—seeking a solution to another kind of personal addiction—founded Alcoholics Anonymous.[15] This program has since gone on to help millions of men and women around the world overcome alcohol-related problems. Combating the drug scourge also requires community initiative, innovative healthcare approaches, and smart law enforcement. And nothing creates a greater climate for success in these areas than healthy economic conditions.

Circumstances shape people. People create events. And events change circumstances. The cycle or spiral can be vicious or virtuous. Human beings have long known that positive economic circumstances don't guarantee happy lives, but they offer a much better starting point. The question remains whether or not Ohio will be able to continually achieve against its 200-plus-year mission of "growing things and making things" even as things continue to change and as national administrations come and go.

If it can, then Ohio's experience may be a good sign for the whole country.

ACKNOWLEDGMENTS

The "spark" for this idea was really not a spark at all but rather a slow, glowing ember. For that I credit my numerous teachers in the Ottawa Hills, Ohio, school system during the 1970s, including Robert O'Connell, Don Fontaine, Barbara Wagner, Ron Stewart, Vance McCarter, Russ Smith, and others who in some measure or another got me to thinking that I was lucky to be both American and Ohioan. Of course, there were several history teachers I had the pleasure to learn from at Bowling Green State University, including Jeff Welsh, a graduate assistant during the time I took a course called "US History (From 1877–Present)."

My greatest teachers were my parents, Ed and Mary Ann Rohr, and they are still at it well into their eighties—both providing a measure of assistance and support with this project, which I dedicate to them.

Many other people have helped out with input, "guest reading," and other assistance. These include Kristin McCarthy, Tom Rohr, Tim Kneeland, Charles Benoit, Jean Kinney, Lauren Fox, Tim Stanford, Kathleen Carmichael, Nancy Kilkenny, Bob Arrighi, Jim Kropp, Paul Schumacher, Christine Brennan, Greg Litz, Brian Klafehn, Dan Steinberg, Tom Weigelt, Kathy Wallace, and the staff of Ohio State University Press. Tom Laemlein offered early advice when I was first considering this project, and his wife, Jennifer, assisted with proofreading an early draft. Kathy Warner created early design work for the cover.

Finally, Karen, and our children, Douglas, Anna, and John, are and always will be central to my experience as an Ohioan (even from afar).

NOTES

Note on endnotes: The best research for writing *The United States of Ohio* was the 29 years I spent growing up and beginning my professional career in the state. Much content is taken from that experience. Numerical facts and figures have been drawn from a variety of print and online sources but could be subject to change (population figures, for example). Facts that are common knowledge or easily ascertainable via online sources such as Wikipedia (example: the fact that Owens-Illinois Inc. is headquartered in Toledo/Perrysburg) are generally not covered in the notes. In addition, notes and complete references in the bibliography are provided for some inclusions that approach the point of being common knowledge. These are given primarily to point readers to sources where more detail or background can be found.

NOTES TO THE INTRODUCTION

1. Bush won Ohio by about 130,000 votes in 2004. Kerry is correct in that changing 75,000 of the 130,000 to his column would have given him a win in Ohio and thus the presidency. See: Rosenthal.
2. Good online resource for reviewing and comparing electoral counts and popular vote totals: Leip.
3. Early NFL: "NFL-1920 Regular Season."
4. Ohio as part of all geographies: I have not been able to find the Columbus promotional brochure. A magazine, however, offers a very similar quote from Mansfield author Louis Bromfield. See: Beasley.
5. Automotive output: "The Ohio Motor Vehicle Industry."

NOTES TO CHAPTER 1

1. Story about St. Joseph School in Fremont, Ohio: Personal discussion with my father, Edward C. Rohr, occurring in early 2009.
2. First capital: Goodman.
3. St. Clair and Worthington: "Thomas Worthington."
4. The Western Reserve: "Sufferers' Land."
5. Indians' 1997 World Series loss: Miles.
6. Roots of Michigan rivalry: "The 'Toledo War.'"
7. Yogurt production: Englehart.
8. Grant's desire to not become a Michigan resident: Grant, 193.
9. Hayes's teams overnighting in Toledo hotels: Naldrett, 134.

NOTES TO CHAPTER 2

1. America writ small: You will see the phrase associated with other states but these typically involve specific issues in which the state figures as a major part of the story. Ohio references typically come at election time. See: Quest.
2. On laws and township establishment traditions moving west: Boorstin, 51–63.
3. Tocqueville on Ohio compared to Kentucky: Tocqueville, 345–47.
4. Whig Party in Ohio: Holt, 34.
5. Railroads in Ohio: "Railroads."
6. Ohio's "late entry" to the union: "The Admission of Ohio as a State."

NOTES TO CHAPTER 3

1. State Population: "Ohio Population 2018
2. Polaris centers: "The History of Polaris."
3. Interstate miles and other statistics: "Traffic Congestion in Ohio."
4. Ohio Interstate miles and port statistics: "Shipping, Ferry and Port Information."
5. Cedar Point statistics: "Roller Coasters."
6. Cedar Point's ValRavn: "Cedar Point Unleashes ValRavn."
7. Ohio land area. This is a figure cited numerous places. Here is one of them: Butler, "Ohio Zip Code Listings."
8. Farms in Ohio: Woods.
9. Climate conditions for agriculture: Bill White, personal interview and email exchange, 10–12 April 2017.
10. Prime farmland, dairy leadership areas: Bonzar and Vidika.

11. Bob Evans, the man and the restaurant chain: Lafferty. Also: "Bob Evans Obituary."
12. Origins of the Bob Evans business: "The Farm."
13. Bob Evans company background information: McConnell.
14. Wendy's philosophy: Shook.
15. Life of Wendy's founder R. David Thomas: Martin.
16. White Castle and dining out: "The White Castle Story."
17. White Castle Restaurant differentiation: Kotler.
18. Number of cars on US roads: Hirsch.
19. State Fair attendance: K. Gray.
20. Fair's early days: "The History of the Ohio State Fair." Also: "Our History."
21. Honda in Ohio: "Fifty Years of Honda in America."
22. Diebold Nixdorf: "Thriving in a Consumer-Centric Global Ecosystem."

NOTES TO CHAPTER 4

1. I should point out that although I was working as a copywriter for the agency, I was not the author of the headline that is mentioned.
2. Hall of Fame and I. M. Pei. Henderson, 17.
3. Wynonie Harris debut: Marion. Also: James Miller, 25–33.
4. Alan Freed's early success in Cleveland: James Miller, 57–61.
5. Alan Freed and the Moondog Coronation Ball: Fong-Torres.
6. The Heart of Rock & Roll: Colla and Lewis.
7. Well-known Ohio bands: Todd.
8. Michael Stanley Band: "The 80s."
9. The "Cleveland Rocks" song itself: Hunter.
10. "Cleveland Rocks" and Cleveland: "Ian Hunter with Mick Ronson."

NOTES TO CHAPTER 5

1. Author of Dixie: McWhirter.
2. Almost all written material published at the time refers to the war as "rebellion." US Grant's memoirs, published 20 years after the war continue to use the term "rebellion" rather than "Civil War." See: Grant.
3. My great-great-grandfather's written English was free and unstructured. For example, he spelled the word *sausages* "sasiges." His actual writing says "tha dident shot with sasiges but with led and iron bulitts that did make ruff music." My family is fortunate to have both a tintype photo of our Civil War ancestor and his diary and many of his letters. My uncle, Tom Rohr, has compiled these into a book. See: T. Rohr.
4. Rankin and the story of Eliza: DeLuca. Also: "John Rankin."

5. Background on *Uncle Tom's Cabin* author: "Harriet Beecher Stowe." Also: "Harriet B. Stowe."
6. Mrs. Stowe's book: Stowe.
7. *Uncle Tom's Cabin*'s impact. Many sources document the acceptance and readership success of the book, including: Winship.
8. Slavery in Kentucky, free labor in Ohio: Tocqueville, 345–46.
9. Sheridan's life: "Philip Henry Sheridan." Also: "Philip Sheridan, General."
10. Philip Sheridan service: Hickman.
11. Sherman in the Civil War: "William Tecumseh Sherman."
12. Sherman's march to the sea and dispiriting the South: "Sherman's March."
13. Damage done by northern troops: Foote, vol. 3, 645.
14. General Grant's drinking: Foote, vol. 2, 217–19.
15. Garfield military and political service: "The Election of President James Garfield."
16. Stowe meeting Lincoln: Ostwinkle. Also: Foote, vol. 3, 972.

NOTES TO CHAPTER 6

1. Early Porkopolis: Ford and Ford, 18–75.
2. Pigs in the street: Cockburn.
3. Millionaires among the hogs: "A Walking Tour."
4. Pork as protein: Coffman.
5. Quote relating to "Porkopolis": "Cincinnati: Quotations."
6. P&G company background: "Our History—How It Began." Also: *Procter & Gamble: The House That Ivory Built*, 9–20.

NOTES TO CHAPTER 7

1. Company background: "Procter & Gamble."
2. Creating the soap that floats: *Procter & Gamble: The House That Ivory Built*, 9–10. Also: "Birth of an Icon: Ivory."
3. Ivory brand status: Ng.
4. Soaps and soap operas: *Procter & Gamble: The House That Ivory Built*, 185–89.
5. P&G "moon and stars" logo: Witt, 3.
6. Tide history and continuing development: "Birth of an Icon: Tide."
7. Procter & Gamble facts and figures: "2015 Annual Report."

NOTES TO CHAPTER 8

1. Early life of John D. Rockefeller: White. Also: "Biographies: Rockefeller, John D."
2. Rockefeller controlling the production process: "John D. Rockefeller: The Ultimate Oil Man."
3. Rockefeller oil business: "Financier's Fortune in Oil."
4. Rockefeller and oil transport: "John D. Rockefeller."
5. Rockefeller controlling the production process: "John D. Rockefeller: The Ultimate Oil Man."
6. Standard Oil specialization and business innovation: "John D. Rockefeller: The Ultimate Oil Man."
7. Standard Oil breakup: "May 15 1911: Supreme Court Orders."
8. Rockefeller life and death: Crowell.
9. Rockefeller fortune and charity: "Financier's Fortune in Oil."

NOTES TO CHAPTER 9

1. Edison's early career at Procter & Gamble: Thomas.
2. Edison boyhood: Abrams.
3. Charles Brush and the illumination of Cleveland: "Charles F. Brush, Sr. Papers."
4. McCormick and Hussey: "Early Industrialization."
5. Wilbur Wright on Ohio opportunity: Cayton, 176.
6. NCR and Dayton: Barry.
7. Barcode tests in Troy, Ohio: Shih.
8. Charles Brush: "Charles F. Brush."
9. Chester Carlson's invention: Crawford.
10. Electrophotography and cat's fur: Brooks, 172–73.
11. Commercialization and naming of Xerox: *The Story of Xerography*, 9–13.

NOTES TO CHAPTER 10

1. Steel in Ohio: "The History of Steel in Ohio."
2. Libbey and glass in Toledo: Fauster, 3–57. Also: "The New England Glass Company."
3. Michael Owens and Toledo: S. Smith.
4. Glass industry centered in Ohio: Russell.
5. Charles Hall and Oberlin: "Charles Martin Hall Had a Purpose."
6. Charles Hall and aluminum: "Production of Aluminum."

7. Rubber in Akron: "A Look Back at the Early Days."
8. Gasoline and "cracking": Sherer.
9. First concrete-paved road in Bellefontaine, Ohio: Snell and Snell, 72–74.
10. Honda Motors in America: Krebs.
11. Kettering inventiveness and other industries: Jeffries.
12. Anti-knock fuel: Kittman.
13. Charles Kettering life and patents: Kittman. Also, "1876. Charles F. Kettering Is Born."

NOTES TO CHAPTER 11

1. Ohio and North Carolina debate: Kleiman. Also: Jonsson.
2. Da Vinci's early flight insight: Stimson, "Da Vinci's Aerodynamics."
3. Lighter-than-air flight and Thaddeus Lowe: Salvatore.
4. Early interest in flight: Wright and Wright.
5. Cooperation with Octave Chanute: "Octave Chanute—A Champion of Aviation." Also: Salvatore.
6. The Wright brothers' own story and years at Kitty Hawk: Wright and Wright. Also: C. Gray.
7. Early Kitty Hawk experiments: Stimson, "Two Crazy Nuts."
8. Charlie Taylor's value to the Wright brothers: B. Taylor.
9. First flights in December 1903: C. Gray.
10. Excellent source of information on the Wright brothers and the birth of aviation: Salvatore.

NOTES TO CHAPTER 12

1. 1995 Dayton peace negotiations: "Dayton Peace Accords at 20."
2. Wright-Patterson AFB: "Wright-Patterson Air Force Base."
3. Eddie Rickenbacker: "Eddie Rickenbacker Papers."
4. Cleveland Air Races: "History of the Cleveland National Air Races." Also: "This Land of Ours (Ohio)."
5. NASA Glenn Information: Bob Arrighi (NASA Glenn Research Center), email communication.
6. Buckeye space explorers: "Ohio Astronauts."
7. Glenn's "taste for flying": Carpenter et al., 29.
8. Armstrong as research pilot: Bob Arrighi (NASA Glenn Research Center), email communication.
9. GE Engine manufacturing: "GE Aviation." Also: Kellner, "GE Started Testing."
10. Crawler-transporter: "Marion Power Shovel."

NOTES TO CHAPTER 13

1. Significance of the French & Indian War: "Washington and the French & Indian War."
2. Plains of Abraham in Quebec: "Clash of Empires."
3. Ohio's Underground Railroad: "Underground Railroad in Ohio." Also: "Aboard the Underground Railroad."
4. Weller Pottery and author's ancestor: McDonald, 100.
5. My great-great-grandfather Carl Weigelt's quote about "getting kids" in America was relayed to us numerous times by my grandfather, Henry C. Weigelt.
6. Ohio's "American Americans": Will, 111.
7. McGuffey and his readers: Lynch.
8. Mormonism in Kirtland, Ohio: Lindbloom.
9. Canal system: "History & Hydraulics."
10. American Party: "Know-Nothing Party."
11. Allegheny and Ohio Rivers: "Ohio River Basin Facts."
12. Fallen Timbers: "Battle of Fallen Timbers."
13. Ohio dialects: Hunt.
14. The Ohio accent: Tomasky.
15. Mid-Atlantic Accent: T. Taylor.
16. Earliest recorded presidential voice: "Former President Harrison Recording."
17. Presidential "r-ful" and "r-less" pronunciation: Metcalf, 143–49.

NOTES TO CHAPTER 14

1. Baseball's beginning: Ward and Burns.
2. Cincinnati Red Stockings founder: "Wright and the Reds."
3. End of baseball editorial: Dess, McNamara and Eisner, 41.
4. Ban Johnson and the American League: Ward and Burns.
5. Judge (and Commissioner) Landis: "Kenesaw Mountain Landis."
6. NFL is born: Klein.
7. Pro football as it began: "NFL-1920 Regular Season."
8. Oorang Indians: "History 1921–1930." Also: Willis.
9. Fritz Pollard in the early days of the NFL: McClellan, 318–22.
10. Washington Redskins: Basan.
11. The Cleveland Rams and Cleveland Browns: Reed. Also: Pierson.
12. Player Bill Willis on Paul Brown's integration of football: Steinberg, 163.
13. Integrating the NFL: Gelhar.
14. Branch Rickey: Lamb. Also: Bona.

15. Larry Doby of the Cleveland Indians: "Larry Doby."
16. Paul Brown legacy: Pierson, 36.
17. Other Branch Rickey innovations: McMurray.
18. Sid Gillman: S. Farmer.
19. Rockne and Cedar Point: Phinizy.
20. Paul Brown as a builder of men: Steinberg, 1–4.
21. Ohio's production of football coaches: Everson. Also: Hartman.
22. Bill Walsh's desire to coach the Cincinnati Bengals: "Paul Brown: A Football Life."

NOTES TO CHAPTER 15

1. Snow Bowl: "OSU–Michigan 1950."
2. Dr. James Lipson: Personal discussion with Dr. Lipson, who hosted an Ohio State–Michigan game viewing party in Rochester, New York, 2004.
3. Vic Janowicz: "Ohio State to Retire No. 31."
4. Snow Bowl—game clips available online including YouTube: "1950: Michigan 9, Ohio State 3."
5. Engineering: OSU engineering background, programs: "Ohio State University College of Engineering."
6. Melvin DeGroote patents: "Innovation at Ohio State."
7. Edison patents: Morris.
8. Teflon inventor: Lyons.
9. Wikipedia cofounder: Gallagher.
10. Steinbrenner involvement with Ohio State: Lyttle.
11. Rutherford Hayes and OSU: "The Other Famous Hayes at Ohio State University."
12. Michigan inventing "Script Ohio:" Bovenzi.

NOTES TO CHAPTER 16

1. Cleveland murders and kidnappings: Urbina and Maag.
2. Burning river: "Cuyahoga River Fire."
3. Cuyahoga River catching fire: Alder.
4. LeBron to Miami Heat: Heisler.
5. Cleaveland and Cleveland: "Moses Cleaveland."
6. Connecticut Western Reserve and Moses Cleaveland: Rich.
7. Population loss: Exner.
8. Population loss and its impact: Larkin.
9. 2010 Most Miserable Cities: Badenhausen.
10. Lakefront construction: Jarboe.

11. Orchestra locations: "Cleveland Orchestra in Miami."
12. Cleveland Orchestra style: Hewett.
13. Cleveland's cultural appeal: Glaser.
14. Biomed industry in Cleveland: R. Smith.
15. Cleveland Clinic mission: "Mission, Vision, Values."
16. Cleveland Clinic: "2016 Year-End: Facts and Figures."
17. The Clinic in Florida: "2016 Year-End: Facts and Figures." Also: "Cleveland Clinic Florida | Highest Ranked."
18. Flagler and building Florida: "Henry Morison Flagler Biography."

NOTES TO CHAPTER 17

1. O'Reilly's *Killing* series: L. Miller.
2. Cleveland in the 1950s: "This Land of Ours (Ohio)."
3. Sheppard murder timeline: "Chronology of a Murder."
4. Officer's accusation: C. Cooper and Sheppard, 54.
5. *Cleveland Press* headlines and coverage: C. Cooper and Sheppard, 36–165.
6. Coroner thoughts about Sheppard case: J. Neff, 90–92. Also: Cooper and Sheppard, 54–65.
7. Sheppard verdict: J. Neff, 88–169.
8. Kirk involvement in Sheppard case: J. Neff, 173–87.
9. Sheppard trial background: "*Sheppard v. Maxwell* (1966-490)."
10. Eberling murders: Affleck. Also: J. Neff, 299–306.
11. Sheppard and Eberling DNA: Butterfield.
12. Eberling and his death: C. Cooper and Sheppard, 299–328.
13. Maxwell Supreme Court decision: "*Sheppard v. Maxwell,* 384 US 333 (1966)." Also: Ewinger.

NOTES TO CHAPTER 18

1. Nixon on Cambodia: "Richard Nixon: 144—The President's News Conference."
2. Unrest in the 1950s and '60s: "The Civil Rights Movement in the 1950." Also: Morgan.
3. A&T Four: Lee, E1. Also: "The A&T Four: February 1st, 1960."
4. March on Washington: Hansan. Also Joyce, C8.
5. Worldwide protests in the '60s: Michener, 467–68.
6. Chicago and other 1960s riots: Fearon et al.
7. 1968 Democratic Convention: Johnson.
8. Bernadine Dohrn and Kent: Michener, 146.
9. Ohio lyrics: Young, *Ohio,* Audio record single.

10. Governor James Rhodes and Kent State: Hayden.
11. Shootings at Kent State: Kifner, 1.
12. Kent event timeline: "Kent State: May 1–4."
13. Rhodes primary election loss: Rudin.
14. Kent State photo: Shapiro.
15. Voting rights for those 18 and over: "The 26th Amendment."
16. Haldeman's observations about Nixon: Lewis and Hensley. Also: Hayden.

NOTES TO CHAPTER 19

1. Electoral College winners in Ohio: "Historical Presidential Elections."
2. 2012 presidential race: Rowland.
3. Maine, bellwether states: Glass.
4. As a perennially close election challenge: Rove, 7–11.
5. Harry Truman campaigning in Ohio: Truman.
6. Test marketing: Sullivan.
7. Social judgment theory: Griffin, Ledbetter and Sparks, 177–85.

NOTES TO CHAPTER 20

1. Garfield home: "James A. Garfield National Historic Site."
2. Garfield speech-making: Garfield.
3. Ohio Presidents: W. Neff.
4. Assassinated Ohio presidents: Farquhar.
5. First Harrison presidency: "William Henry Harrison."
6. Evolution of political campaigning: Holt, 89.
7. 1840 campaigning and slogans: "American History: 1840 U.S. Presidential Campaign."
8. Lincoln on Grant's taste for whiskey: Foote, vol. 2, 217–19.
9. Grant and his memoirs: Grant, both volumes, all pages.
10. Lucy Hayes: Geer.
11. Presidencies and national stability: Independence Hall Association.
12. Garfield assassination: Farquhar. Also: "Stalwarts, Half Breeds."
13. Garfield House of Representatives service and election: "The Election of President James Garfield."
14. Benjamin Harrison life and achievements: "Benjamin Harrison Dead." Also: "Championing the Values."
15. Mark Hanna and William McKinley: "November 3, 1896." Also: Rove, 8–272.
16. Hawaii in the Union: "Annexation of Hawaii."
17. McKinley assassination: Farquhar. Also: Kingseed.

18. Prompt execution of McKinley's assassin: "Czolgosz's Body."
19. Ambitions of others for Taft: Goodwin, 575.
20. Taft vs. Roosevelt: Garber.
21. Harding scandals: Folsom.
22. Harding shoe size: Zhou.
23. Harding fiscal moves: Folsom.
24. Coolidge quote about business: Coolidge.

NOTES TO CHAPTER 21

1. President Hayes as a young clairvoyant: Cayton, 48.
2. Ohio economy: Williams.
3. Ohio gets quiet days prior to 2016 election: Gomez. Also: Zaru.
4. Early general election polls: Salvanto.
5. Michael Moore's prediction: Moore. Also: Guerrasio.
6. Trump yard signs: Hiltner.
7. Ohio pre-election polling: "Ohio: Trump vs. Clinton."
8. Marion Ohio opiate admissions: "Unduplicated Admissions for Opiate Abuse."
9. Ohio drug overdose deaths: "Ohio Leads Nation in Overdose Deaths."
10. Trump blue-collar appeal: M. Cooper.
11. Trump and Sanders: Ball.
12. Belmont County cracking facility: Newpoff.
13. Ohio economic diversity: James Brock, personal interview, 28 March 2017. Also: Bill White, personal interview and email exchange, 10–12 April 2017.
14. Ohio anti-drug legislation: Cass.
15. Alcoholics Anonymous founding: "Over 80 Years of Growth."

BIBLIOGRAPHY

"1876. Charles F. Kettering, Inventor of Electric Self-Starter, Is Born." *History Channel*, n.d., http://www.history.com/this-day-in-history/charles-f-kettering-inventor-of-electric-self-starter-is-born. Accessed 13 January 2013.

"1950: Michigan 9, Ohio State 3 (The Snow Bowl)." *YouTube*, 7 September 2009, www.youtube.com/watch?v=tP1ZfZMbarI. Accessed 3 March 2012.

"2015 Annual Report." *Procter & Gamble*, 28 August 2015, http://news.pg.com/blog/annual-report/released-today-pgs-2015-annual-report. Accessed 11 November 2015.

"2016 Year-End: Facts and Figures," *Cleveland Clinic*, n.d., https://my.clevelandclinic.org/-/scassets/files/org/about/who-we-are/cleveland-clinic-facts-and-figures-2016.ashx. Accessed 10 January 2018.

"The 26th Amendment." *History Channel*, n.d., https://www.history.com/topics/the-26th-amendment. Accessed 5 August 2014.

"The 80s." *The Official Michael Stanley Band Website*, n.d., http://www.michaelstanley.com/THE_80S.html. Accessed 22 August 2015.

"Aboard the Underground Railroad." *National Park Service*, n.d., https://www.nps.gov/nr/travel/underground/states.htm. Accessed 31 August 2014.

Abrams, Michael. "Thomas Edison." *American Society of Mechanical Engineers*, May 2012, http://www.asme.org/engineering-topics/articles/energy/thomas-edison. Accessed 11 March 2013.

"The Admission of Ohio as a State: August 7, 1953." *US House of Representatives,* n.d., http://history.house.gov/Historical-Highlights/1951-2000/The-admission-of-Ohio-as-a-state/. Accessed 12 October 2010.

Affleck, John. "Evidence Disputed in Sheppard Case: State Resists Other Suspects Crimes." *Cincinnati Enquirer,* 15 February 2000: 4. Print.

"Alan Freed Biography." *Rock & Roll Hall of Fame,* n.d., https://www.rockhall.com/inductees/alan-freed. Accessed 30 July 2015.

Alder, Jonathan H. "The Fable of the Burning River, 45 Years Later." *Washington Post,* 22 June 2014, https://www.washingtonpost.com/news/volokh-conspiracy/wp/2014/06/22/the-fable-of-the-burning-river-45-years-later/?utm_term=.989e3047573b. Accessed 20 November 2015.

Allen, Frederick L. *Only Yesterday: An Informal History of the 1920s.* New York: Wiley, 1997 (Reprint of 1931 Harper & Row edition. Ebook via University of Virginia Library), http://xroads.virginia.edu/~hyper/allen/ch6.html. Accessed 13 November 2015.

"American History: 1840 U.S. Presidential Campaign," *HistoryNet,* n.d., http://historynet.com/american-history-1840-us-presidential-campaign.htm. Accessed 18 October 2013.

"Annexation of Hawaii, 1898." *US Department of State,* n.d., https://2001-2009.state.gov/r/pa/ho/time/gp/17661.htm. Accessed 12 July 2013.

"Archives and History." *Alcoholics Anonymous,* n.d., http://www.aa.org/pages/en_US/archives-and-history. Accessed 17 April 2017.

"The A&T Four: February 1st, 1960." *North Carolina A&T State University,* n.d., http://www.library.ncat.edu/resources/archives/four.html. Accessed 3 September 2014.

Badenhausen, Kurt. "America's Most Miserable Cities." *Forbes,* 18 February 2010, https://www.forbes.com/sites/kurtbadenhausen/2012/02/02/americas-most-miserable-cities/. Accessed 29 May 2018.

Ball, Molly. "What Trump and Sanders Have in Common." *The Atlantic,* 6 January 2016, https://www.theatlantic.com/notes/2016/01/what-bernie-sanders-and-donald-trump-have-in-common/422907/. Accessed 30 March 2017.

Barry, Dan. "In a Company's Hometown, the Emptiness Echoes." *New York Times,* 24 January 2010. http://www.nytimes.com/2010/01/25/us/25land.html. Accessed 18 March 2013.

Basan, Ryan. "Fifty Years Ago, Last Outpost of Segregation in N.F.L. Fell." *New York Times,* 6 October 2012: SP1. Print.

"Battle of Fallen Timbers." *Ohio History Central,* n.d. http://www.ohiohistorycentral.org/w/Battle_of_Fallen_Timbers. Accessed 3 October 2014.

Beasley, Bob et al. "35 Reasons to Celebrate Ohio." *Ohio Magazine,* April 2013, https://www.ohiomagazine.com/about/archive/issue/april-2013-issue. Accessed 15 October 2015.

"Benjamin Harrison Dead." *New York Times,* 4 March 1901. Print.

Bernstein, Mark. "Charles F. Kettering—A Self-Starter Who Gave Us the Self-Starter." *Smithsonian Magazine* (On Dayton Innovation Website), July 1988, http://www.daytoninnovationlegacy.org/kettering.html. Accessed 2 February 2014.

"Biographies: Rockefeller, John D." *Free Info Society,* n.d., http://www.freeinfosociety.com/article.php?id=64. Accessed 14 October 2013.

"Birth of an Icon: Ivory." *Procter & Gamble,* 5 November 2012, http://news.pg.com/blog/heritage/birth-icon-ivory. Accessed 11 November 2015.

"Bob Evans Obituary." *Legacy.com,* n.d., http://www.legacy.com/ns/bob-evans-obituary/89406329. Accessed 9 September 2009.

Bona, Marc. "Ohio Ties Strong to Jackie Robinson Story, Movie '42.'" *The Plain Dealer,* 12 April 2013, http://www.cleveland.com/entertainment/index.ssf/2013/04/ohio_ties_strong_to_jackie_rob.html. Accessed 14 November 2014.

Bonzar, Eric and Ron Vidika. "Northeast Ohio Farmers Look to a Future of Promise, Doubt." *Lake County News-Herald,* 28 May 2014, http://www.news-herald.com/article/HR/20140528/NEWS/140529710. Accessed 11 December 2015.

Boorstin, Daniel J. *The Americans: The National Experience.* New York: Random House, 1965. Print.

Bovenzi, Giustino. "The Unlikely History Behind "Script Ohio:" One of College Football's Most Iconic, Longstanding Traditions. *Sports Illustrated,* 20 November 2015, https://www.si.com/college-football/2015/11/20/history-behind-ohio-states-legendary-script-ohio-routine. Accessed 30 May 2018.

Brooks, John. *Business Adventures: Twelve Classic Tales from the World of Wall Street.* New York: Open Road Integrated Media, 2014. Print.

Butler, Rhett, ed. "Ohio Zip Code Listings." *Mongabay,* updated 29 December 2015, https://data.mongabay.com/igapo/zip_codes/OH.htm. Accessed 14 November 2015.

Butterfield, Fox. "DNA Test Absolves Sam Sheppard of Murder, Lawyer Says," *New York Times,* 5 March 1998: 4. Print.

Caldwell, Leigh Ann and Matt Rivera. "In Hard-Hit Ohio Steel Town, Trump and Sanders Resonate." *NBC News,* 16 March 2016, https://www.nbcnews.com/politics/2016-election/hard-hit-ohio-steel-town-trump-sanders-resonate-n536746. Accessed 1 April 2017.

Caniglia, John. "Ariel Castro Files: Documents Offer Greater Details into Castro's Torture of Women." *The Plain Dealer,* http://www.cleveland.com/court-justice/index.ssf/2014/05/ariel_castro_files_documents_0.html. Accessed 5 May 2014.

Carpenter, M. Scott, Gordon L. Cooper, John H. Glenn, Virgil L. Grissom, Walter M. Schirra, Alan B. Shepard, and Donald K. Slayton. *We Seven: By the Astronauts Themselves.* New York: Simon & Schuster, 1962. Print.

Cass, Andrew. "Kasich Signs Bill Combating Opioid Abuse." *Lake County News-Herald,* 5 January 2017, http://www.news-herald.com/article/HR/20170105/NEWS/170109700. Accessed 27 March 2017.

Cayton, Andrew R. L. *Ohio: A History of a People.* Columbus: The Ohio State University Press, 2002. Print.

"Cedar Point Unleashes ValRavn, the World's Tallest, Fastest & Longest Dive Coaster." *Coaster Insantiy,* 9 September 2015, http://coasterinsanity.com/?p=440. Accessed 1 December 2015.

"Championing the Values and Legacy of the 23rd President." *Benjamin Harrison Presidential Site.,* n.d., http://www.presidentbenjaminharrison.org/learn/benjamin-harrison-1. Accessed 4 November 2015.

"Charles F. Brush." *Ohio History Central,* n.d., http://www.ohiohistorycentral.org/w/Charles_F._Brush. Accessed 8 May 2015.

"Charles F. Brush, Sr. Papers: Online Exhibit." *Kevin Smith Library at Case Western Reserve University,* n.d., http://library.case.edu/ksl/collections/special/manuscripts/brush/archive/. Accessed 14 April 2015.

"The Charles Goodyear Story." *Goodyear Tire & Rubber Company,* n.d., http://corporate.goodyear.com/en-US/about/history/charles-goodyear-story.html. Accessed 20 January 2013.

"Charles Martin Hall Had a Purpose to His Life. And It Wasn't a Small One, Either." *Investor's Business Daily* (on Alcoa.com), 6 October 2005, https://www.slideshare.net/GMC_Visions/awj14charlesmartinhall. Accessed 21 February 2013.

Chinni, Dante. "What Do OH, PA and WI Have in Common? Trump Needs 'Em." *NBC News*, 20 March 2016, http://www.nbcnews.com/meet-the-press/what-do-oh-pa-wi-have-common-trump-needs-em-n542176. Accessed 28 March 2017.

"Chronology of a Murder." *PBS*, n.d., http://www.pbs.org/wgbh/nova/sheppard/chronology.html. Accessed 8 August 2014.

"Cincinnati: Quotations Concerning Pigs, Lard and Legacy." *Porkopolis.org*, n.d., http://www.porkopolis.org/quotations/cincinnati/. Accessed 3 March 2015.

"The Civil Rights Movement in the 1950s and 1960s." *Familyeducation*, n.d. https://www.familyeducation.com/civil-rights-movement-1950s-1960s. Accessed 3 August 2014.

"Clash of Empires and the Battle of the Plains of Abraham." *Canadian War Museum*, n.d., http://www.warmuseum.ca/cwm/exhibitions/gallery1/clash3_e.shtml. Accessed 24 September 2014.

"Cleveland Clinic Florida | Highest Ranked Hospital in Broward County." *Cleveland Clinic*, n.d. https://my.clevelandclinic.org/florida. Accessed 6 May 2017.

"Cleveland Orchestra in Miami." *Cleveland Orchestra*, n.d., https://www.clevelandorchestra.com/Tickets/miami-concert-series/. Accessed 1 May 2015.

Cockburn, Alexander. "The March to Porkopolis." *Counterpunch*, 17 August 2005, https://www.counterpunch.org/2005/08/17/the-march-to-porkopolis/. Accessed 9 April 2010.

Coffman, Melodie. "How Much Protein Is in Pork?" *Healthy Eating*, n.d., healthyeating.sfgate.com/much-protein-pork-5369.html. Accessed 1 December 2015.

Colla, Johnny and Huey Lewis. *The Heart of Rock & Roll* (song performed by Huey Lewis and the News). Chrysalis, 1984. Audio record single.

Coolidge, Calvin. "Address to the American Society of Newspaper Editors, Washington, D.C." *American Presidency Project*, 17 January 1925, http://www.presidency.ucsb.edu/ws/?pid=24180. Accessed 14 November 2015.

Cooper, Cynthia L. and Sam Reese Sheppard. *Mockery of Justice: The True Story of the Sheppard Murder Case*. Boston: Northeastern University Press, 1995. Print.

Cooper, Mathew. "Donald Trump: The Billionaire for Blue-Collars." *Newsweek*, 23 June 2015, http://www.newsweek.com/2015/07/03/donald-trump-billionaire-blue-collars-345677.html. Accessed 25 March 2017.

Crawford, Mark. "Chester Floyd Carlson." *American Society of Mechanical Engineers*, April 2012, https://www.asme.org/engineering-topics/articles/technology-and-society/chester-floyd-carlson. Accessed 12 March 2013.

Crowell, Paul. "John D. Rockefeller Dies at 97 in His Florida Home; Funeral to Be Here." *New York Times*, 24 May 1937: 1. Print.

Curtain, Christina and Elizabeth Naab. "Commercialization of Aluminum." *American Chemical Society*, n.d., http://www.acs.org/content/dam/acsorg/education/whatischemistry/landmarks/aluminumprocess/commercialization-of-aluminum-commemorative-booklet.pdf. Accessed 2 March 2013.

"Cuyahoga River Fire." *Ohio History Central*, n.d., http://www.ohiohistorycentral.org/w/Cuyahoga_River_Fire. Accessed 4 April 2015.

"Czolgosz's Body to Be Destroyed at Auburn." *New York Times*, 29 October 1901. Print.

"Dayton Peace Accords at 20." *University of Dayton*, n.d., https://udayton.edu/m/daytonpeaceaccordsat20/. Accessed 12 November 2015.

DeLuca, Leo. "Carry Me Home." *Ohio Magazine*, August 2014, https://www.ohiomagazine.com/travel/article/carry-me-home. Accessed 3 November 2015.

Dess, Gregory G., Gerry McNamara and Alan Eisner. *Strategic Management: Text and Cases* (8th ed.). New York: McGraw-Hill Education, 2016. Print.

"Early Industrialization." *Ohio History Central*, n.d., http://www.ohiohistorycentral.org/w/Early_Industrialization. Accessed 4 March 2013.

"Eddie Rickenbacker Papers, RG 101. Finding Aid." *Auburn University Special Collections and Archives*, n.d., http://www.lib.auburn.edu/archive/flyhy/101/eddie.htm. Accessed 2 February 2010.

"The Election of President James Garfield of Ohio: November 02, 1880." *US House of Representatives*, n.d., history.house.gov/Historical-Highlights/1851-1900/The-election-of-President-James-Garfield-of-Ohio/. Accessed 12 July 2013.

Englehart, Laura. "Dannon Plant in Minster Continues Rapid Expansion." *Dayton Business Journal*, 23 March 2012, https://www.bizjournals.com/

dayton/print-edition/2012/03/23/dannon-plant-in-minster-continues.html. Accessed 4 November 2015.

Everson, Darren. "College Football; Why Ohio Makes the Best Coaches— From Shula and Hayes to Stoops and Meyer—Ohioans Rule Football with a Lunchbucket Approach." *The Wall Street Journal,* 26 December 2008: W4. Print.

Ewinger, James. "Sheppard Trials Still Offer Lessons for Legal Minded." *The Plain Dealer,* 15 November 2015: A10. Print.

Exner, Rich. "Cleveland Now Ranks 45th among U.S. cities, down from 33rd." *The Plain Dealer,* 15 April 2011, http://www.cleveland.com/datacentral/index.ssf/2011/04/cleveland_now_ranks_45th_among.html. Accessed 31 March 2015.

"The Farm." *Bob Evans, LLC,* n.d., https://www.bobevans.com/aboutus/the-farm. Accessed 2 November 2015.

Farmer, Gene and Dora Hamlin. *First on the Moon.* Boston: Little, Brown, 1970. Print.

Farmer, Sam. "Sid Gillman 1911–2003; Coach Revolutionized Offenses in Football." *Los Angeles Times,* 4 January 2003: D1. Print.

Farquhar, Michael. "The Other Assassinations; Lincoln and JFK Are Remembered, But What about Garfield and McKinley?" *Washington Post,* 12 January 2000. Print.

Fauster, Carl U. *Libbey Glass since 1818.* Toledo, OH: Len Beech Press, 1979. Print.

Feagler, Linda. "Great Ohio Road Trips: Literary Tour." *Ohio Magazine,* March 2017, https://www.ohiomagazine.com/travel/article/great-ohio-road-trips-literary-tour. Accessed 26 September 2017.

Fearon, James, David Laitin and Christina Maimone. "The United States Of America," *Stanford University,* n.d., https://web.stanford.edu/group/ethnic/Random%20Narratives/UnitedStatesRN1.1.pdf. Accessed 12 August 2014.

"Fifty Years of Honda in America." *Automobile Magazine,* 7 July 2009, http://www.automobilemag.com/news/fifty-years-of-honda-history/. Accessed 30 August 2010.

"Financier's Fortune in Oil Amassed in Industrial Era of 'Rugged Individualism.'" *New York Times,* 24 May 1937, www.nytimes.com/books/98/05/17/specials/rockefeller-fortune.html. Accessed 1 November 2013.

Folsom, Burton. "The Strange Presidency of Warren G. Harding." *Foundation for Economic Education,* 28 March 2012, https://fee.org/articles/the-strange-presidency-of-warren-g-harding/. Accessed 13 December 2016.

Fong-Torres, Ben. "Biography." *Alan Freed Official Website,* n.d. http://www.alanfreed.com/wp/biography/. Accessed 10 September 2014.

Foote, Shelby: *The Civil War: A Narrative.* 3 vols. New York: Random House, 1974. Print.

Ford, Henry A. and Kate B. Ford. *History of Cincinnati Ohio, with Illustrations and Biographical Sketches.* Cleveland: L. A. Williams & Co., 1881. Print.

"Former President Harrison Recording." *YouTube,* 7 June 2007, https://www.youtube.com/watch?v=u1ykiZk4fE8. Accessed May 12, 2014. Video.

Gallagher, Paul. "Wikipedia's Co-Founder Says Website Has Been 'Taken Over by Trolls.'" *Independent,* 12 November 2015, www.independent.co.uk/life-style/gadgets-and-tech/news/wikipedia-co-founder-larry-sanger-says-website-has-been-taken-over-by-trolls-a6732171.html. Accessed 20 November 2015.

Gammons, Peter. "Carlton Fisk's Home Run in 12th Beats Reds, 7–6." *Boston Globe,* 22 October 1975, https://www.bostonglobe.com/sports/1975/10/22/carlton-fisk-home-run-beats-reds/BlpIMG4goxLVwV-sUarZBNI/story.html. Accessed 12 December 2012.

Garber, Kent. "Teddy Roosevelt, on the Bull Moose Party Ticket, Battles Incumbent William Howard Taft." *U. S. News,* 17 January 2008, https://www.usnews.com/news/articles/2008/01/17/three-way-race-of-1912-had-it-all. Accessed 18 May 2013.

Garfield, James. "James Garfield Speech Inaugural Address." *Famous Speeches and Speech Topics,* 4 March 1881, http://www.famous-speeches-and-speech-topics.info/presidential-speeches/james-garfield-speech-inaugural-address.htm. Accessed 20 September 2013.

"GE Aviation." *GE.com,* General Electric, n.d., https://www.geaviation.com/. Accessed 11 November 2011.

Geer, Emily Apt. "Lucy Webb Hayes and Her Influence upon Her Era." *Rutherford B. Hayes Presidential Center,* n.d., https://www.rbhayes.org/hayes/lucy-webb-hayes-and-her-influence-upon-her-era/. Accessed 13 December 2015.

Gelhar, Alex. "'Forgotten Four' Artfully Depicts Pro Football Integration in 1946." *NFL.com,* National Football League, 10 September 2014, http://www.nfl.com/news/story/0ap3000000392534/article/forgotten-four-artfully-depicts-pro-football-integration-in-1946. Accessed 31 March 2015.

Glaser, Susan. "Cleveland Named to National Geographic Traveler's 'Best of World' List." *The Plain Dealer,* 17 November 2017, http://www.cleveland.com/travel/index.ssf/2017/11/cleveland_named_to_national_ge.html. Accessed 17 November 2017.

Glass, Andrew. "As Maine Goes, So Goes the Nation, Sept. 8, 1958." *Politico,* 8 September 2016, https://www.politico.com/story/2016/09/as-maine-goes-so-goes-the-nation-sept-8-1958-227727. Accessed 31 December 2017.

Gomez, Henry J. "Battleground Ohio Gets a Quiet Saturday as Hillary Clinton and Donald Trump Enter the Home Stretch." *The Plain Dealer,* 5 November 2016, http://www.cleveland.com/politics/index.ssf/2016/11/battleground_ohio_gets_a_quiet.html. Accessed 26 March 2017.

Goodman, Rebecca. "Marietta: First Capital of the Northwest Territory." *Cincinnati Enquirer,* 9 July 2003, http://www.enquirer.com/editions/2003/07/09/loc_ohiodate0709.html. Accessed 8 December 2011.

Goodwin, Doris Kearns. *The Bully Pulpit: Theodore Roosevelt, William Howard Taft and the Golden Age of Journalism.* New York: Simon & Shuster, 2013. Print.

Grant, Ulysses. *Personal Memoirs of U. S. Grant, Vol. 1.* New York: Charles L. Webster & Company, 1885. Print.

Gray, Carroll F. "The Five First Flights: The Slope and Winds of Big Kill Devil Hill—The First Flight Reconsidered." *Wrightbrothers.org,* Pioneer Aviation Group, 2002, http://www.thewrightbrothers.org/fivefirstflights.html. Accessed 8 April 2015.

Gray, Kathy L. "State Fair Sets another Attendance Record." *Columbus Dispatch,* 15 August 2015, http://www.dispatch.com/article/20150810/NEWS/308109871. Accessed 10 November 2015.

Greenberg, Daniel S. *Science, Money and Politics: Political Triumph and Ethical Erosion.* Chicago: University of Chicago Press, 2001. Print.

Griffin, Emory A., Andrew Ledbetter and Glenn Grayson Sparks. *A First Look at Communication Theory* (9th ed.). New York: McGraw-Hill Education, 2015. Print.

Guerrasio, Jason. "Michael Moore Predicted Trump's Path to Victory Exactly Right." *Business Insider,* 12 November 2016, www.businessinsider.com/michael-moore-predicted-trump-path-to-win-2016-11. Accessed 31 March 2017.

Hansan, John. "March on Washington, D.C. August 28, 1963." *Virginia Commonwealth University Libraries,* 13 December 2013, https://socialwelfare.library.vcu.edu/eras/march-on-washington-august-28-1963/. Accessed 23 November 21 November 2015.

"Harriet B. Stowe." *Ohio History Central,* n.d., http://www.ohiohistorycentral.org/w/Harriet_B._Stowe. Accessed 9 September 2013.

"Harriet Beecher Stowe." *Touring Ohio,* n.d., http://touringohio.com/profiles/harriet-stowe.html. Accessed 9 November 2015.

Hartman, Marcus. "Ohio State Has a Long History of Producing Future Coaching Stars." *Dayton Daily News,* 9 December 2016, https://www.daytondailynews.com/sports/ohio-state-has-long-history-producing-future-coaching-stars/RoU3A7IddmYUDhBxYaIvdK/. Accessed 26 December 2016.

Hayden, Tom. "Closure at Kent State?" *The Nation,* 15 May 2013, https://www.thenation.com/article/closure-kent-state/. Accessed 14 September 2014.

Heisler, Mark. "Lebron James Chooses Miami." *Los Angeles Times,* 9 July 2010: C1. Print.

Henderson, Laura. "Rockin' Good Times at AMM 2010 in Cleveland." *MRC Courier,* Fall 2010, p. 17. Print.

"Henry Morison Flagler Biography." *The Henry Morison Flagler Museum,* n.d., https://www.flaglermuseum.us/history/flagler-biography. Accessed 28 August 2017.

Hewett, Ivan. "BBC Prom 68/Cleveland Orchestra, Review: 'Fastidious and Understated.'" *The Telegraph,* 8 September 2014, https://www.telegraph.co.uk/culture/music/proms/11081433/BBC-Prom-68Cleveland-Orchestra-review-fastidious-and-understated.html. Accessed 9 May 2015.

Hickman, Kennedy. "American Civil War: General Philip H. Sheridan." *ThoughtCo,* n.d., https://www.thoughtco.com/general-philip-h-sheridan-2360144. Accessed 1 September 2017.

Hiltner, Stephen. "Where the Trump Name Is Emblazoned Now: The Front Yard." *New York Times,* 15 October 2016, https://www.nytimes.

com/2016/10/16/us/politics/donald-trump-signs.html?partner=bloomberg. Accessed 2 April 2017.

Hirsch, Jerry. "253 million Cars and Trucks on U. S. Roads; Average Age is 11.4 Years." *Los Angeles Times,* 9 June 2014, http://www.latimes.com/ business/autos/la-fi-hy-ihs-automotive-average-age-car-20140609-story. html. Accessed 1 November 2015.

"Historical Presidential Elections." *270 To Win,* n.d., https://www.270towin. com/historical-presidential-elections/. Accessed 4 August 2015.

"History 1921–1930." *NFL.com,* n.d., http://www.nfl.com/history// chronology/1921-1930. Accessed 1 April 2014.

"History & Hydraulics of Ohio's Canals." *Ohio Division of Natural Resources,* n.d. http://parks.ohiodnr.gov/canals. Accessed 24 September 2014.

"History of the Cleveland National Air Races." *Cleveland National Air Show,* n.d., http://www.clevelandairshow.com/about-us/national-air-racing-history/. Accessed 30 August 2017.

"The History of Polaris." *Polaris Centers,* NP Limited Partnership, n.d., http://www.polariscenters.com/About/History. Accessed 18 May 2014.

"The History of Steel in Ohio." *Ohio Steel Council,* 2014, http://www.ohio-steel.org/ohio-steel-industry/history/. Accessed 19 December 2015.

"The History of the Ohio State Fair." *Columbus Dispatch,* 20 July 2012, http://www.dispatch.com/article/20120718/NEWS/307189764. Accessed 18 June 2015.

Holt. Michael F. *The Rise and Fall of the American Whig Party: Jacksonian Politics and the Onset of the Civil War.* Oxford: Oxford University Press, 1999. Print.

Hoppert, Melissa. "A Band Shows Flair Even as It Sticks to the Script: Ohio State Musicians Mix Traditions with Dazzling Formations." *New York Times,* 29 November 2015, Sports, p. 3. Print.

Hunt, Spencer. "Dissecting Ohio's Dialects." *The Columbus Dispatch,* 18 November 2012, http://www.dispatch.com/content/stories/science/ 2012/11/18/dissecting-ohios-dialects.html. Accessed 18 October 2014.

Hunter, Ian. *Cleveland Rocks* (Song performed by the writer on *You're Never Alone With A Schizophrenic*). Chrysalis, 1979. LP.

"Ian Hunter with Mick Ronson—Interview" *Paste Magazine*, April 2009, https://www.pastemagazine.com/articles/2009/04/ian-hunter-with-mick-ronson-interview.html. Accessed 10 September 2015.

Independence Hall Association. "Politics of the Gilded Age." n.d., *U.S. History*, http://www.ushistory.org/us/36f.asp. Accessed 4 October 2015.

"Innovation at Ohio State." *Ohio State University*, n.d., https://www.osu.edu/features/2014/innovation.html. 18 August 2016.

"James A. Garfield National Historic Site." *National Park Service*, n.d., https://www.nps.gov/jaga/index.htm. 7 July 2013.

Jarboe, Michelle. "Cleveland Lakefront Construction, Long a Dream, Could Start in September." *The Plain Dealer*, 3 June 2015, http://www.cleveland.com/business/index.ssf/2015/06/cleveland_lakefront_constructi.html. Accessed 1 November 2015.

Jeffries, Zay. "Charles Franklin Kettering 1876–1958." *National Academy of Sciences*, 1960, http://www.nasonline.org/publications/biographical-memoirs/memoir-pdfs/kettering-charles.pdf. Accessed 8 January 2016.

"John D. Rockefeller." *The History Channel*, A&E Networks, n.d., http://www.history.com/topics/john-d-rockefeller. Accessed 14 October 2013.

"John D. Rockefeller: The Ultimate Oil Man." *U.S. History*, n.d., http://www.u-s-history.com/pages/h957.html. Accessed 12 October 2013.

"John Rankin." *National Abolition Hall of Fame and Museum*, n.d., http://www.nationalabolitionhalloffameandmuseum.org/jrankin.html. Accessed 5 August 2013.

Johnson, Haynes. "The 1968 Democratic Convention: The Bosses Strike Back." *Smithsonian*, August 2008. https://www.smithsonianmag.com/history/1968-democratic-convention-931079/. Accessed 14 August 2014.

Jonsson, Patrick. "First in Flight: Ohio or North Carolina?" Christian Science Monitor, 10 March, 2003, https://www.csmonitor.com/2003/0310/p02s01-usgn.html. Accessed 17 April 2015.

Joyce, Lander. "For Me, March Was a Day of Hope, Joy—And Anger." *Washington Post*, 28 August 2013. Print.

Kellner, Thomas. "GE Started Testing the World's Largest Jet Engine." *General Electric*, 22 April 2016, https://www.ge.com/reports/video-ge-started-testing-the-worlds-largest-jet-engine/. Accessed 14 August 2016.

"Kenesaw Mountain Landis." *U-S-History.com*, n.d., http://www.u-s-history com/pages/h2074.html. Accessed 24 July 2017.

"Kent State: May 1–4, 1970 Chronology of Events." *May 4 Task Force, Kent State University,* n.d., http://www.may41970.com/chronology.htm. Accessed 19 August 2014.

Kifner, John. "4 Kent State Students Killed by Troops." *New York Times,* 5 May 1970. Print.

Kingseed, Wyatt. "President William McKinley: Assassinated by an Anarchist." *HistoryNet,* 1 October 2001, historynet.com/president-william-mckinley-assassinated-by-an-anarchist.htm. Accessed 30 June 2013.

Kittman, Jamie, L. "The Secret History of Lead." *The Nation,* 20 March 2000, https://www.thenation.com/article/secret-history-lead/. Accessed 22 October 2015.

Kleiman, John. "Dayton Stakes Claim on Wright Brothers' Fame." *Chicago Tribune,* 4 July 2003: 1. Print.

Klein, Christopher. "The Birth of the National Football League." *History Channel,* 4 September, 2014, http://www.history.com/news/the-birth-of-the-national-football-league. Accessed 12 August 2015.

"Know-Nothing Party." *Ohio History Central,* n.d., http://www.ohiohistorycentral.org/w/Know-Nothing_Party. Accessed 2 October 2014.

Kotler, Philip. "Case 6: White Castle System Inc." *Pearson Education,* n.d., http://www.pearsoncustom.com/uop/kotler/pdfs/casesix.pdf. Accessed 22 May 2014.

Krebs, Michelle. "A Short History of Japanese Luxury Cars." *Bloomberg Business,* 22 May 2006, https://www.bloomberg.com/news/articles/2006-05-22/a-short-history-of-japanese-luxury-cars. Accessed 5 January 2013.

Lafferty, Mike. "Bob Evans Dies at 89." *Columbus Dispatch,* 22 June 2007, http://www.dispatch.com/content/stories/local/2007/06/21/bob_evans.html. Accessed 9 September 2009.

Lamb, Chris. "Catcher's Tears Were a Likely Inspiration for Rickey." *New York Times,* 15 April 2012: SP10. Print.

Larkin, Brent. "Why Population Loss Is Costing Cleveland—And Why It Matters." *The Plain Dealer,* 14 June 2014, http://www.cleveland.com/opinion/index.ssf/2014/06/what_population_loss_is_costin.html. Accessed 22 May 2015.

"Larry Doby." *National Baseball Hall of Fame,* n.d., https://baseballhall.org/hof/doby-larry. Accessed 19 March 2012.

Lee, Felicia R. "Demanding Lunch, Sparking Action." *New York Times*, 1 February 2005. Print.

Leip, David, ed. "United States Presidential Election Results," *U.S. Election Atlas*, 2012, https://uselectionatlas.org/RESULTS/national.php?year=201 2&off=0&elect=0&f=0. Accessed 1 January 2013.

Lewis, Jerry and Thomas Hensley. "The May 4 Shootings at Kent State University: The Search for Historical Accuracy." *Kent State University*, n.d., https://www.kent.edu/may-4-historical-accuracy. Accessed 3 May 2016.

Lindbloom, Sharon. "The Demise of the LDS Church in Kirtland." *Mormon Research Ministry*, n.d., http://www.mrm.org/kirtland. Accessed 1 August 2017.

"List of the Most Populous Cities in the United States by Decade." *Wikipedia*, n.d., https://en.wikipedia.org/wiki/List_of_most_populous_cities_in_ the_United_States_by_decade. Accessed 8 January 2016.

"A Look Back at the Early Days of the Akron Rubber Industry." *Tire Review*, 6 October 2014, http://www.tirereview.com/early-akron-rubber-industry/. Accessed 12 December 2015.

Lynch, Mathew. "The Story of American Education and the McGuffey Readers." *The Edvocate*, 2 September 2016, www.theedadvocate.org/ story-american-education-mcguffey-readers/. Accessed 19 June 2017.

Lyons, Richard D. "Roy J. Plunkett Is Dead at 83; Created Teflon While at Du Pont." *New York Times*, 15 May 1994: A44. Print.

Lyttle, Eric. "The Amazing Mister Steinbrenner." *Columbus Monthly*, September 2001, http://www.columbusmonthly.com/content/stories/ Classics/the-amazing-mister-steinbrenner-1930---2010.html. Accessed 1 July 2015.

Marion, J. C. "Mr. Blues: Wynonie Harris." *Jamm Up Website*, 2006, http:// home.earthlink.net/~v1tiger/wynonie.html. Accessed 11 November 2015.

"Marion Power Shovel & NASA Crawler-Transporter." *Marion Made!* 2 February 2017, https://www.marionmade.org/2017/02/marion-power-shovel-nasa-crawler-transporter/. Accessed 29 May 2018.

Martin, Douglas. "Dave Thomas, 69, Wendy's Founder, Dies." *New York Times*, 9 January 2002, https://www.nytimes.com/2002/01/09/business/ dave-thomas-69-wendy-s-founder-dies.html. Accessed 18 April 2010.

"May 15 1911: Supreme Court Orders Standard Oil to Be Broken Up." *New York Times Learning Network Blog*, 15 May 2012, https://learning.

blogs.nytimes.com/2012/05/15/may-15-1911-supreme-court-orders-standard-oil-to-be-broken-up/. Accessed 12 October 2015.

McClellan, Keith. *The Sunday Game: At the Dawn of Professional Football.* Akron, OH: University of Akron Press, 1998. Print.

McConnell, Kitty. "Q&A: Bob Evans' CEO Steven Davis." *Columbus CEO,* March 2014, http://www.columbusceo.com/content/stories/2014/03/steve-davis.html. Accessed 12 November 2014.

McCullough, David. *The Wright Brothers.* New York: Simon & Schuster, 2015. Print.

McDonald, Ann G. *All about Weller: A History and Collector's Guide to Weller Pottery, Zanesville, Ohio.* Marietta, OH: Antique Publications, 1989. Print.

McEntyre, Glenn. "Marion Residents Discuss Heroin Issue Following Sign Campaign." *WBNS/10TV,* 5 February 2013, https://www.10tv.com/article/marion-residents-discuss-heroin-issue-following-sign-campaign. Accessed 1 April 2017.

McMurray, John. "Branch Rickey Revolutionized Baseball in More Ways Than One." *Investor's Business Daily,* 12 April 2017, https://www.investors.com/news/management/leaders-and-success/branch-rickey-revolutionized-baseball-in-more-ways-than-one/. Accessed 7 September 2017.

McWhirter, Christian. "The Birth of 'Dixie.'" *New York Times,* 31 March 2012, https://opinionator.blogs.nytimes.com/2012/03/31/the-birth-of-dixie/. Accessed 5 April 2012.

Metcalf, Allan. *Presidential Voices: Speaking Styles from George Washington to George W. Bush.* New York: Houghton Mifflin Harcourt, 2004. Print.

Michener, James A. *Kent State: What Happened and Why.* New York: Random House, 1971. Print.

Miles, Scott. "11 Years Later, Indians' Loss to Marlins Still Hurts." *Bleacher Report,* 11 June 2008, http://bleacherreport.com/articles/28986-open-mic-11-years-later-indians-world-series-loss-to-marlins-still-hurts. Accessed 5 March 2012.

Miller, James. *Flowers in the Dustbin: The Rise of Rock and Roll, 1947–1977.* New York: Simon & Schuster, 1999. Print.

Miller, Jay. "Cleveland Hopkins International Airport Can Soar Again." *Crain's Cleveland Business,* 1 February 2015, http://www.

crainscleveland.com/article/20150201/SUB1/302019971/cleveland-hopkins-international-airport-can-soar-again. Accessed 21 March 2015.

Miller, Laura. "Bill O'Reilly Makes a *Killing*." *Slate Book Review,* 17 December 2015, http://www.slate.com/articles/arts/books/2015/12/bill_o_reilly_s_killing_reagan_and_his_other_historical_thrillers_reviewed.html. Accessed 20 December 2015.

"Mission, Vision, Values." *Cleveland Clinic,* n.d., https://my.clevelandclinic.org/about/overview/who-we-are/mission-vision-values. Accessed 28 April 2015.

Morgan, Edward P. "What America in the '90s Can Learn from the '60s." *Chicago Tribune,* 20 August 1992, http://articles.chicagotribune.com/1992-08-20/news/9203150894_1_john-kennedy-democratic-party-bill-clinton. Accessed 10 May 2018.

Moore, Michael. "5 Reasons Why Donald Trump Will Win." *Michael Moore,* n.d., https://michaelmoore.com/trumpwillwin/. 1 April 2017.

Morris, Jerry. "Edison's Home in Florida Still Aglow with the Spirit of Inventive Genius." *Chicago Tribune,* 10 February 1985: 10. Print.

"Moses Cleaveland." *Cleveland Historical,* 22 July 2011, https://clevelandhistorical.org/items/show/280. Accessed 9 June 2015.

"The Most Important 10 Pages in the History of Aviation are Missing." *GE Reports,* 22 May 2014, https://www.ge.com/reports/post/86230911910/the-most-important-10-pages-in-the-history-of/. Accessed 5 September 2014.

Naldrett, Alan. *Forgotten Tales of Michigan's Lower Peninsula,* Charleston, SC: History Press, 2014. Print.

Natali, Alan. *Woody's Boys: 20 Famous Buckeyes Talk amongst Themselves.* Wilmington, OH: Orange Frazer Press, 1995. Print.

Neff, James. *The Wrong Man: The Final Verdict on the Dr. Sam Sheppard Murder Case.* New York: Random House, 2001. Print.

Neff, William. "8 U.S. Presidents Came from Ohio: 90-Second-Know-It-All." *The Plain Dealer,* 2 November 2012, http://www.cleveland.com/pdq/index.ssf/2012/11/90-second-know-it-all_8_us_pre.html. Accessed 22 September 2013.

"The New England Glass Company 1818–1888." *Toledo Museum of Art,* 1963, https://archive.org/stream/newenglandglasscootole/newenglandglasscootole_djvu.txt. Accessed 21 January 2013.

Newpoff, Laura. "Thai Company Confirms Massive Investment for Ohio Cracker Plant Design Work." *Columbus Business First,* 3 September 2015, https://www.bizjournals.com/columbus/news/2015/09/03/thai-company-confirms-massive-investment-for-ohio.html. Accessed 28 March 2017.

"NFL-1920 Regular Season." *NFL.com,* National Football League, n.d., https://www.nfl.com/history/standings/1920. Accessed 29 May 2018.

Ng, Serena. "Floating an Idea: Would P&G Sell Ivory Soap?" *Wall Street Journal,* 17 August 2014, https://www.wsj.com/articles/floating-an-idea-would-p-g-sell-ivory-1408318299. Accessed 19 October 2014.

"November 3, 1896. Mark Hanna and the 1896 Election." *US Senate,* n.d., https://www.senate.gov/artandhistory/history/minute/Hanna_1896Election.htm. Accessed July 22, 2015.

"Octave Chanute—A Champion of Aviation." *U.S. Centennial of Flight Commission,* n.d., http://www.centennialofflight.net/essay/Prehistory/chanute/PH7.htm. Accessed 14 August 2010.

"Ohio Astronauts." *NASA Glenn Research Center,* n.d., https://www.nasa.gov/centers/glenn/about/bios/ohio_astronauts.html. Accessed 5 August 2015.

"Ohio Leads Nation in Overdose Deaths." *Columbus Dispatch,* 29 November 2016, http://www.dispatch.com/news/20161129/ohio-leads-nation-in-overdose-deaths/1. Accessed 27 March 2017.

"The Ohio Motor Vehicle Industry: Contribution and Economic Concentration." *Ohio Development Services Agency,* November 2014, https://development.ohio.gov/files/research/motorvehiclesnapshot.pdf. Accessed 29 October 2015.

"Ohio Population 2018." *World Population Review,* n.d., http://worldpopulationreview.com/states/ohio-population. Accessed 4 January 2018.

"Ohio River Basin Facts." *Pennsylvania Department of Conservation & Natural Resources,* n.d. http://www.docs.dcnr.pa.gov/cs/groups/public/documents/document/dcnr_20031262.pdf. Accessed 9 October 2014.

"Ohio State to Retire No. 31 in Honor of Vic Janowicz." *Ohio State Buckeyes,* n.d., http://www.ohiostatebuckeyes.com/sports/m-footbl/spec-rel/122104aah.html. Acccessed 21 December 2014.

"Ohio State University College of Engineering." *Ohio State University,* https://engineering.osu.edu/about-college. Accessed 4 April 2013.

"Ohio: Trump vs. Clinton." *RealClear Politics,* n.d., https://www.realclear-politics.com/epolls/2016/president/oh/ohio_trump_vs_clinton-5634.html. Accessed 1 April 2017.

Ostwinkle, Jennifer. "Harriet Beecher Stowe, 'the Little Woman Who Wrote the Book that Started this Great War.'" *U.S. History Scene,* n.d., http://ushistoryscene.com/article/harriet-beecher-stowe/. Accessed 10 November 2017.

"OSU–Michigan 1950: Wolverines Battle Through Raging Blizzard, Buckeyes for 9–3 Victory, Rose Bowl Bid." *The Plain Dealer,* 25 November, 2013, http://www.cleveland.com/osu-michigan/2012/02/osu-michigan_1950_wolverines_b.html. Accessed 20 November 2015.

"The Other Famous Hayes at Ohio State University." *Rutherford B. Hayes Presidential Center,* https://www.rbhayes.org/estate/the-ohio-state-university. Accessed 4 May 2015.

"Our History." *Ohio State Fair,* n.d., http://www.ohiostatefair.com/memory-wall. Accessed 8 August 2013.

"Our History—How It Began." *Procter & Gamble,* n.d., https://www.pg.com/en_US/downloads/media/Fact_Sheets_CompanyHistory.pdf. Accessed 29 August 2016.

"Over 80 Years of Growth." *Alcoholics Anonymous,* n.d., https://www.aa.org/pages/en_US/aa-timeline. Accessed 17 April 2017.

Page, Clarence. "Looking Back at America's Era of Mayhem." *Chicago Tribune,* 7 August 2005. Print.

"Paul Brown: A Football Life." *NFL Network,* 6 November 2015. Television. Accessed July 31, 2017.

"Philip Henry Sheridan (1831–1888)." *The Latin Library,* n.d., http://www.thelatinlibrary.com/chron/civilwarnotes/sheridan.html. Accessed 9 August 2013.

"Philip Sheridan, General." *Civil War Trust,* n.d., www.civilwar.org/learn/biographies/philip-sheridan. Accessed 9 August 2013.

Phinizy, Coles. "We Know of Knute, Yet Know Him Not." *Sports Illustrated,* 10 September 1979, https://www.si.com/vault/1979/09/10/823950/we-know-of-knute-yet-know-him-not-fact-the-real-knute-rockne-was-the-most-successful-of-football-coaches-fancy-the-rockne-of-books-and-film-was-largely-myth. Accessed 24 January 2018.

Pierson, Don. "Paul Brown Dies But the Paul Brown Memories and Anecdotes Live." *Chicago Tribune,* 11 August 1991: 36. Print.

"Procter & Gamble." *Ohio History Central*, n.d., http://www. ohiohistorycentral.org/w/Procter_%26_Gamble. Accessed 10 November 2015.

Procter & Gamble: The House That Ivory Built. By the editors of *Advertising Age*. Lincolnwood, IL: NTC Business Books, 1988. Print.

"Production of Aluminum: The Hall–Héroult Process." *American Chemical Society*, n.d., https://www.acs.org/content/acs/en/education/ whatischemistry/landmarks/aluminumprocess.html. Accessed 2 March 2013.

Quest, Richard. "Ohio: A Microcosm of the U.S." *CNN*, 30 August 2004, http://www.cnn.com/2004/ALLPOLITICS/08/30/quest.ohio/index.html. Accessed 8 April 2009.

"Railroads." *Ohio History Central*, n.d., http://www.ohiohistorycentral. org/w/Railroads. Accessed 14 February 2015.

Rank, Adam. "Fritz Pollard: A Forgotten Trailblazer." *NFL.com*, 1 February 2014, http://www.nfl.com/news/story/oap2000000325958/article/fritz-pollard-a-forgotten-trailblazer. Accessed 12 April 2015.

"Ravages of Heroin Addiction Haunt Friends, Families and Whole Towns." *NPR*, 23 August 2015, https://www.npr.org/2015/08/23/433575293/ ravages-of-heroin-addiction-haunt-friends-families-and-whole-towns. Accessed 30 March 2017.

Reed, Tom. "How Moving a Franchise from Cleveland to L.A. Benefited the Browns and Fostered Social Change." *The Plain Dealer*, 3 February 2014, http://cleveland.com/browns/index.ssf/2014/02/cleveland_rams_browns_move_to_los_angeles.html. Accessed 19 March 2014.

Rich, Bob. "Moses Finds the Promised Land." *The Plain Dealer* (via teachingcleveland.org), 9 July 1995, http://teachingcleveland.org/category/ the-western-reserve-1796-1820/moses-cleaveland/. Accessed 11 October 2014.

"Richard Nixon: 144—The President's News Conference, May 8, 1970." *The American Presidency Project*, n.d., http://www.presidency.ucsb.edu/ ws/?%20pid=2496. Accessed 8 August 2012.

Rohr, Thomas D. (Ed.). *Civil War Letters and Diary: Charles Roahr, 105th O.V.I*, CreateSpace/Amazon, 2014. Print.

"Roller Coasters." *Cedar Point*, n.d., https://www.cedarpoint.com/play/rides-coasters. Accessed 8 August 2016.

Rosenthal, Steve. "Okay, We Lost Ohio. The Question Is Why." *Washington Post*, 5 December, 2004: B3. Print.

Rove, Karl. *The Triumph of William McKinley: Why the Election of 1896 Still Matters*. New York: Simon & Schuster, 2015. Print.

Rowland, Darrell. "Dispatch Poll: Ohio's a Toss-up." *Columbus Dispatch*, 4 November 2012, http://www.dispatch.com/content/stories/local/2012/11/04/dispatch-poll-shows-ohio-a-toss-up.html. Accessed 12 August 2015.

Rudin, Ken. "40 Years after Kent State: Remembering Ohio Gov. James Rhodes." *NPR*, 3 May 2010, https://www.npr.org/sections/politicaljunkie/2010/05/03/126474013/40-years-after-kent-state-remembering-ohio-gov-james-rhodes. Accessed 5 July 2014.

Russell, Rose. "Toledo Still Proudly Wears Title of 'Glass City.'" *Toledo Blade*, 10 June 2012, http://www.toledoblade.com/Culture/2012/06/10/Toledo-still-proudly-wears-title-of-Glass-City.html. Accessed 21 February 2013.

Salvanto, Anthony. "Poll: Hillary Clinton Extends Lead in Ohio." *CBS New,* 21 August 2016, https://www.cbsnews.com/news/poll-hillary-clinton-extends-lead-ohio-iowa-donald-trump/. Accessed 27 March 2017.

Salvatore, Susan C. et al. "American Aviation Heritage: Identifying and Evaluating Nationally Significant Properties in U.S. Aviation History." *National Park Service,* March 2011, https://www.nps.gov/nhl/learn/themes/Aviation.pdf. Accessed 10 September 2014.

"Sand Dunes to Sonic Booms." *National Park Service,* n.d., https://www.nps.gov/aboutus/news/release.htm?id=437. Accessed 4 October 2014.

Shapiro, Stephanie. "For Three People, Kent State Remains a Haunting Memory." *Baltimore Sun,* 4 May 1995, http://articles.baltimoresun.com/1995-05-04/features/1995124172_1_john-filo-ann-vecchio-kent. Accessed 8 July 2015.

"*Sheppard v. Maxwell* (1966-490): 384 U.S. 333 (1966)." *Cleveland Memory Project,* n.d., http://www.clevelandmemory.org/legallandmarks/sheppard/index.html. Accessed 7 April 2015.

"*Sheppard v. Maxwell,* 384 U. S. 333 (1966)." *Justia* (US Supreme Court), n.d., https://supreme.justia.com/cases/federal/us/384/333/case.html. Accessed 5 November 2015.

Sherer, F. M. "Standard Oil as a Technological Innovator." *Harvard University Kennedy School,* January 2011, research.hks.harvard.edu/publications/getFile.aspx?Id=644. Accessed 1 March 2013.

"Sherman's March." *History Channel,* n.d., https://www.history.com/topics/american-civil-war/shermans-march. Accessed 10 August 2013.

Shih, Gerry G. "Game Changer in Retailing, Bar Code Is 35." *New York Times,* 25 June 2009: B1. Print.

"Shipping, Ferry and Port Information." *Ohio Department of Transportation,* n.d., https://www.dot.state.oh.us/Services/Pages/Water.aspx. Accessed 21 March 2015.

Shook, Carrie. "Dave's Way." *Forbes,* 9 March 1998, https://www.forbes.com/forbes/1998/0309/6105126a. Accessed 19 April 2010.

Smith, Robert L. "Cleveland's Biomedical Industry Growing by Billions." *The Plain Dealer,* 13 April 2014, http://www.cleveland.com/business/index.ssf/2014/04/clevelands_biomedical_industry.html. Accessed 15 April 2015.

Smith, Scott. "Michael Owens' Glass Bottles Changed the World." *Investor's Business Daily,* 10 January 2013, https://www.investors.com/news/management/leaders-and-success/michael-owens-invented-automatic-bottle-making-machines/. Accessed 11 August 2015.

Snell, Luke and Billie Snell. "A Concrete Street in the United States." *Concrete International,* March 2002. Print

"Stalwarts, Half Breeds, and Political Assassination." *Garfield Observer,* 20 November 2012, https://garfieldnps.wordpress.com/2012/11/20/stalwarts-half-breeds-and-political-assassination/. Accessed 10 May 2018.

Steinberg, Donald. *Expanding Your Horizons: Collegiate Football's Greatest Team.* Pittsburgh, PA: Dorrance, 1992. Print.

Stimson, Richard. "Da Vinci's Aerodynamics." *Wright Stories,* n.d., http://wrightstories.com/da-vincis-aerodynamics/. Accessed 8 August 2010.

The Story of Xerography. Xerox Corporation, 1999. Print.

Stowe, Harriet Beecher. *Uncle Tom's Cabin; or, Life among the Lowly.* Boston: John P. Jewett & Co., 1852. Ebook version (iBooks).

"Sufferers' Land." *Firelands History Website,* n.d., https://firelands.wordpress.com/index-of-posts/. Accessed 1 December 2012.

Sullivan, Michelle. "How Columbus Became America's Test Market." *Columbus Monthly,* 26 January 2015, http://www.columbusmonthly.com/content/stories/2015/01/how-columbus-became-americas-test-market.html. Accessed 17 November 2016.

Taylor, Bob. "Charles E. Taylor: The Man Aviation History Almost Forgot." *Federal Aviation Administration,* n.d., https://www.faa.gov/about/office_org/field_offices/fsdo/phl/local_more/media/CT%20Hist.pdf. Accessed 9 September 2014.

Taylor, Trey. "The Rise and Fall of Katharine Hepburn's Fake Accent." *The Atlantic,* 8 August 2013, https://www.theatlantic.com/entertainment/archive/2013/08/the-rise-and-fall-of-katharine-hepburns-fake-accent/278505/. Accessed 4 May 2014.

"The 'Toledo War.'" *Michigan State University Department of Geography,* n.d., http://geo.msu.edu/extra/geogmich/toledo_war.html. Accessed 1 December 2011.

"This Land of Ours (Ohio)." *Dudley Pictures Corporation* (via *YouTube*), 10 January 2009, https://www.youtube.com/watch?v=2uDKVS7xfbc. Accessed 11 November 2015.

Thomas, Mike. "Would Thomas Edison Survive in Your Innovation Group If He Worked There Today?" *Innovation on Purpose,* 17 February 2013, https://innovation-on-purpose.com/2013/02/17/would-thomas-edison-survive-in-your-innovation-group-if-he-worked-there-today/. Accessed 18 September 2015.

"Thomas Worthington." *Ohio History Central,* n.d., http://ohiohistorycentral.org/w/Thomas_Worthington. Accessed 25 July 2017.

"Thriving in a Consumer-Centric Global Ecosystem." *Diebold Nixdorf,* n.d., https://www.dieboldnixdorf.com/en-us/company/about-diebold-nixdorf/overview. Accessed 4 December 2017.

Tocqueville, Alexis de. *Democracy in America.* Translated by George Lawrence; edited by J. P. Mayer. New York: Harper & Row, 1966. Print.

Todd, Donny. "Famous Bands from Ohio We've All Known and Loved." *Like the Record,* 4 December 2014, http://liketherecord.com/famous-bands-ohio/. Accessed 8 August 2015.

Tomasky, Michael. "A Little Bit More on Accents, American This Time." *The Guardian,* 2 June 2010, https://www.theguardian.com/commentisfree/michaeltomasky/2010/jun/02/usa-accents-ohio. Accessed 18 October 2014.

"Traffic Congestion in Ohio." *Ohio Department of Transportation,* 2000, https://www.dot.state.oh.us/policy/SOTS2000/SOTS2000/Congestion. pdf. Accessed 9 September 2015.

Truman, Harry S. "231. Rear Platform and Other Informal Remarks in Ohio." *Harry S. Truman Presidential Library,* 11 October 1948, https:// www.trumanlibrary.org/publicpapers/index.php?pid=1981&st=&st1=. Accessed 1 August 2015.

"Two Crazy Nuts." *Wright Stories,* n.d., http://www.wrightstories.com/kitty-hawk.html#Two%20Crazy%20Nuts. Accessed 8 August 2010.

"Underground Railroad in Ohio." *Touring Ohio,* n.d., http://touringohio. com/history/ohio-underground-railroad.html. Accessed 31 August 2014.

"Unduplicated Admissions for Opiate Abuse and Dependence Ohio MACSIS Data—State Fiscal Year (SFY) 2014." *Ohio Mental Health & Addiction Services,* n.d., http://mha.ohio.gov/Portals/0/assets/Research/Maps/Ohio_ MACSIS_2014_v6.pdf. Accessed 30 March 2016.

Urbina, Lan and Christopher Maag. "After Gruesome Find, Anger at Cleveland Police." *The New York Times,* 6 November 2009: A1. Print.

Vare, Robert. *Buckeye: A Study of Coach Woody Hayes and Ohio State Football Machine.* New York: Harper's Magazine Press, 1974. Print.

Ward, Geoffrey C. and Ken Burns. *Baseball.* Random House Audio, 1994. Cassette tape.

"A Walking Tour Down Historic Dayton Street." *Dayton Street Historic District,* n.d., http://daytonstreethistoric.org/history-architecture-2/. Accessed 5 November 2015.

"Washington and the French & Indian War." *Mt. Vernon Ladies Association,* n.d., http://www.mountvernon.org/george-washington/french-indian-war/ washington-and-the-french-indian-war/. Accessed September 5 2015.

"The White Castle Story: The Birth of Fast Food and the Burger Revolution." *The Consumerist,* 14 July 2015, https://consumerist. com/2015/07/14/the-white-castle-story-the-birth-of-fast-food-the-burger-revolution. Accessed 18 April 2010.

White, Trentwell. "John Davison Rockefeller." *Johndrockefeller.org,* 1920, www.johndrockefeller.org/. Accessed 13 January 2016.

"Wilbur Wright Biography." *A&E Television Networks,* n.d., https://www. biography.com/people/wilbur-wright-20672839. Accessed 8 August 2014.

Will, George F. *Men at Work: The Craft of Baseball.* New York: HarperCollins, 1991. Print.

"William Henry Harrison." *Whitehouse.gov,* n.d., https://www.whitehouse.gov/about-the-white-house/presidents/william-henry-harrison/. Accessed 4 October 2015.

"William Tecumseh Sherman." *History Channel,* n.d., https://www.history.com/topics/american-civil-war/william-t-sherman. Accessed 9 August 2013.

Williams, Mark. "Ohio's Economy Strongest among Great Lakes States But Lags U.S." *Columbus Dispatch,* 10 June 2015, http://www.dispatch.com/article/20150610/NEWS/306109776. Accessed 30 March 2017.

Willis, Chris. "Remembering the Oorang Indians." *Pro Football Researchers Association,* n.d., http://profootballresearchers.com/archives/Website_Files/Coffin_Corner/24-03-943.pdf. Accessed 10 March 2012.

Winship, Michael. "Uncle Tom's Cabin: History of the Book in the 19th-Century United States." *University of Virginia,* June 2007, http://utc.iath.virginia.edu/interpret/exhibits/winship/winship.html. Accessed 31 July 2013.

Witt, Howard. "Procter Symbol Succumbs to Devilish Rumor." *Chicago Tribune,* 25 April 1985. Print.

Wolfe, Tom. *The Right Stuff.* Toronto: Bantam Books, 1983. Print.

Woods, Katie. "Ohio's Organic Farming on the Rise." *Farm and Dairy,* 17 October 2015, www.farmanddairy.com/news/ohios-organic-farming-on-the-rise/291597.html. Accessed 2 November 2015.

"Wright and the Reds." *American Studies at the University of Virginia,* n.d., http://xroads.virginia.edu/~hyper/incorp/baseball/wright.html. Accessed 8 March 2012.

Wright, Orville and Wilbur Wright. "The Wright Brothers Aëroplane." *Century Magazine* (on Wright-brothers.org), September 1908, http://www.wright-house.com/wright-brothers/Century.html. Accessed 29 July 2010.

"Wright-Patterson Air Force Base." *Wright-Patterson,* n.d., http://www.wpafb.af.mil/Welcome/Fact-Sheets/Display/Article/1146061/wright-patterson-air-force-base/. Accessed 4 February, 2015.

Young, Neil. *Ohio* (Song performed by Crosby, Stills, Nash & Young). Atlantic Records, 1970. Audio record single.

Zaru, Deena. "Clinton Campaign Manager Robby Mook Explains Why Clinton Is in Michigan." *CNN*, 7 November 2016, https://www.cnn.com/2016/11/07/politics/hillary-clinton-michigan-robby-mook/index.html. Accessed 3 April 2017.

Zhou, Li. "Ten Fascinating Presidential Facts to Impress on President's Day: Learn a New Side of the Commanders-in-Chief, from Whiskey Séances and Magazine Cover Boys." *Smithsonian*, 13 February 2015, https://www.smithsonianmag.com/smithsonian-institution/ten-fascinating-bits-of-presidential-trivia-180954227/. Accessed 9 October 2015.

ABOUT THE AUTHOR

Born and raised in Ohio, David Rohr spent his working career in the state until the age of 29. Even though he's been a resident of other states since then—New York and Tennessee—David remains a frequent Buckeye State visitor, as most of his immediate family still resides there. He is an enthusiastic fan of Ohio State Buckeye football as well as of many other Ohio college and professional sports teams.

His advertising and marketing communications career includes writing, creative direction, and management for a number of advertising agencies and communications firms throughout Ohio and New York. He has served clients ranging from Fortune 500 firms to smaller companies and human services organizations. He is also an entrepreneur, teacher, and father of three. He has a B.S. in Journalism from Bowling Green State University and an M.S. in Management and an M.A. in Liberal Studies, both from Nazareth College of Rochester.